# Apartheid Israel

# Apartheid Israel

## The Politics of an Analogy

Edited by Jon Soske and Sean Jacobs

Haymarket Books
Chicago, Illinois

© 2015 Jon Soske and Sean Jacobs

Published by
Haymarket Books
P.O. Box 180165
Chicago, IL 60618
773-583-7884
info@haymarketbooks.org
www.haymarketbooks.org

ISBN: 978-1-60846-518-7

Trade distribution:
In the US through Consortium Book Sales and Distribution, www.cbsd.com
In the UK, Turnaround Publisher Services, www.turnaround-uk.com
In Canada, Publishers Group Canada, www.pgcbooks.ca
All other countries, Publishers Group Worldwide, www.pgw.com

This book was published with the generous support of the Wallace Action Fund and
Lannan Foundation.

Cover design by Josh On.

Library of Congress CIP Data is available.

Entered into digital print November, 2020.

All royalties from this book will be donated to the Palestinian Campaign
for the Academic and Cultural Boycott of Israel (PACBI).

To donate to PACBI, please make your check payable to Friends of Sabeel North
America (FOSNA) and indicate PACBI in the reference line:
Norcal FOSNA
PO Box 9301
Berkeley, CA 94709

FOSNA is a nonprofit, tax-exempt organization
www.fosna.org

# Contents

Foreword

# On Palestine

Achille Mbembe

T here is no need to say much more. We have heard it all by now and from all parties.

We all know what is going on—it can't be "occupied territory" if the land is your own. As a result, everyone else is either an enemy, a "self-hater," or both. If we have to mask annexation, so be it. In any case, there is no need to take responsibility for the suffering inflicted on the other party because we have convinced ourselves that the other party does not exist.

Thus thuggishness, jingoism, racist rhetoric, and sectarianism.

Thus every two or three years, an all-out, asymmetrical assault against a population entrapped in an open-air prison.

We each know why they do what they do—the army, the police, the settlers, the pilots of bombing raids, the zealots, and the cohort of international Pharisees and their mandatory righteousness, starting with the United States of America.

We all know what is going on: by any means necessary, they must be purged from the land.

I am willing to bet on the following:

- In Palestine, it would be hard to find one single person who has not lost someone—a member of the family, a friend, a close relative, a neighbor.

- It would be hard to find one single person who is unaware of what "collateral damage" is all about.

- It is worse than the South African Bantustans.

To be sure, it is not apartheid, South African style. It is far more lethal. It looks like high-tech Jim Crow-cum-apartheid.

The refusal of citizenship to those who are not like us. Encirclement. Never enough land taken. It is all a gigantic mess. Rage, resentment, and despair. The melding of strength, victimhood, and a supremacist complex. No wonder even the Europeans are now threatening Israel with sanctions.

Israel is entitled to live in peace. But Israel will be safeguarded only by peace in a confederal arrangement that recognizes reciprocal residency, if not citizenship.

The occupation of Palestine is the biggest moral scandal of our times, one of the most dehumanizing ordeals of the century we have just entered, and the biggest act of cowardice of the last half-century.

And since all they are willing to offer is a fight to the finish, since what they are willing to do is to go all the way—carnage, destruction, incremental extermination—the time has come for global isolation.

Introduction

# Apartheid/Hafrada

## South Africa, Israel, and the Politics of Historical Comparison

Jon Soske and Sean Jacobs

D uring the 2015 Israeli electoral campaign, Benjamin Netanyahu announced in no uncertain terms that a Palestinian state would not come into existence on his watch. While he later recanted in the midst of an international outcry, the prime minister's statement removed any lingering doubts about the Israeli government's strategy regarding the so-called peace process: the interminable and Byzantine series of negotiations has coincided with a series of Israeli actions that seek to render a truly independent Palestinian state impossible. This strategy has hardly been subtle. In the first instance, it has proceeded through forced removals, land seizures, and the construction of an extensive system of settlements, including roads reserved for settlers only, designed to fragment the West Bank (already separated from Gaza) into dozens of disconnected units.[1] Secondly, the Israeli government has erected an enormous military and surveillance apparatus, including the Separation Wall and permanent checkpoints, which makes movement across Palestinian areas time-consuming and difficult. In practice, this infrastructure has entrenched and fortified the occupation, undermining the Palestinian economy and rendering everyday life precarious and, in many cases, almost unbearable.[2] Within the same geographic space, one regime of Israeli military law applies to Palestinians, while some half million Jewish settlers (many from countries such as Russia and the United States) enjoy their rights as Israeli citizens and unimpeded travel to Israel. The situation is further defined by a complete asymmetry of power. The Israeli government and army exercise extensive control over most aspects of life in the occupied territories (from residency permits to the planting of vegetables), while Palestinians lack meaningful political rights—most importantly, a democratic and sovereign state with control over its own borders, airspace, finances, and contiguous territory. Protest and resistance, including nonviolent political activities, are met with repression, imprisonment, and extrajudicial assassination. The long-term trend of Israeli policy appears to be the territorial annexation of the West Bank and the "voluntary transfer" of the Palestinian population, that is, their gradual ethnic cleansing through economic and military attrition.[3]

Although comparisons between Israel and South Africa stretch back to the 1970s, the past decade has seen a growing recognition that Israel's policies and practices toward the Palestinian people should be characterized as apartheid. The term *apartheid* (Afrikaans for separation or apartness) gained currency among Afrikaner racial theorists in the 1930s and became the basis of government policy with the election of the National Party in 1948. The Nationalists did not introduce white supremacy to South Africa. They assumed power over a country shaped by three hundred years of settler-colonialism and institutions such as pass laws restricting African mobility, reserved areas for African residency and landownership, a political economy reliant on the exploitation of African migrant labor, and voting restrictions that virtually eliminated the Black population's few existing political rights. As a policy, apartheid sought to reorganize and rationalize these mechanisms of segregation on a national scale in defense of the ethnonationalist ideal of a white South Africa. In order to realize this vision, the state categorized the population into three major groups (later extended to four: Native, white, Coloured, and Indian), zoned South Africa into areas of racially exclusive residence, and introduced a systematic program of land seizures and forced relocations. The government stripped Black Africans of citizenship and assigned them to ethnically defined "homelands," the so-called Bantustans. In theory, the Bantustans allowed for the realization of African self-determination: they were self-governing, and four of them "achieved" independence. In practice, they were composed of impoverished, dispersed territorial fragments directly and indirectly under the control of the Pretoria government.

In reaction to antiapartheid struggle and growing international outrage, the 1965 International Convention for the Elimination of All Forms of Racial Discrimination declared apartheid a crime. Crucially, this and subsequent treaties did not limit the term *apartheid* to southern Africa, but provided a general definition with delineated components.[4] According to the 1975 International Convention on the Suppression and Punishment of the Crime of Apartheid, apartheid consists of "inhuman acts committed for the purpose of establishing and maintaining domination by one racial group of persons over any other racial group of persons and systematically oppressing them."[5] These acts include denial of life or liberty; the imposition of living conditions designed to cause the destruction of the group in whole or part; legislative or other measures designed to prevent a group from participating in the economic, social, political, or cultural life of the country; measures that divide the population along racial or ethnic lines and create separate reserves or ghettos; exploitation of labor; and the persecution of political opposition. As legal scholars John Dugard and John Reynolds observe, the definition of apartheid in international law centers on its systematic and legal-structural aspects: "It is this institutionalized element, involving a state-sanctioned regime of law, policy, and institutions, that distinguishes the practice of apartheid from other forms of prohibited discrimination."[6] In its essentials, the Rome Statute of the International Criminal Court reiterated this understanding in 1998.

In recent years, two separate debates have developed—and have sometimes become confused—regarding the idea of Israeli apartheid. The first is a dispute about legal definitions: Do Israeli actions in the occupied territories (or, in some formulations, the Israeli state's policy toward the Palestinian population, including refugees and Palestinian Israelis) amount to apartheid and colonialism under the relevant international treaties? When the official statements of the boycott, divestment, and sanctions (BDS) campaign use the term *apartheid*, they are *not* making a direct analogy with the South African regime.[7] They are arguing that Israeli policies should be condemned as the crime of apartheid under international law. In advancing this case, activists and lawyers are motivating a paradigm shift in the international community's approach to the conflict: a change from viewing the situation as a territorial dispute between two peoples (one under temporary military occupation) to a general assessment of the goals and consequences of the Israeli state's long-term policies.[8] The significance of this discussion is that the prohibition against apartheid is a peremptory (absolute) norm under international law. In other words, a legal finding of apartheid would obligate the international community to end any aid that perpetuated the crime and to cooperate actively to bring the violation to an end.[9]

The second debate concerns the broader comparison between Israel and South Africa: To what extent can the histories of these two countries be juxtaposed? Do South Africa's experiences of settler-colonialism and apartheid provide insights that can sharpen our understanding of Israeli politics and society? Are there meaningful lessons from the antiapartheid struggle—for example, from the global cultural and academic boycott— for Palestinian solidarity work? Does the South African political transition and the achievement of a democracy based on "one person, one vote," whatever its considerable shortcomings, offer lessons for Israel/Palestine? What are the most significant differences between the two cases, and what consequences might these have for the future of the Middle East? This book is primarily concerned with this second set of questions.

We have invited seventeen writers and scholars of Africa and its diasporas to reflect on the South Africa/Israel analogy. On one level, the parallels are unmistakable. Apartheid South Africa and Israel both originated through a process of conquest and settlement justified largely on the grounds of religion and ethnic nationalism. Both pursued a legalized, large-scale program of displacing the earlier inhabitants from their land. Both instituted a variety of discriminatory laws based on racial or ethnic grounds. In South Africa itself, the comparison is so widely accepted (outside a small coterie of Zionist groups) that it is generally uncontroversial. Leading members of the antiapartheid struggle, including the Archbishop Desmond Tutu and Jewish activists such as Ronnie Kasrils, have repeatedly averred that the conditions in the West Bank and Gaza are "worse" than apartheid.[10] At the same time, no historical analogy is ever exact. Comparisons reveal differences even as they underline similarities. If South Africa emerged through a centuries-long process of European settlement and colonial warfare, the foundation of Israel in 1948 was preceded by one of the most singular atrocities in humanity's history, the Holocaust. While the South African economy continues to rely overwhelmingly on the exploitation of African workers, early Zionists consciously sought to displace Arab labor and managed to build a far more closed, ethnically unified economy. However politically important South African exiles were during the apartheid period, nothing existed that approached either the scale of the Palestinian refugee population or the global Jewish diaspora, which today is increasingly divided over Israel's claim to speak in its name.

The importance of the apartheid comparison, obviously, is not that the cases are "identical" (a straw man argument that could be used to discredit any analogy). Several contributions to this volume explore the divergences at some length. The importance of the comparison is that it has assisted in fundamentally changing the terms of debate. Until recently, the Israeli government and its partisans, especially in the United States, had largely succeeded in depicting Israel as a besieged democracy defending its very existence against the threat of outside terrorism. Framing Israel/ Palestine as an international conflict between two equivalent sides (Jews and Arabs), this narrative suggests that peace will only be achieved by guaranteeing Israel's security and then adjudicating claims over "disputed" territory.[11] Along these lines, subsequent Israeli governments have contended that their actions in the occupied territories—including the land seizures, mass arrests, settlements, checkpoints, and the Separation Wall— are defensive measures driven by military necessity and the exceptional circumstances of a long-term (but nonetheless temporary) occupation.[12] Israel cannot reasonably be accused of apartheid, the argument continues, because the West Bank and Gaza lie outside of Israel proper. Insistently conflating the state's actions with defense of its Jewish population, this entire mode of debate sets up any criticism of Israel's policies as being in and of itself "anti-Semitic."

In challenging this account, the comparison with South Africa returns the discussion to Israel's colonial origins and the settler project of consolidating a nation-state through the expropriation and expulsion of Palestinians. By emphasizing the strategic aims of current Israeli policies (the fragmentation and annexation of Palestinian territory), the comparison underlines that resistance does not somehow come from "outside," but is the inevitable and justified response to occupation and forced displacement. The apartheid analogy also illuminates the circularity of Israel's security argument: since occupation and settlement generate resistance, there can be no resolution to the "conflict" short of Israel's withdrawal from the occupied territories and the dismantling of its colonizing infrastructure. It highlights the mendacity of the Israeli government's pretense of negotiating for "peace" while attempting to construct a permanent regime of military control. After almost five decades of occupation, it is unfathomably cynical to claim immunity from the charge of apartheid on the basis of a territorial separation that the Israeli government, military, and supreme court have actively worked to undermine. Perhaps most important, the apartheid analogy has helped to insert the staggering human costs of the occupation at the center of global attention. In place of the Palestinian "terrorist," the world is increasingly confronted with images of Israeli bulldozers destroying houses and olive trees, Israeli soldiers harassing and humiliating civilians at checkpoints, and the Israeli army's indiscriminate shelling of civilians in Gaza. This shift is taking place not only in North America and Europe but also, tentatively and on a much smaller scale, within Israel itself.[13]

In response, apologists for Israel's policies have attempted to relocate the comparison. When measured against the civil rights records of other Middle Eastern countries, they respond, the Palestinian minority within Israel enjoys significant political rights and civic protections. Palestinian Israelis vote, participate in national elections through legal political parties, and sit in the Knesset—all things that would have been unthinkable for Black South Africans under apartheid. When forces like the Islamic State are perpetrating systematic atrocities against minorities in Iraq and Syria, they pose, why are pro-Palestinian activists focusing so narrowly on Israel, the "only democracy" in the region? It is tempting to respond that this vindication tries to have it both ways by asserting that Israel upholds (if imperfectly) the standards of liberal democracy while measuring its record against regimes that are almost universally condemned for their disregard of basic human rights. But there is another motivation at work. South Africa's apartheid government also accused its critics of selectivity by invoking the record of governments such as Idi Amin's Uganda, which imprisoned internal opposition, expelled almost the entirety of its South Asian population, and murdered tens of thousands of its own citizens. In doing so, it represented the white settler colony as an island of civilization and modernity surrounded by "primitive" societies and cultures unprepared for—if not organically hostile to—Western democracy. Its defenders could therefore imply that segregationist institutions and repressive actions, while perhaps genuinely regrettable, were necessary given the internal and regional threats that the country faced. Apartheid's opponents, it followed, were naïve idealists who did not grasp the realities of building a liberal civil society in a "backward" region.

When Israel's apologists recycle this style of argument today, they are trafficking in similar forms of racism. Today, it is "terrorism," "radical Islam," or "Arab anti-Semitism." The problem here is not that fundamentalism and popular anti-Semitism don't exist. Of course they do—although the Western media's frequent depiction of these phenomena as intrinsic to Arab culture is both false and self-serving. The basic hypocrisy of this position is that the Israeli state (not unlike South Africa during the Cold War) has supported corrupt, antidemocratic regimes in the face of popular movements that might challenge the regional status quo by presenting a radical alternative to both Islamicism and military rule. The Netanyahu government's unembarrassed loyalty to the Egyptian dictatorship during the Tahrir Square uprising is only the most vivid example. The realpolitik is, in the abstract, understandable: a popularly elected government in Egypt or Jordan, secular or Islamic in ideology, might well be less friendly to Israeli interests than the existing, US-backed strongmen. Nevertheless, Israel's direct subvention of these regimes undercuts the image of a lone protagonist struggling to uphold democracy in a region hostile to human rights.

The attempt to shift the comparison from Israel/South Africa to Israel/Syria or Israel/Iran deserves scrutiny on two other levels. The first concerns the argument that the BDS campaign singles out Israel unfairly by failing to call for a boycott of Syria and Lebanon as well—countries that have long histories of marginalizing Palestinians, repressing Palestinian organizations, and denying civil rights to refugees. Why then, critics ask, focus solely on Israel and not on these countries as well? This particular strategy of comparison conflates cause and effect. As many historians now acknowledge, the origin of the Palestinian refugee crisis was the policy of expulsion or "transfer" pursued by Zionist forces in 1947–48. The continued existence of almost three million refugees in surrounding countries is the direct result of the fact that Palestinian claims to land and citizenship within the borders of post-1948 Israel have not been resolved. The refugee issue is complex and the Palestine Liberation Organization (PLO) has arguably manipulated the limbo status of Palestinian refugees as a negotiating tool.[14] Be that as it may, it is misleading to equate the underlying cause of the problem (the ethnic cleansing of Palestinians and the

denial of their right to return) and its immediate consequences (the existence of disenfranchised refugees across the region and their treatment by
Arab governments).

Second, it is true that Palestinians currently living in Israel (that is,
those who were not expelled in 1948) possess civil rights and participate
openly in the spheres of sport, culture, and the economy. This fact is often
cited as a prima facie refutation of the claim that Israel is an apartheid
state. More sophisticated pundits will acknowledge that Israeli Arabs face
discrimination but then depict it as prejudice within a common civil society—that is, something very different from apartheid. These claims are
deceptive on multiple levels. Israeli law institutionalizes the distinction between the Jewish population and other groups. As codified in its Basic Law
and affirmed by the supreme court in 1970, Israel is the state of the Jewish
people: non-Jewish Israeli citizens do not enjoy the same status under civil
law. (It is, in fact, illegal for a political party to run for the Knesset if it
questions this principle.) In contrast to Israel's strong equal rights legislation regarding women and the disabled, more than fifty laws discriminate
directly or indirectly against the Palestinian minority of Israel.[15] Reflecting these legal disparities, Palestinian Israelis face staggering levels of poverty (in 2011, 50 percent); workforce discrimination and higher rates of
unemployment; extensive restrictions on land ownership and residency;
and numerous forms of educational, linguistic, and cultural marginalization.[16] The claim that Arab Israelis enjoy full civil rights further ignores
the phenomenon of "unrecognized" Palestinian Bedouin villages. By declaring settlements illegal under laws such as the 1965 National Planning
and Building Law, the Israeli state has deprived some 75,000 to 90,000
people of basic services, facilities, and political representation.[17] Nor do
these claims address the situation of Palestinians in occupied East Jerusalem (unilaterally and illegally annexed by Israel after the 1967 War). In
addition to an aggressive program of settlement designed to transform the
ethnic composition of the city, the Israeli state has stripped over 14,000
Palestinians of their residency since 1967.[18]

Ultimately, the trumpeting of minority rights falsely *detaches* the discrimination endured by Arab Israelis from the earlier expulsion of Palestinians and its political, ideological, and legal justification on the basis that
Israel is a Jewish state. This point is key. Zionism's postulation of a Jewish
national identity for Israel is inseparable from the denial of Palestinian

rights in much the same way that apartheid's assertion of a white South Africa presupposed the displacement and disenfranchisement of the African majority. If the apartheid regime enfranchised a limited number of Black South Africans, this eventuality would have altered neither the original acts of population transfer nor the status of those living in the Bantustans or in exile—that is, outside the country's "official" borders. Indeed the apartheid government, which from the late 1950s spoke in terms of "separate development" for different groups and rejected accusations of white supremacy, experimented with the partial enfranchisement of the Black population. In the 1980s, the state offered selective voting rights to Coloureds and Indians in separate chambers of its national parliament. The same era witnessed the introduction of Black local authorities in African areas. Additionally, each Bantustan had its own legislature. These "democratic reforms" were roundly rejected and provoked the formation of a national mass movement, the United Democratic Front. The enfranchisement of some Palestinians resolves neither the forced division of the Palestinian nation between exile, the fragmented occupied territories, and Israel nor the denial of self-determination to the Palestinian people as a whole.

In approaching the debates over the apartheid/Israel analogy, the essays in this volume strive for attentiveness to the singularity of the individual cases even as they attempt to place multiple histories of oppression and resistance in dialogue. They highlight the interwoven histories of South Africa and Israel/Palestine as well as the distance between the present historical moment and the period of the antiapartheid struggle. They seek to make the work of comparison explicit, therefore creating open spaces for critical self-reflection rather than "objectively" tallying similarities and differences—an exercise that, invariably, raises the question of how the terms of comparison were originally defined. While all the authors accept (to different degrees and in varying ways) the utility of the apartheid analogy, they also emphasize the complexity of South African history and the antiapartheid struggle. Taken as a whole, they suggest that while there are many lessons to be learned from South Africa, the most important are neither simple nor easily translatable into other contexts. Although the 1994 transition dismantled legal white supremacy, South Africa remains a profoundly divided society, convulsed by unresolved questions of race, class, and gender inequality. The work of fully understanding the historical experience of apartheid—and addressing its continuing legacies—is still far from complete.

In this respect, these essays also provide a corrective to reductive depictions of the antiapartheid struggle that sometimes circulate among
pro-BDS activists. While simplifications are an inevitability of activism,
instrumentalist uses of South African history can shut down much-needed
debate. There is, for example, a tendency to exaggerate the impact of North
American cultural and academic boycott. On occasion, US activists go so
far as to suggest that the boycott movement itself brought about the end
of apartheid—a position that comes dangerously close to what Teju Cole
has called the "white saviour industrial complex."[19] There is no question
that the academic boycott and university divestment helped raise public
awareness and force debate regarding foreign support for the South African regime. But it was one part of a much wider movement that included
the massively influential sports boycott, the International Defense and Aid
Fund, direct action by trade unions, and the Free Mandela campaign. This
solidarity was not centered in the West, but truly global in scope: it was
arguably the largest civil society movement of the twentieth century.[20] And
it was supplemental to a mass, democratic movement within South Africa
itself. In many cases, global solidarity drew strength from its close connections with local political struggles. Given the prominence of Cold War alliances, opposition to apartheid was also a means of defying Pinochet's military junta in Chile, Thatcher's assault against trade unions and "urban" (in
other words, immigrant and minority) communities in England, and Reagan's anti-Black and aggressively neoliberal agenda.[21] In the 1980s, Mandela was not yet the feel-good symbol of liberal reconciliation. (In fact, he
was on a US terrorism watch list until 2008.) Denounced by mainstream
parties in the United States and United Kingdom, Mandela embodied the
struggles of oppressed and working-class people around the world.

Today, the BDS campaign is growing—in considerable part—through
building these kinds of alliances between the Palestinian solidarity movement and struggles around questions such as racism, education, and the
prison industrial complex. Rather than "singling out Israel," as pro-Zionist voices often allege, activists are highlighting the parallels and very
real connections between Israeli apartheid and forms of oppression and
inequality at work in American society. They are targeting companies such
as G4S (a controversial security firm involved in Israeli, US, and South
African prisons), highlighting the increased connections between American domestic police and Israeli security services since 9/11, and responding

to attacks against academic freedom by Zionist groups.[22] In the process, they are confronting those aspects of US political culture—ranging from the American mythology of settler manifest destiny to the ideology of "antiterrorism"—that have normalized support for both South African apartheid and Zionism as political projects. They are also challenging the powerful coalition of interests behind the US government's diplomatic, military, and financial support of Israel, including the Christian right, the massive arms and "security" industries, and substantial sections of mainstream liberal opinion.[23] By tracing historical and contemporary linkages between Israel, South Africa, and the United States, this collection seeks to aid this process. It is only possible to treat the question of Israeli apartheid as "something over there" by ignoring its intimate connection with forms of racism, militarization, and censorship at work in North America.

If this book accomplishes one thing, it should help refute the claim that the comparison between South Africa and Israel is "anti-Semitic." In the wake of recent victories by the BDS movement, pro-Zionist forces are increasingly leveling this accusation to shut down further discussion. In some cases, they are being assisted by the fact that actual anti-Semites are indeed employing both Israel's actions and the boycott call as pretexts for organization. Few movements have denounced anti-Semitism more consistently and forcefully than the BDS campaign. The analogy with the South African antiapartheid struggle only underscores this position. At the ideological heart of apartheid was the program of building an (ultimately impossible) "white South Africa," based on an ethnonationalist appeal to self-determination. Apartheid's forced removals, the creation of the Bantustans, and the stripping of African citizenship rights were directed to this end. Whatever its many shortcomings, the defeat of apartheid represented the historic triumph of an inclusive vision of South Africa over a racially exclusive conception of nation. In drawing a comparison between the two cases, the apartheid analogy is clearly targeting a set of *state* practices and policies—not the Israeli Jewish population as a group of people.

As these essays suggest, any lessons the South African transition offers for the future of Israel and Palestine are far from simple. A coalescence of factors—internal and external, economic and geopolitical—led to the white minority's abandonment of political power in 1994. For some activists, South Africa speaks to the possibility of a one-state solution based on universal citizenship and equal rights for all. Others see the negotiations of the early 1990s as a model for the realistic and painful compromises that would be necessary to enact a truly just two-state solution. At this level, historical comparison is more useful in sharpening questions rather than providing meaningful answers. Significantly, Palestinian civil society's call for BDS has left the form of a future settlement open. It advances the general demand for a truly equitable solution for both Israelis and Palestinians that corresponds with international law.[24] However, one lesson from South Africa is clear enough. Whatever other factors contributed to the timing and circumstances of its demise, the destruction of South African apartheid would not have occurred without a powerful, international movement dedicated to freedom for all South Africans. In retrospect, "above the fray" experts might try to untangle and isolate the different strands of liberation struggle, arguing that one tactic or another was decisive. At the time, the African National Congress and other liberation organizations encouraged diverse forms of resistance and continuously searched for new methods of linking internal opposition to international solidarity. They understood that different modes of struggle strengthened and reinforced each other in ways that cannot always be predicted in advance. Their lesson is clear: we must multiply the forms and points of cultural, economic, and political pressure.

Chapter 1

# Palestine Journey

Ishtiyaq Shukri

**London, Sunday 11th September 2005**
In his foreword to Arundhati Roy's collection of essays *The Algebra of Infinite Justice*, John Berger writes,

> On 11 September 2001, the pilots who attacked New York and Washington put an end forever to a "normalcy," and thus to a sense of security, which had prevailed in the First World since the disintegration of the Soviet Union. (Let us note in passing how the rich are called the First.) This "normalcy" lived hand in glove with extremities of humiliation, poverty, and suffering which were and still remain each day comparable in their extremity to what happened that morning when the Trade Center, the hub of the new world economic order, crumbled.[1]

I am reminded of Berger's comments, writing as I am at my desk in London on the fourth anniversary of the attacks on New York and Washington. I am aware that the site of the World Trade Center has been cleared and is ready for redevelopment. But Kabul? The London Underground is now fully operational following the blasts of 7th July 2005. Baghdad? "Normalcy" restored? Here. In the Rich World. Perhaps. But I have just returned to London from Palestine where "extremities of humiliation, poverty and suffering" continue to govern the daily grind. For Palestinians, "normalcy" continues to mean the brutal Israeli occupation, now entering its thirty-ninth year. And for Palestinians in what remains of the West Bank, "normalcy" now also includes the towering Apartheid

Wall—as illegal, as decimating, as it is monstrous. This is how I came to be in Palestine. This is what I saw.

## Amman, Sunday 7th August 2005

In 1996, I found myself in a new city, visiting its ancient sites by day, savouring the pages of the longest contemporary novel in English, Vikram Seth's *A Suitable Boy*, by night. The more I read, the more I loved. The more I loved, the slower I read—a futile attempt to forestall the dreaded two words on the last page of a story that has swept you over: The End. When it came it was like a kind a death. And I entered a kind of mourning. I wandered the streets of my adopted ancient city with Mrs. Rupa Mehra, Lata, Maan—no longer in my hands but always in my head. I could not read anything new. For weeks all visits to bookshops ended with my scanning *A Suitable Boy* for my favourite scenes. Eventually one visit did end in a purchase, though not of a novel but of a writing pad. Faced with an intimidating blank page, I started with what intrigued me most—air travel and aeroplanes—on my balcony overlooking the Nile with the echoes of a thousand minarets marking the course of the day. I have just retrieved the writing pad. The entries are dated. The first is for 28th March 1996, the day I started scratching the story that would become *The Silent Minaret*.

On 9th September 2001, I boarded a flight from Cape Town to London, welcoming the opportunity again to study carefully the layout of the craft, its route, everything about the journey, and the machine. I did not know that in the United States nineteen young men had been doing the same. Two days later, on the morning after my trans-African flight had set me down in London, I stood mute in front of pictures of New York, Washington, and the realization of what nineteen young men and four planes could do.

No time for stories. The world had buckled. I bailed out of fiction, abandoned my manuscript, and watched an eternal war of infinite retribution unfold. Until the night the war found me. I reached for the manuscript. Everything had changed. Nothing worked. *When cities crack, do stories too, their scaffolding collapsing?* I had to start from scratch, now no longer writing on a balcony by the Nile but in London, secretly, where mosques were being raided as Britain's rulers took up their seats as co-pilots in the "War on Terror."

Readers will be aware that *The Silent Minaret* culminates at the Apartheid Wall, which Israel is rushing to complete around the West Bank despite an Advisory Opinion by the International Court of Justice on 9th July 2004 finding it and Israeli settlements in the West Bank illegal. One of the novel's characters, Karim, challenges sceptics of the Palestinian struggle to visit Palestine, if only for "just one day."[2] Tonight, I am writing from Amman, mountainous capital of the Hashemite Kingdom of Jordan. I will leave at dawn to cross the Jordan River into Palestine to take up Karim's challenge.

## Amman to Jerusalem, Monday 8th August 2005

The early morning ride from Amman to the lowest border crossing on earth is as beautiful as any, through the glowing golden Moab Mountains of the Jordan Valley with views of the Dead Sea shimmering like a mirage on the approach. Jordanian departure procedures at King Hussein Bridge are swift and efficient, even polite. But when our coach draws near to the fortified Israeli-controlled border on the west bank of the River Jordan, a silent air of trepidation descends on the passengers. Those who know the drill warn of an arduous procedure ahead, then reach for their bags with a collective sigh. I have not arrived anywhere with more foreboding than here.

They are right. Four stages lie ahead. First, you join a queue to deposit your luggage (to be collected on the other side, if you are allowed through). Then another queue for security screening. At the far end of the room, a machine looms, pumping bursts of air through valves that look like showerheads. What, I wonder, would the grandparents of those young Israelis on duty here be reminded of if they were shuffled into this ominous chamber? My face must betray the workings of my mind. I am quickly singled out and called aside for the first set of questions from "security," the same questions that will be asked repeatedly by different agents during the course of the day. I answer the questions. Then I am led to the ominous machine. I am told, without irony by the guard armed with a huge automatic rifle, that it will detect even the finest traces of ammunition. Fine. Put me through a test that you yourself will fail. Around the corner, a third queue—passport control—and yet more questions. This is where I will spend most of the day, waiting. My passport disappears behind a closed door on which is written in Hebrew, Arabic, and English: No Entry. I am told to take a seat. The slow tick and grinding tock of the clock begins. At the fourth queue, if you reach it, is luggage collection. Even though you have officially passed through immigration, yet more questions await here.

By the time I finally collect my bag and step outside, it is twilight in the Judean Desert, eight hours since I left the bag at the front of the building. I wonder, when was the last time you spent eight hours getting through one building?

Today I left Amman at seven in the morning to travel seventy kilometers to Jerusalem. It took me twelve hours. When was the last time it took you twelve hours to travel seventy kilometers?

Waiting. Answering questions. What was your great-grandfather's name? Sending text messages: "Stil w8ing." And writing, on slips of immigration paper. Waiting, until one begins to doubt oneself. Waiting, until I thought I must have done something wrong. Waiting. And remembering. In April 2003, just weeks after the invasion of Iraq, I travelled from Damascus to the border of Iraq, to enter Iraq if possible. It was an unfulfilled journey and Iraq remains an elusive destination. *At moments like this, when destinations, glimpsed, just there, at the bottom of the road, slip away, all you have is the journey, the not-much-deliberated, unfulfilled attempt to get there.* Waiting until one feels powerless. Receiving text messages: "Cant settle 2 do anything here. Everybody is waiting with you." Waiting until you realize that all there is to do is wait.

And write. During the course of the afternoon, I saw one Palestinian, now living in Cyprus and visiting the West Bank for the first time, made to read out all the numbers stored on his mobile phone. Another, now living in the States, was told he would not be allowed in because he did not have the necessary paperwork. He argued in frustration that the documentation had been confiscated at the same border when he passed through at the end of his last visit. The Israeli officials were demanding documentation they had themselves confiscated. Yet another Palestinian was asked how long he intended to stay in "Israel."

"Two days," he said. "I have work. I must return to Amman tomorrow." He only wanted to see his sick mother.

Despite having all his paperwork and a letter from his mother's physician, he was made to wait.

So we wait.

It is after four before he is eventually allowed to pass though. The day is gone. He will spend one night with his mother and tomorrow he will face departure procedures—known to be as arduous if not worse—in this same building.

Palestinians around me whisper that they face these procedures daily: "When we enter Palestine, inside Palestine, when we leave Palestine. What do we do? When we leave, we're wrong. When we arrive, we're wrong. When we stay, we're wrong. No matter what we do, we're wrong."

We wait till we're exhausted for the saddest scene of the day to un-fold. Young woman. Palestinian. Travelling alone with her three young sons: eight, five, and three. The young family has, like everybody else, been called several times to answer questions then made to sit down again. Each time they are summoned, the mother has to gather the boys. They take it as a game—she manages to find one, another slips away to hide—anything for a bit of distraction. But it is late now. We're tired. No time for games. She watches the boys dart around the room. Which one to grab first? She makes several false starts. Then stops. Buries her face in her hands, the only privacy she can find, and weeps. But only for a moment. She wipes her face hurriedly then dashes after the five-year-old, grabs hold of him, spanks him, pulls him to the counter. But what's happening now? The im-migration official is vacating her desk. She's approaching the woman. She starts shouting at her. For spanking her child. Everybody looks. The young mother falls to her knees. Her boys freeze. Game's up. But the immigra-tion officer is still shouting. "How dare you spank a child?" I can still see the mother, the faces of each of her boys, the immigration official shout-ing, shouting at a Palestinian mother for spanking her Palestinian child, when the official works for a government that shoots them.

That was when he came to get me, the captain, to ask the same ques-tions I had already answered to his subordinates. But this time, I must answer to him. He takes me aside. The questions go like this. I wonder, how would you answer them?

> "Are you a Muslim?"
> "Are you religious?"
> "Do you go to the mosque?"
> "Are you married?"
> "Is your wife a Muslim, too?"
> "What do you do?"
> "Do you have evidence to prove your job?"
> "Why did you go to Syria?"
> "Do you have friends there?"
> "Did you meet any Muslims there?"
> "Why do you travel in the Middle East?"

"Why are you coming to Israel?"
"Will you be going to the West Bank and Gaza?"
"Do you know people there?"
"Are they Muslim?"

Waiting with me are French, Italian, Australian, Japanese, Indian, and South African travelers. We compare stories to find a common denominator that makes us suspect. We have all travelled around the Middle East. We have all been asked whether we "know Muslims." I start to hear the message: if you want unhindered access through borders controlled by Israel, do not be Palestinian. Do not know Arabs. Do not know Muslims. As my shared taxi departs the border for Jerusalem, it is hard not to feel that I am entering a country decidedly ill at ease and scornful of its closest neighbours. I find my mobile phone: "I'm through. In taxi to Jerusalem. Passing Jericho. No walls here."

I am in Palestine to observe the impact of the Apartheid Wall on rural Palestinian communities in the remote northern areas of the West Bank. A leading Palestinian nongovernmental organization, the Palestinian Agricultural Relief Committees (PARC), is facilitating my journey. PARC is a nonprofit organization that works toward ensuring long-term food security, empowering rural women and increasing their profile in society, training and research development, enhancing the role of civil society and institutions, and promoting the ethos of voluntary work. As part of my journey I will participate in the annual summer camp based at Zababdeh in the Jenin District. The camp unites international and Palestinian volunteers to work together at both manual and research projects in rural Palestinian villages. This year's camp is organized around the theme of the Apartheid Wall and provides volunteers with direct access to the remote rural communities whose lives have been sliced through by the wall.

Barriers. My history is littered with them. All South Africans with any lived experience of apartheid know them, the divisions within, between, and amongst. And even if the barriers were more often intangible, we know that they were never ineffective. I don't know the points on the map at which the avenues of my youth—Transvaal Road in Kimberley, Klipfontein Road in Athlone, Modderdam Road in Bellville—changed from being Black, a part of town in which I could live, to being white, a part of town in which I could not. But I knew those invisible markers existed. We all did. And that knowing, as we grasped at ordinary lives from separated existences forged around imperceptible cordons, was enough. In apartheid South Africa, "normalcy" was a carnival of the macabre. In Palestine, the carnival marches on.

To those young new South Africans who ask the question: How come? Let me point you to one very literal root: *Brabejum stellatifolium*, still growing in Cape Town's Kirstenbosch Gardens. Dutch settlers planted that wild almond hedge in 1660, making it the first official boundary between the Cape Colony and the indigenous Khoi population. From the moment it took root, so too did the notion of division, which flourished to become the most defining feature of our society for the next 326 years. Over time the idea of separation took such root it transcended all need for tangible manifestation. One testimony to its surreptitious power lay in its invisibility—in South Africa, barriers governed our lives in absentia. In Palestine, they don't.

There is nothing invisible about Israel's Apartheid Wall. My first glimpse of it is as we approach Jerusalem on a road that, our driver informs us, is for Israelis only.

"Palestinians cannot use this road."

"How would they know?" I ask, jotting down our exact location from a road sign as it flashes by: Maale Adummim.

"Easy," he says. "Israeli cars have yellow plates, Palestinians have green plates."

"And what would happen if a Palestinian car were found on this road."

"It would be stopped here. This road accesses that huge settlement on the hill there, Maale Adummim. Actually, it's not a settlement anymore," he sighs. "It's a city of seventy-five thousand now."

I look ahead at déjà vu. Do you remember the entrance to the University of the Western Cape during "states of emergency"—fortified encampments patrolled by young men, young men with big guns? Drive into Jerusalem today and that is what you'll see.

"Look!" our driver exclaims when we have left behind the checkpoint. "Look, there to our left!" We follow his pointing finger and there it is, the wall, cutting through the hillsides around Jerusalem. I have seen many pictures and read countless articles on the wall, but none has prepared me for my first glimpse of the grey, snaking monster and the sinking feeling that comes with the realization that, yes, it actually exists. The sight, seconds later, of the magnificent golden Dome of the Rock, glowing in the setting sun, is too confounding a leap to process. I don't remember the rest of the journey, only being dropped off at Damascus Gate, the heart of Arab East Jerusalem, aware, as I reach for my bag, that something has changed. Can an upbringing of religious association with the "Eternal City" be undone in the blink of an eye? Somewhere between concrete wall, golden dome, and ancient city gate, Jerusalem loses its holiness for me. In the two days I spend in the city, I strain to find any will to visit the sacred places that surround me. All I can see is guns. You have to be a very blinkered pilgrim not to notice them.

So I seek out a bookshop. I buy a writing pad. In the Middle East, I am usually drawn to the streets at night, often wandering the ancient alleyways till dawn. Not in Jerusalem. One night three young Israeli soldiers outside Damascus Gate take me for a Palestinian. I answer their questions, barked in Arabic. They search me, digging their hands intrusively into my pockets. By the time they realize I am foreign and try to temper their approach—"Welcome to Israel. Enjoy your stay"—it is too late; they've already revealed their procedures. In fiction, to juxtapose this event with what happened next would be overbearing. But this is not fiction. Walking back to my hostel, I hear bleating sounds coming from a car parked across the road. I glance at the car, full of young Israelis. They are bleating at me. In Jerusalem, Israelis treat me like a Palestinian because of my looks. On 10th August, I pass through the Qalandia checkpoint to enter the occupied West Bank knowing a little what that treatment feels like.

Before we leave Jerusalem, water bottles are filled for the journey to Ramallah via Qalandia checkpoint. Many things surprise me about the journey: that I am here, making it; that the soldiers I saw from a distance are, up close, young women; that a painting (on the Palestinian side of The Wall) by London's most famous graffiti artist, Banksy, is right there, next to the Qalandia checkpoint; that when it comes to our turn, our car (full of "internationals") is waved through the checkpoint, while there, just over there, long queues of Palestinians are made to walk through a series of turnstiles not unlike cattle chutes at abattoirs, in the land of their birth. Whatever the logic, this is not how people treat people: without respect, forget compassion.

"You have passports," our driver says, handing them back. "They have permits. You should know what that means," he says to me, holding out my passport, open on the first page: In the Name of the President. The president of the Republic of South Africa requests all whom it may concern to allow the bearer of this passport to pass freely without let or hindrance and to afford the bearer all necessary assistance and protection. "You all have passports and countries. They have nothing." When we stop, it's not for fuel or to wait for the other cars in our convoy. We stop because, well, we've arrived.

"In Ramallah?"

"Yes. This is Ramallah. Ahlan wa sahlan."

Water bottles are still mostly untouched, the water in them still cold. Geographically, we've travelled almost no distance at all—not even Johannesburg to Pretoria—but mentally, ideologically, politically, the journey through the Apartheid Wall into the occupied territory of the West Bank spans a galaxy. When I return to Ramallah from Jenin District two weeks later, a young Palestinian friend will tell me a story over beer and *nargile* (hookah). The story is set in a Ramallah wine bar down the road from the one we're in. It is compelling, punctuated with intriguing plot points and surprising twists. The ending is hilarious. When my laughter subsides, my host elaborates. Last December he told the same story in Milan to a group in which a young Israeli was present. When the story ended, all the Israeli asked was: "You can buy beer in Ramallah?"

My friend turns to me. "You've seen it for yourself now. This land is small. Palestinians and Israelis are not held separate by large open spaces. Tel Aviv is down the road. We live next to one another, like antagonistic neighbours. But we don't know one another. I can travel to Milan, Paris, Johannesburg tomorrow, just like that. But I can't go to Jerusalem, just over there." He shakes his head. "We don't know one another at all."

From Ramallah, our convoy heads north into deepest Palestine for our camp in Zababdeh, a small village outside Jenin. Here the economy is almost entirely agricultural with few of the economic cushions that bolster the more prosperous south. As we wind our air-conditioned way through a mountainous landscape entirely covered by olive trees cultivated on terraced slopes, I am aware of our Palestinian counterparts waiting to receive us at the camp. Many of them will have made this same journey, not like this, but through the back routes, avoiding areas from which their permits restrict them; avoiding Jerusalem, where most Palestinians cannot go; avoiding checkpoints, vulnerable to gangs of settlers vexed by the "Gaza withdrawal"; creeping, on tiptoe, through their own country.

The welcome is embracing, the camp a sanctuary, completely surrounded by olive groves. My mobile phone loses its signal.

Strangers become friends. The camp speaks like central London, in French, Arabic, Spanish, Italian, and English. It branches out into multilingual working groups to conduct field trips to decimated villages by day. By night, it shares stories over nargile pipes, beats derbouka drums, strums guitars, and dances Debke, Palestine's mesmerising traditional dance form and demonstration of resistance. Inside the camp, the cruel occupation is kept at bay. Goodbyes ten days later will be the saddest I've seen. Somewhere in the heat, perhaps while we wait together for no apparent reason at yet another choking checkpoint, somewhere on a farm cut through by the wall, maybe while we study the contemptuous military order—handwritten, left under stones or pinned to olive trees—dispossessing farmers of their land, somewhere along the path back to the camp when your footsteps fell in time with mine and you told me about your village, Beit Foureeq, where three villagers—twenty-three, sixty-five, and eighty—were killed by settlers during the olive harvest of October 2002, the eighty-year-old bludgeoned with a rock. How dare he harvest his own olives from his own tree on his own land? Somewhere in the back of a bus when you point to the serial number in your ID and say, "This means I can't go to Jerusalem. What's it like? I long to see it. Did you go to Al Aqsa?" Somewhere in the night, while we look up at the stars and you ask, "Can you spot the satellites?" Somewhere during the course of ten decisive days, friends become family. And Palestine personal.

In rural areas, "the barrier," as Israel prefers to call it, consists of an electrified fence—two, in fact—running along either side of a military buffer zone and bordered by razor wire. The fence, like the wall, is an excessive structure; it measures 250 meters from side to side. Paths of fine sand, regularly swept, run along the inside of the electrified fences to show trespassing footprints. Palestinian footprints trespassing on Palestinian sand. The consequences are as horrifying as the structure.

In Zboubah, 20 kilometers north of Jenin, more than 250 dunams of land were cleared in 2002 for wall construction and a military base on village land. Residents of Zboubah are exposed to continuous shooting from the military training camp, and raw sewage flows from the camp through the village. Seerees, 22 kilometers south of Jenin, has a population of 5,500 people. Villagers used to depend on work inside Israel but are no longer able to access their jobs because of the wall. As in other villages in the region, unemployment has soared to between 75 and 80 percent as a direct consequence of the wall. Nazlet Issa, 13 kilometers from Tulkarem, is a village of 3,000 people. The wall effectively divides this village in half, separating Palestinians from Palestinians. Nazlet Issa used to be an important trade center, but 400 shops were destroyed to build the wall. Villagers were not allowed to salvage their products, and the shops were levelled with the goods inside. The village has lost $15 million in trade since construction of the wall began. The local economy here lies in ruins. What security purpose does that serve? In Deir al-Ghsoun, a village of 10,000 people entirely reliant on agriculture, we are escorted along the path of the wall (whether fence or concrete, that is what Palestinians call it) by the chairperson of the local farmers, Mahmoud Abu Saa. "At least we can still see our land," he says, pointing to the other side. "In Qalqilya, they can't even do that."

Being able to see one's land on the other side of an electrified fence may bring some comfort, but it brings no income. Deir al-Ghsoun has traditionally relied on olive production, but the wall has taken 2,000 dunams, which has decimated the olive industry. One of the few remaining soap factories in Nablus, once a thriving industry in the city, imports the primary ingredient in the manufacture of soap—olive oil—from Italy. Palestine is covered in olive trees, but the dynamics of the occupation have rendered local supply unreliable.

In Deir al-Ghsoun 70 percent of villagers no longer have access to their land. Of the 194 members in the Deir al-Ghsoun Farmers Union, only 25 qualified for permits to access their land on the other side of the wall, the criteria for qualification set by Israel:

- The land should be in the name of the applicant. Sons who work the land for aged parents or grandparents do not qualify.
- Permits need to be renewed every two years but the majority are only issued for six months.
- If there is a "security situation" inside Israel, all permits are cancelled and applications start from scratch.

In March 2005, 1,050 farmers applied for permits in the village of Kafeen. Only sixty were granted. There is method to the bureaucratic madness:

land not cultivated for three years is viewed by Israel as surrendered, and is permanently seized. Watch the snaking, winding path of the wall. See the "fingers" that grab into the West Bank. Ask, What lies between the path of the wall and the internationally recognised Green Line from which it deviates, cutting deep into Palestinian territory? Land. Wells. Fertile.

As in other villages affected by the wall, unemployment in Deir al-Ghsoun has soared to an estimated 75 percent, and debts owed to the already cash-strapped local municipality have reached 1,800,000 New Israeli Shekels (NIS), nearly half a million dollars. And even as Israel withdraws from the Gaza Strip, there are plans for new settlements in Deir al-Ghsoun. An additional 1,600 dunams will be confiscated to build an Israeli-only road to serve the proposed new settlements. Withdrawal from Gaza is matched by new settlements in the West Bank.

Across the West Bank, the military occupation does not only touch every aspect of civilian life. It also exploits natural resources, especially water, penalising Palestinians and privileging settlers. It restricts Palestinians to digging wells between 150 and 180 meters. Settlers can dig as deep as they like. In Deir al-Ghsoun, one well now lies outside the wall, leaving farmers with only one viable well. The military visits this well every two to three months to measure usage. The thoroughfare of military vehicles frequently damages underground pipes, causing leaks. Israel puts a unilateral limit on amounts to be used—350,000 meters squared for the years 2004 and 2005. Settlers have no limit. When usage exceeds the stipulated amount, a more severe ration is imposed for the following year. In Deir al-Ghsoun the well for drinking water is no longer viable. Farmers are certain that usage will exceed the imposed limit, which means that in 2006 they will only be allowed 300,000 metres squared. This is not an endless religious conflict. It is an escalating humanitarian disaster.

A South African travelling in Palestine will immediately be struck by the genuine affection and high regard that the country enjoys in the eyes of Palestinians. Everywhere I go I encounter admiration and interest in South Africa's political procedures and a willingness to emulate its achievements. Palestinians draw comparisons between the permits they are forced to carry and the passbooks for which South Africa was notorious. They see similarities between the map of their shrinking terrain and the maps of South Africa's former Bantustans. These comparisons are not contrived: identity cards with serial numbers severely restrict the movement of people around the West Bank; drivers negotiate back routes to avoid checkpoints so that Palestinians are forced to creep around their own country; in the state of Israel itself, thirty-three separate pieces of legislation discriminate against Palestinians-Arab citizens of Israel.

When I met in Ramallah with Sisa Ncwana, South Africa's Diplomatic Representative to the Palestinian Authority, he asked me to say this to South Africans, wherever I have an audience: "Palestinians look to no country more than South Africa as an example of an amicable democratic settlement. They are keen to foster relations with South Africa and to build bridges between our two countries. The longer we ignore them, the sooner we will lose all credibility."

**Date: Thu, 25 Aug 2005 7:32:18 +100 (BST)**
**From: palestinejourney@yahoo.co.uk**
**To: South Africa**

Time to leave. I woke this morning dreading the border. I have had to scratch through my bag, looking for . . . for what, exactly? For things that will be confiscated at the border. My notebook, my words, photographs, Israeli military orders confiscating Palestinian land, Palestinian permits, all need to be sent by courier to London. I have also been told to delete the details of all Palestinians I have met from my mobile phone. The indignity feels like a betrayal. Why? Because in a few hours I will be passing through not an Afghan border, not an Iraqi border, but an Israeli one.

I am tired. So is language. The occupation—an inadequate word, a static word—the Strangulation is suffocating. Its relentless grinding dynamics are no less than protracted, indiscriminate psychological warfare on an entire civilian population. Yet I have only had to negotiate it for three weeks. Palestinians my age know nothing else. When you come, you will find phenomenal hospitality, laughter, and cheer in private homes. But see those same Palestinians when you approach a checkpoint. Watch them as the officials tap pockets searching for permits. Look especially to their eyes. And tell me what you see.

Tonight I will be back in mountainous Amman. It's only down the road. But it seems very, very far away. I will dump my bag at the hostel and walk to the Roman Amphitheatre. The stars seemed nice there. Real stars. Not Israeli satellites. Then I will board a plane for Heathrow. While Miriam (not her real name) boards a coach to Qalqilya. I imagined Qalqilya in

India when I was writing *The Silent Minaret*. But the reality of Qalqilya? I could never have imagined that. And now this is how it ends, me to London then Johannesburg, Miriam to "normalcy" in Qalqilya, where 41,600 people are cut off behind 38 kilometres of wall, concrete in the west, fence in the east, and with only one entrance and exit. Try to imagine just this one thing—the congestion. And now that it is complete, the wall reveals its consequences with every passing day, every passing season. In February of this year, as *The Silent Minaret* was receiving praise, Qalqilya was flooded—in Palestine's macabre carnival, The Wall also masquerades as a dam. After just a few hours of heavy winter rain, the water level reached three metres beside the wall, almost half its eight-meter height. Schools were disrupted, poultry farms destroyed, and greenhouse crops ruined. Israeli soldiers in the towers that punctuate the wall saw the rising water but, despite pleas from municipal officials, refused to open the eastern gate for the water to drain. By the time the gate was opened twenty-four hours later, the damage—five million NIS and forty-five flooded farms—had been done.

"Travel safely, Ishtiyaq," Miriam says to me.

"You too," I say, knowing that safety needs to fold its arms more tightly around her than me.

"Have a nice time," she says, "In London. And South Africa."

"You too," I echo, wondering how one would manage to do that in Qalqilya.

Chapter 2

# Israel, the Apartheid Analogy, and the Labor Question

Ran Greenstein

W hy engage in a comparison of Israel/Palestine and apartheid South Africa? In principle, any society can be compared to any other society, but these two countries share features that make the comparison particularly interesting. Both came into being in the course of conflict between indigenous people and settler immigrants. The process of settlement took place as part of the overall expansion of European political and economic domination over the globe, albeit at different historical periods. The majority of settlers, especially in Israel/Palestine, did not come from the ranks of the principal colonizing power, the British Empire. In this sense, both processes were instances of surrogate colonization.

Perhaps of most significance is that in both places indigenous people never ceased to pose a challenge to settler domination. In many colonies the indigenous population was wiped out almost completely (the Caribbean, North America, and Australia) or merged to varying degrees with settlers (Central and South America). In other places, European powers conquered overseas territories but later withdrew without leaving behind permanent populations: the French in Algeria and Indochina, for example, and the Portuguese in southern Africa. Only in few places did the conflict continue as intensely as ever beyond the historical moment of global decolonization that started in the late 1940s. The originating violence that generally marks the foundation of new states and nations repeats itself on a daily basis in Israel/Palestine, but less so in South Africa since 1968, even if the demise of political apartheid has not led to a reduction of social inequalities.

Against this background of similarities there are also differences. I focus here on one issue that serves to set the two cases apart: the labor question. This refers both to labor's crucial role in molding the respective social orders and in shaping possibilities of resistance. The focus on labor is particularly necessary in view of the exclusive concern with political and legal issues in much of the comparative literature. A sociological approach can enhance our understanding of the operation of underlying and more profound social forces beyond obvious but superficial political and diplomatic events. We need to add this dimension to the analysis.

In conducting this comparison, we have to distinguish between two questions: 1) Is the notion of apartheid, which seems unique to South Africa, applicable to Israel/Palestine? and 2) Does the comparison between Israeli/Palestinian and South African societies help us to understand them better?

The first question prompts us to engage international law while the second leads us to examine social and political developments in South Africa and Israel/Palestine against each other, make sense of their evolution, outline their similarities and differences, and draw analytical and practical-political conclusions. It is this latter task that is the focus of this chapter.

## What Is Apartheid?

What precisely is apartheid? The answer seems simple: a system of political exclusion and domination that was in place in South Africa from 1948 to 1994. The apartheid era centered on attempts to impose legal, social, and geographical distinctions between people on the basis of race. At the same time, state policy sought to ensure that Black people continued to work for and serve white people, a principle that shaped the white-dominated economy and society for centuries of South African history.

Two major attempts have been made to expand the notion of apartheid beyond South African boundaries, with the International Convention on the Suppression and Punishment of the Crime of Apartheid, adopted by the UN General Assembly in 1973; and the Rome Statute of the International Criminal Court, which dates to 2002. The 1973 International Convention regards apartheid as "a crime against humanity" and a violation of international law. Apartheid is defined as "similar policies and practices of racial segregation and discrimination as practised in southern Africa . . .

committed for the purpose of establishing and maintaining domination by one racial group of persons over any other racial group of persons and systematically oppressing them."[1]

A long list of such practices ensues, including measures to prevent a racial group from "participation in the political, social, economic and cultural life of the country" and creation of conditions that prevent full development "by denying to members of a racial group or groups basic human rights and freedoms, including the right to work, the right to form recognized trade unions, the right to education, the right to leave and to return to their country, the right to a nationality, the right to freedom of movement and residence, the right to freedom of opinion and expression, and the right to freedom of peaceful assembly and association."[2] This includes policies "designed to divide the population along racial lines by the creation of separate reserves and ghettos for the members of a racial group or groups, the prohibition of mixed marriages among members of various racial groups, the expropriation of landed property belonging to a racial group or groups or to members thereof."[3]

This definition draws on apartheid in South Africa but cannot be reduced to it. A further step away from that historical case was taken with the Rome Statute of the International Criminal Court, which omitted all references to South Africa in its definition of "the crime of apartheid."[4] In its Article 7, addressing crimes against humanity, the Rome Statute defines the crime of apartheid as inhumane acts committed in the context of "an institutionalized regime of systematic oppression and domination by one racial group over any other racial group or groups and committed with the intention of maintaining that regime."[5] These acts include "deportation or forcible transfer of population" and "persecution against any identifiable group or collectivity on political, racial, national, ethnic, cultural, religious, gender . . . or other grounds that are universally recognized as impermissible under international law."[6] Persecution, in turn, is defined as "intentional and severe deprivation of fundamental rights contrary to international law by reason of the identity of the group or collectivity."[7]

With the passage of time and the unfolding transformation of South Africa, apartheid is becoming a more legal and less descriptive term. While its association with South Africa remains strong, it has acquired a general meaning of systematic oppression and discrimination on the basis of origins. It is premature to delink it from its historical foundations, however. In the minds of many people, it continues to evoke a specific system rather than an abstract concept. For this reason, the best comparative strategy would pursue two tracks simultaneously: examine Israeli social practices by comparing them to their South African equivalents (and vice versa) and examine independently the applicability of international law to these practices.

If we use the international legal definition of apartheid, we do not need to retain a focus on South African racial policies and practices. And yet it would be useful to keep a focus on comparing South Africa and Israel, in order to highlight crucial features of Israeli/Palestinian history. We must keep in mind that the point of a comparative analysis is *not* to provide a list of similarities and differences for its own sake, but to use one case in order to reflect critically on the other and thus learn more about both.

Back in the 1960s, the South African Communist Party coined the term *colonialism of a special type* to refer to a system that combined the colonial legacies of racial discrimination, political exclusion, and socioeconomic inequalities with political independence from the British Empire. It used this novel concept to devise a strategy for political change that treated local whites as potential allies rather than as colonial invaders to be removed from the territory. Making analytical sense of apartheid in South Africa was relatively straightforward, since it was an integrated system of legal-political control. Different laws applied to different groups of people, but the source of authority was clear.

Making sense of the way apartheid as a legal concept may apply in Israel/Palestine is more complex. The degree of legal-political differentiation is greater, as it includes an array of military regulations in the 1967 occupied territories and policies delegating powers and resources to nonstate institutions (the Jewish Agency, Jewish National Fund) that act on behalf of the state but are not open to public scrutiny. That much of the legal apparatus applies beyond Israeli boundaries—to all Jews, regarded as potential citizens, and to all Palestinians, regarded as prohibited persons—adds another dimension to the analysis. For this reason, we may talk about "apartheid of a special type"—a regime combining democratic norms, military rule, and exclusion or inclusion of extraterritorial populations.

What are some of the characteristics of this regime?

- It is based on an ethnonational distinction between Jewish insiders and Palestinian Arab outsiders. This distinction has a religious dimension—you can join the Jewish group only through conversion—but is not affected by the degree of religious adherence.

- It uses this distinction to expand citizenship beyond its territory, potentially to all Jews, and to contract citizenship within it: Palestinians in the occupied territories cannot become Israeli citizens. Israel is open to all nonresident members of one ethnonational group, wherever they are and regardless of personal history and links to the territory. It is closed to all nonresident members of the other ethnonational group, wherever they are and regardless of personal history and links to the territory.

- It is based on the permanent blurring of physical boundaries. At no point in its sixty-seven years of existence has its boundaries been fixed by law, nor are they likely to become fixed in the foreseeable future. They are thus permanently temporary, porous in one direction, through expansion of military and civilian forces into neighboring territories, and impermeable in another direction: severe restrictions or prohibition on entry of Palestinians from the occupied territories and the diaspora into its territories.

- It combines different modes of rule: formal democratic institutions to the west of the Green Line and military authority with no democratic pretensions across it. In times of crisis, the military mode of rule tends to spill over the Green Line to apply to Palestinian citizens of Israel. At all times, civilian rule spills over the Green Line to apply to Jewish settlers (in the West Bank). The distinction between the two sides of the line is constantly eroding as a result, and norms and practices developed under the occupation filter back into Israel—as the phrase goes, the "Jewish democratic state" is "democratic" for Jews and "Jewish" for Arabs.

- It is in fact a "Jewish-demographic state." Demography— the fear that Jews may become a minority—is a prime concern behind the policies of mainstream forces. All state structures, policies, and efforts aim to meet the concern for a permanent Jewish majority exercising domination in the state of Israel.

How do these features compare with historical South African apartheid?

- The foundation of apartheid was a racial distinction between whites and Blacks (further divided into Coloureds, Indians, and Africans, with the latter subdivided into ethnic groups), rather than an ethnonational distinction. Racial groups were internally divided on the basis of language, religion, and ethnic origins and externally linked in various ways across the color line. This can be contrasted with Israel/Palestine, in which lines of division usually overlap: potential bases for cross-cutting affiliations existed early on—Arabic-speaking Jews in the region, indigenous Palestinian Jewish communities—but were undermined by the simultaneous rise of the Zionist movement and Arab nationalism in the twentieth century.

- In South Africa then, there was a contradiction between the organization of the state around the single axis of race and a social reality that allowed for some diversity in practice and multiple lines of division as well as cooperation. This opened up opportunities for change. The state endeavored to eliminate this contradiction by entrenching residential, educational, religious, and cultural segregation, but its capacity was limited and eroded over time. In Israel/Palestine there is tighter fit between the organization of the state and social reality, with one exception: Palestinian citizens are positioned between Jewish citizens and Palestinian noncitizens. They are the only population segment that is fully bilingual, familiar with political and cultural contexts across the ethnic divide. They have enough freedom to organize but not enough rights to support the oppressive status quo. They may thus act as crucial catalysts for change.

- A key goal of the apartheid state was to ensure that Black people performed their role as providers of labor without presenting difficult social and political challenges. The strategy for that focused on externalizing them. They were physically present in white homes, factories, farms, and service industries but were absent, politically and legally, as rights-bearing citizens. Those no longer or not yet functional for white employers were prevented from living in the urban areas: children, women—especially mothers—and old people. Able-bodied Blacks working in the cities were supposed to commute—daily, monthly, or annually, depending on the distance—between the places where they had jobs but no political rights and places where they had political rights but no jobs.

- This system of migrant labor opened up a contradiction between political and economic imperatives. It broke down families and the social order, hampered efforts to create a skilled labor force, reduced productivity, and gave rise to crime and social protest. The effort to control people's movements created a bloated and expensive repressive apparatus, which put a constant burden on resources and capacities. Domestic and industrial employers faced increasing difficulties in meeting their labor needs. It went from an economic asset (for white people) to a liability. It simply had to go.

- The economic imperative of the Israeli system, in contrast, has been to create employment for Jewish immigrants. Palestinian labor was used by certain groups at certain times because it was available and convenient, but it was never central to Jewish prosperity in Israel. After the outbreak of the first intifada in the late 1980s, and under conditions of globalization, it could easily be replaced by politically unproblematic foreign workers. A massive wave of Russian Jewish immigration in the 1990s helped this process. The externalization of Palestinians, through denial of rights, ethnic cleansing, and *hafrada* (Hebrew for "separation"), has presented limited economic problems for Israeli Jews. Its impact will not undermine Israeli apartheid as it did apartheid in South Africa.

- Apartheid was last in a series of regimes in which European settlers dominated indigenous Black people in South Africa. People of European origins were a minority, relying on military force, technology, and divide-and-conquer strategies to entrench their rule. Demography was not a major concern as long as security of person, property, and investment could be guaranteed. When repression proved counterproductive, a deal exchanging political power for ongoing prosperity became acceptable to the majority of whites. Israeli Jews, for whom a demographic majority is seen as the guarantee of political survival on their own terms, are not likely to accept a similar deal.

In summary then, Israel's "apartheid of a special type" is different from apartheid in South Africa in three major respects:

- At its foundation are consolidated and relatively impermeable ethnonational identities, with few crosscutting affiliations across the principal ethnic divide in society.

- It is relatively free of economic imperatives that run counter to its overall exclusionary thrust, because it is not dependent on the exploitation of indigenous labor.

- Its main quest is for demographic majority as the basis for legal, military, and political domination.

How can we account for these three points of difference? To answer that, we have to examine them from a historical perspective, with a focus on patterns of settlement and resistance during the colonial period.

## Israel/Palestine: The Dynamics of Exclusion

By the time the state of Israel was established in 1948, Mandate Palestine had been transformed over the preceding decades from a predominantly rural society, where people engaged in agricultural production for subsistence and to some extent for the local markets, into a much more urbanized and industrialized society. This process was initiated by indigenous social forces—merchants, landlords, and peasants—who took advantage of opportunities created by Palestine's greater integration into the world market since the mid-nineteenth century. Economic development was further accelerated under the impact of Zionist settlement, which attracted into the country large amounts of capital, advanced technology, and production methods as well as many skilled immigrants.

By increasing internal inequalities, this pattern of economic growth proved a mixed blessing for the indigenous Arab population. A minority managed to prosper as a result of commodification of land, growing commercialization of production, and the creation of large urban markets for agricultural goods. The majority, however, became less secure in their position as the impact of these same processes undermined social stability and made their hold on the land more tenuous. Despite these disruptive forces, throughout the pre-1948 period Palestinians retained control over most of the productive land in the country *as a community* and did not fall under the domination of settlers. Although many lost their land *as individuals*, only a small percentage were engaged in the service of settlers. The rest were largely self-employed (primarily on the land) or employed by other Palestinians as well as by state and international companies.

The capacity before 1948 of Palestinians to hold their ground; retain access to land, labor, and capital; and participate in economic development on relatively solid foundations was a major reason for the exclusionary direction taken by class relations. It coincided with the dominant settler strategy of building a self-sufficient economic sector that would not be dependent on the indigenous labor force and would provide for minimal contact between the two ethnonational communities. This exclusionary trend was facilitated by the British authorities, which made little effort to encourage intercommunal relations. Communal disengagement was never complete, but the overall tendency was toward ever greater separation between Jews and Arabs, to the point that in 1947 the UN Special Committee on Palestine (UNSCOP) likened the relations between the communities to trade between nations.

The same period saw the consolidation of mutually exclusive national identities, Palestinian-Arab and Israeli-Jewish, and corresponding sets of separate political institutions. Arabs and Jews became distinct from each other in terms of language, history, religion, and ethnic identity. They entered the period with few overlapping affiliations, and, in the course of their encounters, even the little they had had in common did not survive. The local Jewish community, which had shared some cultural characteristics with indigenous Arabs (such as language and residential patterns), diminished numerically and was marginalized politically. Affiliation to external foci of identity—the Arab nation and Islamic world and the worldwide Jewish people, respectively—reinforced their separation.

When the final clash of 1947–1948 broke out, two distinct groups, which had established their own systems of class relations, national identities, and political institutions, confronted one another. The coherence and capacity of Zionist-led structures and their degree of organization were far higher than their Palestinian equivalents, and, as a result, they emerged victorious from the conflict. In the process of consolidating their control, they evicted hundreds of thousands of Palestinians from the territories that became the state of Israel and prevented those who fled under duress, or were expelled, from returning to their homes (a process known as the *Nakba*).

Emptying the territory of 80 percent of its indigenous residents left a huge gap, geographically and socially, that was filled in the early 1950s by Jewish immigrants from Eastern Europe, the Middle East, and North Africa. Palestinian workers had been marginal to the Jewish economy before 1948 and were not missed as a source of labor. On the contrary, their displacement was deemed beneficial, perhaps essential, for a successful absorption of immigrants, who were (re)settled by the state onto land that had belonged to Palestinians. A new Jewish working class thus developed, consisting of immigrants who moved into recently vacated neighborhoods in the big cities (Jaffa, Haifa, Jerusalem), depopulated towns (such as Ramle, Lydda/Lod, Beersheba, and Beisan), and newly established "development towns," formed in areas where many Palestinian communities used to live or along the borders.

With the 1948 *Nakba*, the majority of Palestinians found themselves excluded from participation in Israeli social and economic structures, either because their areas fell under Arab foreign rule (Jordan in the West Bank and Egypt in Gaza) or because they became refugees in other Arab countries. Only a minority of 15 percent became citizens of Israel. After an initial period of military closure and restrictions on movement and employment, from the late 1950s Palestinian Israelis started joining the labor force in growing numbers but never reached the central position occupied by Black workers in the white-dominated economy in South Africa. They remained a minority, geographically marginal, largely employed in nonstrategic industries (agriculture, construction), with limited capacity to defend their own interests, let along bring about change in the society at large.

The 1967 War and the subsequent occupation reestablished unified rule over the entire country. But, unlike Palestinians under Israeli rule since 1948, who were granted citizenship as a small and subordinated minority, Arab residents of the West Bank and Gaza remain without basic social and political rights to this day. For a period of twenty years, they were employed in the lowest-paid positions in the labor market, commuting between their homes and workplaces. Like Palestinian citizens before them, they were restricted to agriculture, construction, and sanitation, while more lucrative positions in industry and services remained in the hands of Jewish workers. An ethnic hierarchy saw Ashkenazi Jews at the top, followed by Mizrahim, then Palestinian citizens, and occupied Palestinians at the bottom. Unlike in South Africa, Jewish settlers remained the largest segment of the working class as well as those best positioned strategically to fight for rights and resources.

In other words, Palestinian workers after 1967 were visible and important in some sectors, but they never became central to the Israeli labor market as a whole. With the uprising of 1987—the first intifada—followed by the Gulf War of 1991 and the Oslo process, even that limited role as suppliers of labor was curtailed. Frequent military closures imposed on the occupied territories, and the growing integration of the Israeli economy into global markets, encouraged the replacement of Palestinian laborers with foreign workers (from Eastern Europe and Southeast Asia in particular). Over the last twenty-five years, the role of Palestinian labor declined to such an extent that it practically disappeared from the Israeli scene in economic or political terms.

Beyond the obvious economic implications, this state of affairs has had an impact on resistance politics as well: the central role played by the labor movement in the struggle against apartheid in South Africa cannot be replicated in Israel/Palestine. Palestinian workers do not possess the crucial strategic leverage deployed by their South African counterparts. The link between race and class shaped Black politics for decades and provided the social foundation for the alliance between the main liberation movement (African National Congress [ANC]), Black-led trade unions (South African Congress of Trade Unions, Congress of South African Trade Unions), and the Communist Party. We cannot imagine opposition to apartheid without it. And yet, apartheid of a special type in Israel/Palestine has experienced nothing like that, nor is it likely to in the future. Why has South Africa moved in a different direction?

## South Africa: The Dynamics of Incorporation

Contemporary South Africa is the product of a long history that saw groups of imperial powers and settlers (the Dutch East India Company, the British Empire, Afrikaner and English settlers, missionaries, farming and mining capitalists), collaborate and compete over the control of indigenous groups, themselves divided by language, religion, political affiliation, territory, and social conditions. A prolonged period of expansion, stretching over 250 years from the mid–seventeenth century to the late nineteenth century, witnessed many micro-level interactions between these forces and created a multilayered system of domination, collaboration, and resistance. Numerous political entities—British colonies, Boer republics, independent African kingdoms, autonomous missionary territories—emerged as a result, accompanied by different social relations, including slavery, indentured labor, communal production, various forms of land and labor tenancy, sharecropping, and wage labor.

By the late nineteenth century, a more systematic approach had begun to crystallize. It was used to streamline the preexisting multiplicity of conditions and policies into a more uniform mode of control. Between 1903 and 1979, a series of official commissions of inquiry, focusing on the "native question," proposed policies to improve control and stabilize white rule. Apartheid was one link in that chain, seeking to close existing loopholes and entrench white domination while continuing to use Black labor as the economic foundation of the system. Even under apartheid, the rhetoric about segregation and separation could not disguise the need for using Black workers not only on farms and mines but also, increasingly, in industry and services as well.

During the same period, the nature of resistance changed as well, from attempts to ward off settler attacks and retain or regain independence in the nineteenth century to a struggle for incorporation on an equal basis in the Union of South Africa that came into being in 1910. The ANC, formed in 1912, became the most important movement to pursue that goal. Since the 1930s most Black political movements aimed to take over and transform the existing state rather than create their own independent institutions and state structures. National liberation was defined as the key goal, but it was seen largely as a way to allow Black people to access their birthright on an equal basis in their homeland rather than return to a real or imaginary free and unified precolonial past.

By the late 1970s, it had become clear to white business and political leaders that apartheid was counterproductive to ensuring white prosperity. The system began to crack because it was too costly and cumbersome and increasingly irrational from an economic point of view: it hampered the creation of an internal market and prevented a shift to a technology-oriented growth strategy. The resistance movement that grew in strength after the 1976 Soweto uprising, combined with international pressure and increasing stress on the state's resources, gave the final push toward a negotiated settlement. That settlement took the form of a unified political framework, within which numerous social struggles continue to unfold.

It is important to realize that the South African postapartheid state, which grants equal rights to all citizens, was made possible by specific historical circumstances outlined above: a diversity of groups brought together in a long process that involved a multiplicity of local circumstances and interactions. This was accompanied by the formation of intimate—but highly unequal—relations between racial groups through the employment of Black laborers in the white-dominated economy as well as domestic and childcare workers in most white households. It is this "insider" position that allowed Black South Africans to organize in order to change the system from within, an option not open to the bulk of Palestinians.

## Why Are These Differences Important?

Given these different histories, the South African "rainbow nation," based on the multiplicity of identities and the absence of a single axis of division to bring them all together and bind them—*unity in diversity*—is unlikely to be followed as a model in Israel/Palestine. Elements such as the mutual dependency between white business and Black labor; the shared use by all groups of the English language as the medium of political communication, business, and higher education; and Christianity as a religious umbrella for the majority of people from all racial groups do not exist in Israel/Palestine. These features emerged in South Africa through a long process of territorial expansion, conquest of indigenous people, and their incorporation as "hewers of wood and drawers of water" in the growing economy. They cannot be created from scratch by using attractive slogans that are not historically grounded.

This difference aside, if we consider pre-1967 Israel in isolation, some elements similar to the South African experience can be identified. People of all backgrounds—Ashkenazi and Mizrahi Jews, Russian and Ethiopian immigrants, and Palestinian citizens—use Hebrew in their daily interactions and share similar social and cultural tastes. In mixed towns, such as Haifa, Jaffa, and Acre, neighborhoods exist in which Jews and Arabs live together with little to distinguish their lifestyles except for their home language. One does not have to idealize the situation to recognize that these

people have much more in common with one another than white subur-
banites have with rural Black South Africans, during apartheid or today.

Politically, this means a focus on working for a "one-state solution"
within pre-1967 Israel's borders as a state for all its citizens, at least in the
immediate-to-medium term: not an easy task in light of recent right-wing
campaigns to enhance the Jewish character of the state and the return, in
the 2015 elections, of the hard right to power, possibly in an ever harsher
form. This means a need to campaign for making Israel a proper democratic state in which ethnoreligious affiliation confers no political privileges. Can the antiapartheid movement in South Africa provide lessons
for the struggle to democratize Israel, terminate the occupation, and extend equal rights to all Israelis and Palestinians?

Yes, it can, provided we understand the core strength of the movement:
its grounding in local conditions and reliance on mass mobilization in the
streets, factories, schools, townships, and communities. The ability to generate support overseas was based on the movement's widely recognized
claim to represent the masses and lead them in struggle, above all through
the trade union movement and the United Democratic Front, which
brought together hundreds of community organizations, unions, women
and student constituencies, progressive religious movements, white draft
resisters, and so on. The slogan "one person, one vote" provided a banner
behind which people inside and outside the country could march together.

The Palestinian solidarity movement sets out to replicate the achievements of the antiapartheid struggle but with no equivalent mass movement that seeks to mobilize people on the basis of labor conditions and
socioeconomic demands. In a sense, it acts as if the cart could pull the
proverbial horse. Activists must consider the implications of the absence
of a grounded mass movement in Israel when aiming to build on the South
African experience. The key difference between the South African apartheid regime, with its massive dependence on Black labor power, and the Israeli regime, which has relied historically on the labor power of immigrant
Jews, is behind this contrast. Labor exploitation in South Africa led to the
creation of a mass movement of workers and township residents, willing
and able to overturn the apartheid regime from within, while Palestinians
have been restricted to a large extent to struggling against the oppressive
regime from the outside. Uplifting slogans that assert the similarity of
conditions and strategies between the two cases cannot disguise this deep

sociopolitical difference.

Identifying Israel as an apartheid regime (of a special type) is just the beginning of the task, then. It is not a substitute for an analysis of the specific features of the regime, its strong and vulnerable spots, its allies and opponents. Strategies used successfully in South Africa may be relevant to struggles in Israel/Palestine only if they can be adjusted to the different context. Perhaps the most important lesson of the South African movement is its originality, having worked with no preconceived models in order to develop a unique combination of passive resistance, mass defiance, marches, popular mobilization, and militant tactics, seeking to involve different segments of the population based on their concrete needs and demands. What activists should emulate then, is this creative attitude rather than any fixed set of tactics (such as boycott, divestment, and sanctions), regardless of the historical background and current circumstances.

Without offering any ready-made recipes for action (they do not exist), it is safe to say that three broad principles can guide the re-examination of political strategies today: the need for internal unity among Palestinians on each side of the Green Line, and between both sides, based on mass action; the need to use such action as a foundation for work with marginalized Israeli-Jewish constituencies to address their own social concerns; and the need for global solidarity efforts. How to translate these principles into concrete strategy will remain the task of scholars and activists on all sides.

## Chapter 3

# Solidarity with Palestine
## Confronting the "Whataboutery" Argument and the Bantustan Denouement

### Salim Vally

The Palestinian struggle does not only exert a visceral tug on many around the world. A reading of imperialism shows that apartheid Israel is needed as a militarized state not only to quell the undefeated Palestinians but also as a rapid response unit (in concert with despotic Arab regimes) to do the Empire's bidding in the Middle East and beyond.

Over the years this has included support for the mass terror waged against the people of Central and South America and facilitation of the evasion of international sanctions against South Africa. Throughout the apartheid years in South Africa, there were individuals and groups who identified and stood in solidarity with the Palestinian people and their struggle for freedom. The Palestine Liberation Organization (PLO) became a symbol of resistance for most South Africans. South Africans struggling against apartheid policies and realities agreed with apartheid prime minister Hendrik Verwoerd back in 1961 when he stated, approvingly in his context, that "Israel like South Africa is an apartheid state."[1] Unlike Verwoerd, they considered this a violent abuse of human rights rather than a reason to praise Israel. In 1976, a watershed year in the resistance against apartheid, then prime minister John Vorster was invited to Israel and received with open arms by the likes of Yitzhak Rabin and Shimon Peres.

In addition to identifying with the struggle of Palestinians, South Africans also recognized that Israel was playing a role in their own oppression.

For instance, Israel was an important arms supplier to apartheid South Africa despite the international arms embargo, and, as late as 1980, 35 percent of Israel's arms exports were destined for South Africa. Israel was loyal to the racist state and clung to the friendship when almost all other relationships with South Africa had dissolved. During the 1970s, this affiliation extended into the field of nuclear weaponry, when Israeli experts helped South Africa develop at least six nuclear warheads. In the 1980s, when the global antiapartheid movement had forced many states to impose sanctions on the apartheid regime, Israel imported South African goods and reexported them to the world in a form of inter-racist solidarity. Israeli companies, subsidized by the South African regime despite the pittance they paid workers, were established in a number of Bantustans.

Today, besides providing a ready supply of mercenaries to terrorize a populace—whether in Guatemala, Iraq, or New Orleans—Israel also trains police forces and military personnel around the world, lending its expertise in collective punishment and terror. For instance, at least two of the four law enforcement agencies that were deployed in Ferguson, Missouri, after the killing of eighteen-year-old Michael Brown in August 2014—the St. Louis County Police Department and the St. Louis Police Department—had received training from Israeli security forces in recent years.

We have to recognize that the Israeli economy was founded on the special political and military role that Zionism then and today fulfills for Western imperialism. While playing its role to ensure that the region is safe for oil companies, today it has also carved out a niche market producing high-tech security essential to the day-to-day functioning of New Imperialism. The weaponry and technology the Israeli military-industrial complex exports around the world are field-tested on the bodies of Palestinian men, women, and children.

## The "Whataboutery" Argument, Revisited

In attempting to isolate the erstwhile South African apartheid regime, we were confronted with responses by apartheid apologists that often ended with diversionary questions, such as "What about Pol Pot?" or "What about Idi Amin?" Once again, supporters of Israel and unfortunately even well-meaning liberals voice similar evasive sentiments, including the indignant cousin of "Whataboutery," the complaint "Why single out Israel?"

Over the years the countries and groups invoked by the "whatabout" critics included Sudan, Iran, Syria, Boko Haram, and now ISIS, or the "Islamic State" group. Sudan was bombed and stiff sanctions implemented; Iran has been under sanctions since 1979, Syria since 2003; atavistic groups such as Boko Haram and ISIS are actively hunted by the United States and other Western powers. Ilan Pappé put it succinctly: "There are horrific cases where dehumanization has reaped unimaginable horrors. But there is a crucial difference between these cases and Israel's brutality: the former are condemned as barbarous and inhuman worldwide, while those committed by Israel are still publicly licensed and approved by Western governments."[2]

So the supporters of Israel miss the point. The Israeli regime is of course not the only one worthy of opprobrium and censure, but in the past it would have been absurd and foolhardy to have a boycott, divestment, and sanctions (BDS) strategy against the genocidal and isolationist Pol Pot regime or today against the horrific Boko Haram or ISIS. BDS is not a universally appropriate strategy—it is a particular tactic chosen because of its potential effectiveness in a particular situation. As the writer and journalist Mike Marqusee explains: "Arguing that one should ignore this specific call for BDS [against Israel] because it is not simultaneously aimed at all oppressive regimes is like arguing you should cross a picket line because the union in dispute is not simultaneously picketing all other bad employers."[3]

The demand of the BDS campaign is not that Israel should be better than other countries, but that it should adhere to the very modest minimum standards of human rights and international law. It is an attempt to end the impunity given to Israel. In fact, Israel is singled out by Western powers for special treatment. The United States provides Israel with massive aid, including military support as well as diplomatic and political cover. The European Union provides preferential trade agreements and even the football body FIFA treats Israel as if it were a European country. The material support the Israeli state has received has not tempered its crimes but has instead made it more vicious. It should be seen in all its nakedness as a pariah state like Israel's dear and unlamented former friend, apartheid South Africa.

## Lessons from the Campaign to Isolate Apartheid South Africa

It will be helpful to draw activists' attention to some of the lessons from the campaign to isolate apartheid South Africa.

First, it took a few decades of hard work before the boycott and sanctions campaign made an impact. Despite the impression given by many government leaders that they supported the isolation of the apartheid state from the outset, this is just not true. Besides the infamous words of Dick Cheney, when as a US senator he called for the continued incarceration of Nelson Mandela because he was a "terrorist," and the support given by US president Reagan and British prime minister Thatcher (together with Pinochet's Chile, Israel, and others), most multilateral organizations and even unions were hesitant for many years to fully support the campaign. The antiapartheid movement (AAM) was formed in 1959 and the first significant breakthrough came in 1963, when Danish dock workers refused to off-load South African goods.

The rise of the AAM must be seen in the general effervescence of liberation struggles and social movements in the turbulent 1960s/early 1970s and in the context of, whatever our opinion was of the USSR and its motivations, a counterweight to the US hegemon. The post-9/11 climate of fear, silencing of dissent, and Islamophobia (together with the viciousness of the pro-Israeli lobby and its opportunistic references to the Holocaust and anti-Semitism) makes the task of isolating apartheid Israel more difficult. Despite these seemingly daunting obstacles, the BDS movement against Israel is gaining momentum, and already some significant gains have been made, gains that would have been difficult to imagine just a few years ago.

Second, opposition to the boycott based on the harm it would allegedly cause Black South Africans was easily rebuffed by lucid and knowledgeable arguments. The disingenuous argument that Black workers in South Africa would be harmed by sanctions was given short shrift by the democratic movement, which argued that if sanctions hastened the end of apartheid then any short-term difficulties would be welcomed. The Israeli economy depends even less on Palestinian labor than the South African economy depended on Black South Africans, so the argument that "Palestinians will also suffer" from a BDS campaign is just not true. The South African regime, like the Israeli regime today, used Bantustan leaders and an assortment of collaborators to argue the case for them. Careful research played an important role in exposing the economic, cultural, and armaments trade links with South Africa to make our actions more effective as well as to "name and shame" those who benefited from the apartheid regime.

Third, sectarianism is a danger about which we must be vigilant, and principled unity must be our lodestar. Some in the AAM favored supporting only one liberation movement—the African National Congress (ANC)—as the authentic voice of the oppressed in South Africa. They also aspired to work largely with "respectable" organizations, governments, and multilateral organizations and shunned the much harder and patient linking of struggles with grassroots organizations. During the South African antiapartheid struggle, sectarian attitudes resulted in debilitating splits. In England, for instance, the London chapter of the AAM (the biggest in the country), which supported the anti-imperialist struggle in Ireland and was part of the "Troops Out" movement, was ostracized by the official AAM. The latter was also keen not to annoy the British government by taking a stronger stance against racism in Britain. At a huge Palestinian solidarity rally in South Africa, members of the Palestinian Solidarity Campaign were asked by officials from the Palestinian ambassador's office to pull down the flag of the Western Sahara Republic because they feared this would alienate the ambassador of Morocco. We refused this request. Similarly, Palestinian solidarity must take a stand against oppression in all its forms and, as far as possible, be active in solidarity with other struggles, locally and globally.

Fourth, we should actively oppose any sign of anti-Semitism, whether overt or covert, and its manifestations should be challenged immediately. Utmost vigilance around this is necessary. There have been attempts by agents provocateurs to encourage and bait people so that the charge of anti-Semitism could be used to discredit our movement. These instances should be studied and the culprits exposed. We remain fully cognizant, of course, that the canard of "anti-Semitism" is used opportunistically by the supporters of Israel against anyone opposed to Israel's policies.

Fifth, the BDS campaign must develop in concert with supporting grassroots organizations in Palestine as a whole and in the Palestinian diaspora. This can take many forms and shapes, including "twinning" arrangements, speaking tours, targeted actions in support of specific struggles, and concrete support.

Finally, the sanctions campaign in South Africa did produce gatekeepers, sectarians, and commissars, but, as Shireen Hassim observes in her contribution to this book (chapter 10), they were also challenged.

**Bantustans Redux**

Palestinian solidarity movements in South Africa as elsewhere are confronted with the mantra of the "two-state" denouement, which allows
various politicians to conveniently portray themselves as even-handed in
their call for "two states for two people, living in peace side by side" without interrogating the nature of the Palestinian state on offer or questioning the Israeli state's deliberate stalling as it expropriates more land. In his
book *Overcoming Zionism*, Joel Kovel argues that Zionism continues the
two-state façade while reserving for itself the intention of total expropriation. So the two-state notion is essentially a code word for the maintenance of the status quo for the Israeli ruling class. Kovel explains:

> Within Israeli discourse the notion of two states simply means
> then the continued aggrandisement of the Jewish state along
> with the more or less negligible other state on an ever-shrinking
> fragment of land. What it does not mean is an equable shar-
> ing of the space of Palestine. The negligibility of the Palestinian
> state is exactly what is happening in reality. More than half a
> century of chewing and gnawing away at Palestinian land has
> left the latter more a rag doll on a stick than the framework for
> a living organism, down to some 8% of the original territory . . .
> laced with Jews-only roads and peppered with hundreds of set-
> tlements that arrogate the water and resources . . . a dumping
> ground for Israeli waste, its fields and olive trees destroyed, its
> land carved up by the apartheid wall, the potential Palestinian
> state is no more than a bad joke.[4]

In the South African version of the Bantustan, there was at least some
coherence. The apartheid regime, despite their racial imaginations, wanted
the Bantustans to be viable and actually built schools, hospitals, and colleges. For the apartheid rulers in Israel, there is no such pretense, rather
an unrestrained zeal to destroy any potential, any capacity to be viable. It
is, as Kovel calls it aptly, more "a concentration camp than a state in waiting, with no viable economy save handouts and no prospect of authentic
foreign relations. . . . It remains only as a false hope and another source of
propaganda allowing Israel to be perceived as a bona fide member of the
community of nations."[5]

Increasingly, many in the solidarity movement believe that the only
viable alternative is a single state in the long term. This would be a society

where people retain recognition of identity but overcome chauvinism (and this is critical) through inclusion within a larger whole where fealty and desire no longer attach to tribal identity. It will of course require immense struggle and there are no illusions that this will be anything but a long march. During the antiapartheid struggle in South Africa, the one state/ many statelets conundrum (and the return of the refugees) was not the main issue, but it is centrally relevant for the Palestinian struggle. While both Israel and apartheid South Africa are instances of states producing racism, Zionism is not identical with apartheid, and the struggle against Zionism requires strategies different from those that we employed.

Twenty-one years after the first democratic elections in South Africa, we know all too well that you cannot transform society if you do not also transform the class structure. This is a salutary lesson we in South Africa can offer. It is thus critical to speak to the social and class nature of the future Palestinian/Israeli state. Unfortunately, even before a "sovereign" state is declared, the Palestinian Authority (PA), according to the political economist Adam Hanieh, has embraced "the fundamental precepts of neoliberalism . . . promoted by the Israeli government, the Palestinian Authority (PA), and their US and European Union (EU) supporter."[6] According to Hanieh, this vision aims to formalize a "truncated network of Palestinian-controlled cantons and associated industrial zones . . . through which a pool of cheap Palestinian labor is exploited by Israeli, Palestinian and other regional capitalist groups."[7] For Hanieh, Pax Americana envisions a Middle East resting upon Israeli capital in the West and Gulf capital in the East, underpinning a low-wage, neoliberal zone that spans the region. If this scenario materializes, then the future Palestinian state might come to resemble the Bantustans that existed in South Africa.

A rich debate during the liberation struggle in South Africa centered around whether the national question should be de-linked from the social question, or, if you like, whether the struggle against apartheid should be separated from the struggle against capitalism. The dominant view in the ANC and the South African Communist Party was that it should be and the struggle should be fought in stages. Others, such as Neville Alexander (in his book *One Azania, One Nation*), instead called for the cultivation, through the struggle against racial capitalism, of a political consciousness conducive to producing the unity necessary for nation-building. He also, like Frantz Fanon before him, cautioned against the "pitfalls of national consciousness." Today, Alexander has been vindicated. In exploring alternatives to ethnic states, his words in a recent essay, entitled "The Moral Responsibility of Intellectuals," are apposite:

> We are building a new historical community in South Africa. The Truth and Reconciliation Commission whatever its virtues and positive legacies could not establish the social basis for this new community. . . . Social reconciliation under conditions of cruel inequality such as we have in South Africa is not only impossible; it is a lie that has to be exposed. We will have to work very hard to bring about social cohesion and national unity. Suffice to say that unless the Gini Coefficient is tackled seriously, all talk of social cohesion and national unity is so much nonsense.[8]

## Palestinian Solidarity in South Africa Today

On August 9, 2014, between 150,000 and 200,000 South Africans marched in Cape Town against the recent atrocities in Gaza and for full sanctions against Israel. It was the biggest march in South Africa's history and a continuation of the intense solidarity activity in support of the Palestinian struggle since the first South African democratic elections in 1994. The highlights of these activities include: a ten-thousand-strong march in Durban during the UN World Conference Against Racism in 2001, where the "second antiapartheid movement" was declared and a BDS campaign against "apartheid Israel" proposed; an equally strong march at the World Summit on Sustainable Development Summit in 2002 in support of the Palestinian struggle and against the presence of an Israeli delegation (including former Israeli president Shimon Peres); the refusal of dock workers in Durban to off-load an Israeli ship in 2009 in the wake of Israel's Operation Cast Lead assault on Gaza; and, in 2011, the decision by the senate of the University of Johannesburg to sever ties with Ben Gurion University.

Despite the ANC's support for a sanctions campaign against apartheid South Africa during our liberation struggle, the postapartheid South African government has facilitated increasing trade with Israel since 1994.[9] In a response to the overwhelming sentiment of South Africans to expel the Israeli ambassador during the latest outrage in Gaza, our deputy president, Cyril Ramaphosa, said: "It's often best when you want to solve problems to remain engaged so that you can have some leverage and this gave our president leverage to be able to send the two special envoys."[10] For many this was a variation on the "constructive engagement" espoused by the likes of Thatcher and Reagan. Rajini Srikanth captures this duplicity:

> In the summer of 2014, for instance, President Jacob Zuma declared that "the country was outraged by the 'continued violence that is claiming scores of lives of civilians in Palestine.'" Two days later, Zuma criticized Hamas, and a spokesperson for the Department of Trade and Industry announced that there were "no plans to impose trade restrictions on Israel amid its conflict with Palestine." Activists consider such statements to be the ANC-led government's way of having it both ways—of providing a seemingly supportive response to the groundswell of clamor to condemn Israel's violation of Palestinian rights and sever all ties with Israel while keeping open the avenues of trade that are seen to benefit South Africa economically.[11]

Many activists are simply fed up with the empty posturing and what they correctly perceive as lucre trumping principle. Trade has increased since then. Bilateral trade between the two countries now stands at 12 billion South African rand, up from 4 billion in 2003. Despite their tremendous respect for South Africans, many Palestinians are increasingly expressing the view that statements and symbolic gestures of solidarity, as have been coming from the South African government, are no longer enough in the face of Israel's acts of terror in Gaza. Resisting the attempts at promoting collective amnesia, some of us remember the outpouring of practical support and succor the Israeli state provided to our erstwhile oppressors, while many Palestinians shared trenches with South African freedom fighters.

The BDS campaign consciously makes connections to the South African struggle. Other writings have justified this strategy, so it will suffice here to quote Virginia Tilley, an American political scientist who lived in South Africa. In the aftermath of the cluster bombing by Israel of Lebanon in 2006, Tilley wrote:

> It is finally time. After years of internal arguments, confusion, and dithering, the time has come for a full-fledged international boycott of Israel. Good cause for a boycott has, of course, been in place for decades, as a raft of initiatives already attests. But Israel's war crimes are now so shocking, its extremism so clear, the suffering so great, the UN so helpless, and the internation-

al community's need to contain Israel's behavior so urgent and compelling, that the time for global action has matured. A coordinated movement of divestment, sanctions, and boycotts against Israel must convene to contain not only Israel's aggressive acts and crimes against humanitarian law but also, as in South Africa, its founding racist logics that inspired and still drive the entire Palestinian problem.[12]

Chapter 4

# Apartheid's "Little Israel"
## Bophuthatswana

Arianna Lissoni

It would be hard for present-day visitors to the city of Mafikeng, the administrative capital of South Africa's North West Province, to miss the sight of its massive stadium, which sits like a white elephant on the otherwise relatively flat landscape. The Olympic-standard football stadium, which can accommodate up to sixty thousand spectators, is currently inactive and was not deemed suitable to host the 2010 FIFA World Cup games.[1] Instead, a brand-new complex, the Royal Bafokeng Stadium, was built in the fast-growing platinum city of Rustenburg for this purpose. This can perhaps be viewed as evidence of the relative decline since the end of apartheid of what was once Bophuthatswana's thriving capital, Mmabatho.[2] Not immediately evident to the eye is that Mafikeng's now defunct stadium—known in its heyday as the Independence Stadium—was designed by Israeli architects and built by an Israeli construction firm during the Bantustan era in apartheid South Africa.

From its inception in the early 1970s, the secret alliance between the Israeli state and apartheid South Africa was the subject of discussion in antiapartheid and pro-Palestinian circles (as part of their efforts to isolate both countries internationally) as well as in scholarly research.[3] Given its sensitive nature, however, much information about this relationship was inaccessible for a long time and therefore could only be inferred. It is only recently that the full extent of the Israeli–South African collaboration on military and nuclear matters has started to be revealed in detail, thanks to the opening of archives in South Africa following the end of apartheid.[4] Whereas the Israeli–South African military alliance had to remain "unspoken" (as the title of Sasha Polakow-Suransky's book suggests), there is another relationship between these two countries that was very public in its day and yet today appears to have been largely forgotten. The relationship in question is the one between Israel and South Africa's former Bantustans, in particular Bophuthatswana.[5]

That this relationship has been forgotten is all the more surprising given the parallels between South Africa's apartheid policy and Israel's treatment of Palestinians, as well as between South Africa's Bantustan strategy and Israel's carving up of the Palestinian territories.[6] One reason may be that the ties between the former Bantustans and Israel do not fit neatly into the analogy between the Bantustans and the Palestinian territories as geographically, politically, and economically unviable "dumping grounds" for Black South Africans and Palestinians, respectively. Rather, these ties twist the analogy into unexpected directions. "Homeland" elites identified their territories not with the Palestinian ones but with Israel itself, as a country driven by a kind of ethnonationalist politics similar to the Bantustans' ethnic foundations.

Israel's dealings with apartheid-era Bantustans suggest a much deeper and more direct implication in the perpetuation of South African apartheid than is commonly assumed. In other words, Israel was not only responsible for selling arms to and sharing nuclear secrets with apartheid South Africa (which Pretoria used, in turn, to continue to oppress the Black majority), it also played a significant role in sustaining one of the very cornerstones of apartheid through its extensive relations with the Bantustans. Primarily shaped by economic interest, rather than ideological considerations, Israeli engagement with the Bantustans also had important political spinoffs.

In light of this, comparisons between apartheid South Africa and Israel cease to have a purely abstract or theoretical value but can begin to be viewed as historically informed. This is not, however, to return to simple equations between South Africa and Israel. As Ran Greenstein has argued, historical apartheid is not the same as the broad notion of apartheid as a system of oppression and discrimination as, for instance, in the UN definition of apartheid as a "crime against humanity."[7] But the relations between Israel and South Africa's Bantustans reveal a close historical association between Israel and apartheid South Africa beyond the level of military and nuclear cooperation, which makes current analogies less misguided than Israel's supporters would like to argue.

## "Home Sweet Homeland"

In 1973, in the aftermath of the Yom Kippur War, the Organization of African Unity (OAU) passed a resolution urging its member states to sever diplomatic ties with Israel in condemnation of its continued occupation of Egypt's Sinai Peninsula. All countries—with the exception of Malawi, Swaziland, Lesotho, and Mauritius—almost immediately complied with the request.[8] By the next decade, Zaire, Liberia, and the Ivory Coast had reestablished ties with the Jewish state, with Zaire's President Mobutu taking the lead in calling for the normalization of relations with Israel and advocating a policy of "positive neutrality" by African states toward the Palestinian–Israeli conflict (based on the view that Israel had withdrawn from the Sinai, and that this was in any case an extracontinental issue).[9]

Apartheid South Africa, like the small group of reactionary African countries headed by Zaire, also had no qualms about establishing relations with Israel—at a time when Israel was beginning to lose international credibility and the majority of African states were breaking off relations. Prime minister John Vorster's famous visit to Israel in 1976 not only placed the diplomatic seal on a "much bigger deal"[10] between the two countries (by 1977 South Africa had become Israel's largest arms customer)[11] but also paved the way for economic relations between South Africa's "homelands" and "independent" Bantustans and their rulers.[12]

After the Venda Bantustan was granted "independence" in September 1979, its president, Patrick Mphephu, and a number of government ministers made a state visit to Israel in 1980. Bophuthatswana's president, Lucas Mangope, followed suit a year later. In late 1982, the Ciskei opened a trade mission in Tel Aviv and employed two Israelis, Yosef Schneider and Nat Rosenwasser, to act as its representatives in Israel. In 1983 representatives of these three Bantustans (including the whole of Venda's chamber of commerce) were in Israel again (in the case of the Ciskei, for the seventh time).[13] George Matanzima, prime minister of the Transkei, and four of his ministers visited Israel in 1984. In 1985, it was the turn of Gatsha Buthelezi, who, the *Jerusalem Post* unashamedly argued in a feature article about the visit, should have been the rightful recipient of the Nobel Peace Prize the previous year—in place of Desmond Tutu—for his role as "the real peacemaker in South Africa."[14]

Heavily reliant on Pretoria's financial handouts for their economic
survival and denied foreign aid because of their lack of international recognition, the Bantustans granted massive tax and customs concessions and
other favors (which were integral to South Africa's policy of industrial de-
centralization) in order to attract foreign investment into their territories.
The absence of organized trade unions, wage refunds, and large supplies of
cheap, unskilled Black labor provided further incentives for foreign companies to do business with the Bantustans. Israeli entrepreneurs were quick
to discover that this was "new 'virgin soil' for high-profit investment."[15]
As the title of an article in the *Rand Daily Mail* aptly described, it was
"Home Sweet Homeland for Israeli Businessmen."[16] Although the Bantustans' economic dependence on Pretoria was never a secret and has been
well documented, the role that foreign (especially Israeli and Taiwanese)
investment played in developing the Bantustans' infrastructure, helping in
turn to prop up their illegitimate governments, is yet to be properly inves-
tigated. Likewise, the extent to which such investment injected new blood
into a suffering Israeli economy—thus contributing to the survival of the
Israeli state—remains an open question. Even if it is unlikely that the profits derived from these "legitimate" business operations ever matched those
involved in the secret arms trade between Israel and South Africa, they
were by no means insignificant. Moreover, they had important political
ramifications and for these reasons should not be too easily dismissed.

## The Only State with an Official Flag of Bophuthatswana

Mangope was thus neither the first nor the last Bantustan leader to establish
ties with Israel. But the relationship between Bophuthatswana and Israel
not only outlasted those with all other Bantustans, it also was one of the
most lucrative and pervasive of the lot—extending well beyond economic
interest. Mangope's 1981 and 1983 visits to Israel marked the beginning
of a prosperous relationship, whose fruits were soon to be reaped. Over
the course of 1983, Israeli investment in Bophuthatswana already totaled
US$250 million, and the amount was predicted to increase in the follow-
ing years.[17] It was probably during Mangope's second visit to Israel, in 1983,
that Shabtai Kalmanowitch was appointed Bophuthatswana's trade representative in Israel. A Russian-born Israeli businessman, Kalmanowitch
had links with an international criminal network of Mossad agents and
was introduced to Mangope by Solomon "Sol" Kerzner (the "uncrowned

king" of the casino and hotel empire in Bophuthatswana). Kalmanow-itch became responsible for arranging and coordinating a wide range of business deals and economic/ diplomatic contacts for Bophuthatswana—while amassing a huge fortune for himself on the side. These activities and contacts, although primarily centered in Israel, eventually extended to at least fourteen other countries as part of a concerted effort both to sell Bophuthatswana to foreign businesses and to gain international political recognition for the Bantustan.[18]

Through Kalmanowitch, Bophuthatswana purchased a four-story building at 194 Hayarkon Street in Tel Aviv to house its trade mission of-fice, which it was hoped would become the Bophuthatswana government's "future head-quarters" in Israel.[19] The building stood "in one of the most beautiful spots in Tel Aviv opposite the Hilton Hotel and the Indepen-dence Park—with a fascinating view of the sea."[20] An Israeli architectural firm, Barchana, was contracted in 1984 to undertake the renovation works under Kalmanowitch's supervision. It is not clear how much the building originally cost, but just for its renovation the Bophuthatswana govern-ment had to cough up at least US$1 million. Bophuthatswana House, as the building was renamed, featured marble floors and decorative ceilings, while its entire western façade was made of glass, aluminum, and travertine marble to allow an uncorrupted view of the scenery. On the ground floor was a large lobby (which could also be used to hold receptions) where an exhibition of "Bophuthatswana's art" was displayed. A number of class-rooms or small conference rooms, two offices, and a small kitchen were also located on this floor. Kalmanowitch's office occupied the sea-facing portion of the first floor. Adjacent to it was the main conference room, his secretaries' office, a telex room, and a waiting room. An additional office and waiting room as well as four smaller rooms took up the rest of the floor. The second floor housed the central dining room, the main kitchen, and three hotel-type rooms with adjoining conveniences, which could each accommodate up to three guests. Facing the sea on the third floor was the presidential suite, which included a bedroom, a study, a dressing room, and two bathrooms (one with shower and the other with Jacuzzi). On the same floor were also a gym (complete with sauna) and two addi-tional rooms with conveniences intended to service the president's family or personal guests.[21] "High-quality Italian furniture" was specially im-ported (and additionally taxed!) to furnish the building.[22]

Israel did not officially recognize any of the Bantustans, including Bophuthatswana. However, Bophuthatswana House in Tel Aviv (which was formally inaugurated by President Mangope in April 1985 and became the only place in the world outside of South Africa to fly the flag of Bophuthatswana) functioned in fact and practice as an embassy, with Kalmanowitch acting as Bophuthatswana's unofficial ambassador. Bophuthatswana House became not only the external headquarters of a wide international network of economic and political relations for Bophuthatswana but also performed consular duties such as the issuing of visitors' and work permits and providing information about business and travel opportunities.[23] The state-owned Israeli telephone company listed Bophuthatswana and the Transkei as foreign nations in the international dialing section of its directory.[24] Polakow-Suransky has argued that the Israeli government was deeply uncomfortable about its private citizens' investments in the Bantustans and the dealings of so-called trade representatives in Israel, although, he admits, "Israel came remarkably close to granting [the Bantustans] de facto recognition."[25] Undoubtedly, these activities may have sometimes turned into a source of international embarrassment for Israel,[26] especially at the UN. But several Israeli officials as well as various members of the Knesset (MKs) and ministers remained closely involved in this network of business and quasi-diplomatic relations. This is not to imply that the Israeli government acted as a monolith. As Polakow-Suransky has documented, there were significant divisions between government departments—especially between the foreign and defense ministries—which sometimes pushed Israeli policy regarding South Africa in opposing directions.[27]

According to the 1984 annual report compiled by the Bophuthatswana trade mission office in Tel Aviv, ninety-eight people from Bophuthatswana visited Israel during that year. The following year the number of visitors to Israel increased to 120. These included representatives from a broad spectrum of Bophuthatswana's government departments (including Public Works, Finance, Prisons and Police, Law and Order, Justice, Public Relations, Agriculture, Sports, Education, and Housing) as well as representatives of the University of Bophuthatswana (UNIBO) and two parastatals, Agricor and the Bophuthatswana National Development Corporation. In 1984, the number of visitors from Israel to Bophuthatswana was eighty-one, reaching ninety in 1985.[28] These trips and the type of personnel (government functionaries and private citizens) involved on both sides point to the large overlap between business and diplomatic interests. At least fifty important contacts were established in Israel in the period between 1984 and 1985. Many of these were "independent" contacts (a large number of them architects), but they also included the mayor and deputy mayor of Tel Aviv, the director of a cultural center and the mayor of the town of Kfar Saba, the head of the Likud Party, members of the Liberal and Labor parties, the head of the ultra-orthodox Jewish party Agudat, the Knesset secretary for Mafdal (or National Religious Party), an ex-chief rabbi, the general managers of First National and Mizrahi banks, MKs, and representatives of several government ministries. Between 1984 and 1985 it was reported that seventy-nine business projects had been submitted to the Bophuthatswana government. These ranged from housing projects, the construction of the stadium, the opening of a tennis center in Mmabatho, irrigation projects, security systems, television programming, the purchase of tractors, aviation,[29] diamond manufacturing, a shoe factory, a meat processing plant, and the establishment of a crocodile farm (called Kwena Gardens) near Sun City.[30] These projects can be viewed as evidence of the significance of Israeli investments for Bophuthatswana's infrastructural development.

Bophuthatswana also found Israel a valuable source of expertise. The trade mission office in Tel Aviv became responsible for recruiting professionals in various fields to work in Bophuthatswana. In 1985, ten working visas were issued in this respect.[31] An Israeli architect, Ilan Sharon, was employed as planning advisor by the Bophuthatswana government.[32] A number of Israeli businessmen and their families moved to Bophuthatswana to set up commercial ventures. Israeli lecturers were recruited to teach at UNIBO, Israeli doctors went to work in Bophuthatswana hospitals, and agricultural specialists were also employed over the years.

In 1984 two additional trade mission offices became operational in Frankfurt and Rome, staffed by a Mr. Jürgen Komischke and Italian hotelier Roberto Sciò, respectively, while plans to open further offices in New York, Bangkok, Milan, and Spain were reportedly under way.[33] The functions of the German and Italian missions, though smaller in scale, were similar to those of their parent office in Tel Aviv. Their central task was that of luring potential investors to Bophuthatswana by establishing new contacts and activating existing ones in the banking, trade, and industry sectors, and arranging meetings with the relevant Bophuthatswana departments. Entertaining local political and financial figures for the purpose of "furthering the Bophuthatswana cause" seems to have been a favored method in achieving such aims—for the year 1984 alone Italian representative Sciò claimed 45 million lire in expenses for private parties and receptions held at his villa in Rome.[34] The costs must have been deemed worthwhile, for in submitting the estimated expenditure for the Israeli, German, and Italian trade missions for the year 1985 to President Mangope, the secretary for economic affairs was able to justify an annual budget of over one million rand: "A lot has been done for the Government [by the trade missions]. Investors have been attracted to the country and many industries have been established at our industrial development points."[35]

## "A Rival to the Pyramids as a Monument to its Ruler"

One of the biggest construction projects undertaken in this period was the building of the "national" stadium in Bophuthatswana's capital, Mmabatho. The Independence Stadium was inaugurated in December 1985, on the occasion of Bophuthatswana's eighth Independence Day celebration, hence the name. Israeli architect Israel Goodowitch and engineer Ben Avrhan planned the "unique stadium," in which 75 percent of its sixty thousand spectators would be seated on elevated platforms, staggered in a diamond shape, "something that is not the normal idea in stadia around the world"[36] (perhaps a reason for its nonqualification for the 2010 FIFA World Cup). Four training centers and a school for football coaches were also part of the US$18 million project. LIAT Finance Trade and Construction Corporation, a company set up by Kalmanowitch, subcontracted the construction of the project. An Israeli soccer player, Amatzia Lefkowitz, landed another contract worth thousands of dollars to run the school for coaches. The negotiations for the deal, which must have exceeded $30,000 a year, were kept "like a military secret," and in 1984 Lefkowitz, who was then coaching a Tel Aviv team, twice traveled to Bophuthatswana under the cover of army reserve service for this hidden purpose.[37] It was alleged at the time that through LIAT Kalmanowitch had given out the contracts for the stadium without tenders being called for. The gross corruption that the stadium deal exposed became one of the contributing factors to the February 1988 attempted coup against Mangope.[38]

Mmabatho, a city literally built from scratch (it did not exist before Bophuthatswana's independence in 1977) was a construction site throughout most of the 1980s. On closer inspection, however, these developments were largely for the exclusive benefit of Bophuthatswana's new political elite—whose vested interest in the Bantustan system simultaneously made it both a product and one of the pillars of South Africa's Bantustan strategy. In the words of a former economic adviser to Mangope, "Nothing is really developing in Bophuthatswana—except the government offices, houses, cars, and the roads for the elite to drive around on. Mmabatho as a capital must surely rival the ancient pyramids as a monument to its ruler."[39] As Jonathan Hyslop has pointed out, Bantustan bureaucracies became fertile soil for corruption and maladministration, which, in turn, provided "a happy hunting ground for shady entrepreneurs from South Africa and abroad."[40] Kalmanowitch is a prime example of this category of individuals with dubious credentials who used the Bantustans for their own personal enrichment. According to a study on sanctions and embargo-busting by Thomas Naylor, writing on Kalmanowitch's company LIAT:

> [Its] main contribution to [Bophuthatswana's] economic development was to win public contracts, sublet the actual work to other companies whose own bids had been lower, then kick back part of the profits to the president. To make sure he got paid, Kalmanowitch also arranged for "Boph" [sic] to borrow abroad, specifically from Kredietbankin Belgium, the institution through which South African intelligence financed its European espionage activities.[41]

As mentioned before, Mangope's alleged acceptance of bribes from Kalmanowitch was singled out as one of the main causes of discontent in a radio broadcast by the leaders of the 1988 coup.[42] By then, however, Kalmanowitch had long disappeared from the Bophuthatswana scene. Kalmanowitch's move was perhaps a preventive measure designed to evade further investigations into the corruption related to the stadium deal, or perhaps it was the prospect of higher profits that drove him to Sierra Leone, where between 1985 and 1987 he became involved in the diamond trade. Kalmanowitch's LIAT encouraged president Joseph Momoh to regularize the mining and marketing of diamonds in Sierra Leone in exchange for a monopoly over these operations. As it turned out, however, Kalmanowitch became implicated in smuggling South Africa's precious stones to the rest of the world and importing machinery and supplies into South Africa by using Sierra Leone as a pass-through point[43] (a practice known as "springboarding" or "backdooring"[44]).

In 1987 Kalmanowitch was arrested, while traveling in London, for forgery he had committed in the United States. He was then extradited to the United States, only to be released on bail (toward which Mangope apparently contributed) and allowed to return to Israel, where he was charged with being a KGB agent and sentenced to nine years in prison. According to some sources, Kalmanowitch's alleged spying for the Soviet Union was intended to cover up his dodgy dealings in Sierra Leone (where he held the title of Israel's "cultural representative") and, in turn, Israel's close relations with apartheid South Africa.[45] Kalmanowitch ended up serving five of his nine-year prison term. He then relocated to Russia, where he capitalized on the new business opportunities afforded by the collapse of the Soviet Union. In 2009 Kalmanowitch was gunned down in a contract killing on the streets of Moscow, as a consequence of his shady business activities and links to the Russian mafia.[46]

## "Africa's Little Israel"

Kalmanowitch's exit to some extent put at bay the crude and rapacious character of early Israeli commercial operations in Bophuthatswana. This, however, did not mean the end of the relations between the two areas. The period that followed was largely one of consolidation of the initiatives started during Kalmanowitch's era and saw their penetration into the cultural and social fabric of the Bantustan. The political implications of this process—especially for Bophuthatswana's survival into the 1990s—were far-reaching.

The late 1980s and early 1990s were a period of dramatic change both in South Africa and internationally. Growing resistance effectively made the country ungovernable, while economic sanctions started to bite and the apartheid government found itself almost completely isolated at the international level, leading to the stalemate that forced the National Party to the negotiating table. Because of the huge economic interests at stake in the secret arms trade with Pretoria, Israel was reluctant to comply with other nations in taking action against South Africa—but eventually it had to, and in 1987 a sanctions resolution was passed. Yet instead of severing Israel's ties with South Africa, "members of the security establishment in both parties sought to preserve the relationship—and derive as much export revenue as they could from it."⁴⁷ It was only on the eve of South Africa's transition to democracy that the sordid affair between Israel and South Africa finally ended.⁴⁸

The future of the TBVC (Transkei-Bophuthatswana-Venda-Ciskei) states and the remaining self-governing "homelands" soon came under the spotlight during the negotiations. With Mandela's release and the lifting of the bans on the ANC and other political parties in 1990, the Ciskei and Venda Bantustans quickly unraveled. In Transkei, the 1986 coup had placed in power Bantu Holomisa, who openly supported the ANC. In May 1990 president F. W. de Klerk announced the abolishment of the policy of granting "independence" to the "homelands." Despite these dramatic changes and increasing internal resistance within the Bantustan, Mangope continued to cling to power, and announced in 1990 that Bophuthatswana would "remain an independent state one hundred years from now."⁴⁹

In its desperate bid to retain its independence at a time when Pretoria's support was withdrawing, Bophuthatswana increasingly looked to the outside world for friends. The early 1990s saw a vigorous expansion of Bophuthatswana's diplomatic efforts as the Bantustan tried to project internationally the image of a stable, moderate, multiracial, Black African country firmly set in the capitalist economy as justification for its continued survival. More trade missions were opened in this period, with the former Soviet Union satellites proving especially receptive to the establishment of ties with the Bantustan.⁵⁰

Israel's friendship with South Africa's Bantustans remained steadfast in the late 1980s and early 1990s, providing Israel and its supporters with "fresh ammunition to use against critics of Israel's relations with South Africa."⁵¹ Israel continued to embrace the Bantustans and their leaders, envisioning them as allies in the future geopolitical reconfiguration of the region (against the prospect of the coming to power of the "pro-Soviet" and "pro-Palestinian" ANC). These relations were used in turn as evidence of Israel's abhorrence of apartheid, while allowing for the illegal trade in arms with South Africa to carry on unabated. Bophuthatswana, on the other hand, looked to Israel as a role model and "an example, similar to their own, of a young country that has achieved independence as a result of their cultural and historical ties to the land."⁵² Bophuthatswana also began to display signs of Israel's (and South Africa's) "siege mentality," with senior officials speaking of their "beleaguered" homeland as "the little Israel of Africa."[53]

It is unclear what happened exactly to Bophuthatswana House in Tel Aviv after 1985, but what is clear is that with Kalmanowitch gone, somehow so was the flashy building. Ms. Tova P. Maori, who had been Kalmanowitch's secretary, took over the leadership of the trade mission office as authorized representative of Bophuthatswana in Israel. A new office was opened in Tel Aviv's city center at the prestigious Asia House[54] (at 4 Weizmann Street), where the Italian, Japanese, Dutch, and Swedish embassies are located today. Under Maori's direction, the new trade mission office started cultivating not only business exchanges but also what were then called "humanitarian exchanges" in fields such as tourism, education, athletics, and culture. All of these activities were, of course, integral to Bophuthatswana's plans to present itself internationally as a healthy, self-reliant democracy.

In 1989, Maori set up the Israel–Bophuthatswana Friendship Society in Israel "as a forum for cultural exchanges and networking between the people of Israel and Bophuthatswana." The first chairman of the Society, Lenny Maxwell, summed up its philosophy as such: "I feel strongly that the road to understanding between nations is paved by the people. Governments are restricted by the terms of understanding, whereas groups like us advocate unconditional acceptance as a prerequisite for our relationship."[55]

Members of the Society in Israel (consisting of approximately 150 individuals) thus took it upon themselves to host Bophuthatswana dignitaries during their stays in Israel. Guests were also invited to address the group on relevant topics. The Society's activities included the awarding of scholarships to students from Bophuthatswana "to enable them to participate in educational programs in agriculture, education management and arts and crafts."[56] In 1991, two students from Bophuthatswana were given bursaries to study agriculture and animal husbandry at Kibbutz Messilot. The following year a similar program was initiated in the "arts and crafts" to allow for two students to share their "native skills" by spending six weeks of intensive training at Givat Haviva Arts Institute in Israel.[57]

Mangope's daughter-in-law Rosemary, who studied in Jerusalem (and went on to become chief director of the Directorate of Arts, Social Development and Youth in the Department of Arts and Culture), drew inspiration from Women's International Zionist Organization programs in Israel when setting up a cultural center (of which she became executive director) called Mmabana—meaning "mother of the children" in Setswana—in Thaba'Nchu in Bophuthatswana. This "oasis of learning and culture" was officially inaugurated by Mangope in October 1991 and offered activities and courses ranging from drawing, sculpture, quilting, and sewing to dance, sports, drama, literature, and music for the young and the old.[58] The center was staffed by experienced people "from around the world." The bulk of the funding for the project came from the Bophuthatswana government, while the remaining balance was obtained from tuition fees, admissions at productions, and donations by businesses and individuals. Driven by the motto, "A people's quest for excellence," Mmabana aimed at allowing "everyone to experience the exhilaration of achievement which leads to the development of self-esteem and confidence."[59] The cultural center defended itself from accusations of being elitist by arguing that its tuition fees were "in the range of most people."[60]

The plans for the construction of a tennis center in Mmabatho that had been initiated in the mid-1980s eventually resulted in the setting up of the Bophuthatswana Tennis Union and of a national junior tennis tournament sponsored by the Standard Bank of Bophuthatswana (STANBO).[61] As with soccer, Israeli tennis coaches contributed their expertise to the development of tennis in Bophuthatswana. In 1992 and 1993 Bophuthatswana's junior tennis champions were invited to participate in the Riklis Tennis Tournaments in Tel Aviv.[62] In a similar way, the soccer developments around the construction of the stadium were instrumental to the establishment of the Bophuthatswana Professional Soccer League (BOPSOL), of which Sol Kerzner's Sun International became a sponsor (to the tune of 500,000 rand per year). To give a sense of the scale of the growth in this field, in the 1991 league season, thirteen first division and twelve second division teams were competing as part of BOPSOL.[63]

## Conclusion

The final collapse of Bophuthatswana and the coming to power of the new ANC government in 1994 at last put a halt to this hive of activities—commercial, sports, educational, cultural, ideological, and ultimately political—between the former Bantustan and Israel. Mangope fought to the bitter end for Bophuthatswana to retain its "independence," and Israeli support played a critical role in helping Bophuthatswana to survive for as long as it did. It can be argued that this relationship was essentially an opportunistic one. To be sure, Israelis made huge profits by doing business with Bophuthatswana (and other Bantustans). Economic ties paved the way for other types of links, which, taken together, contributed to upholding the Bantustans as a political project. Israel's engagement with apartheid practices is rooted in historical precedent and therefore goes much deeper than its present policy-making context. On the other side of the relationship, Bophuthatswana desperately needed allies such as Israel for the development of its infrastructure. This, in turn, provided the foundation on which Bophuthatswana's failed claim to a separate identity in a new South Africa could be based. Israel became a cultural and ideological model on which the Bantustan could draw to shape its own ethnonationalist project and articulate its right to exist.

Chapter 5

# Neoliberal Apartheid

Andy Clarno

In early September 2001, the World Conference Against Racism (WCAR) in Durban, South Africa, placed the Palestinian struggle at the heart of the global movement against racism, neoliberalism, and empire. The NGO Forum issued a powerful declaration that marked Israel as an "apartheid state." Thousands of protesters marched through the streets of Durban wearing t-shirts emblazoned with the slogan "APARTHEID IS/REAL." By no means the first time Israel was likened to South Africa, the WCAR was instrumental, however, in globalizing the discourse of Israeli apartheid.

Since 2001, activists and scholars have increasingly turned to South Africa to make sense of current conditions in Palestine/Israel, to explore strategies of resistance, and to conceptualize possible futures. For many observers, South Africa represents a principled rejection of settler-colonialism, a model of a one-state solution, and a vision of reconciliation and multiracial democracy based on a common humanity. In addition, the boycott, divestment, and sanctions (BDS) campaign has made tremendous gains, building on the tactics of the South African antiapartheid movement. In short, studying the *success* of the South African struggle has been highly productive for the Palestinian freedom movement.

Building on this work, I want to suggest that understanding the *limitations* of liberation in postapartheid South Africa could also prove productive. Overthrowing the apartheid state freed Black South Africans from the confines of the white supremacist regime. This extraordinary victory has been rightfully celebrated, and South Africa has become a beacon of hope for millions. Yet South Africa remains one of the most unequal

67

countries in the world. A small Black elite and a growing Black middle class have emerged alongside the old white elite, which still controls the vast majority of land and wealth in the country. Poor Black South Africans have been relegated to a life of permanent unemployment, informal housing, and high rates of HIV/AIDS in the townships and shack settlements of the urban periphery. While rooted in the history of colonialism and apartheid, these conditions cannot be dismissed as simply the lingering effects of the old regime. Waves of strikes, social movements, and popular uprisings have made clear that the struggle in South Africa continues.

Until now, nearly every comparative study has focused on *apartheid-era* South Africa and *contemporary* Palestine/Israel. Yet the continuing crises and ongoing struggles in South Africa have important implications for the Palestinian struggle. The crises serve as a reminder that democratizing a settler state does not entirely eliminate inequality, segregation, or even racism. And these struggles make it possible to deepen the connections between social justice movements in Palestine/Israel and South Africa today.

The end of formal apartheid in South Africa and the Oslo "peace process" in Palestine/Israel were fundamentally neoliberal projects connected to the restructuring of global political/economic relations at the end of the Cold War. While the South African state was democratized and deracialized, the formation of the Palestinian Authority allowed Israel to introduce a form of indirect rule in the West Bank and Gaza Strip, and to expand its colonial domination over the entire territory. Each of these transitions, however, was closely connected to the rising global hegemony of neoliberal capitalism.

Promoting market-based policies such as privatization, deregulation, entrepreneurialism, and free trade, neoliberal restructuring has enabled the rise of multinational corporations, the growth of finance capital, the concentration of wealth among the elite, the deepening marginalization of the poor, and the expansion of security forces to manage these surplus populations. In both Palestine/Israel and South Africa, neoliberal restructuring has intensified race and class inequality and generated new struggles and social movements.

The transition from apartheid to democracy in South Africa was accompanied by the consolidation of neoliberal capitalism. Building on economic reforms initiated by the apartheid regime, the African National Congress (ANC) adopted a series of market-friendly policies to win the support of the South African and global business elites. Most importantly, the ANC accepted constitutional protections for the existing distribution of private property, despite the fact that it was ultimately acquired through conquest and violent dispossession. Within two years of coming to power, the ANC government adopted an explicitly neoliberal economic strategy. In addition, it took on the debt accumulated by the apartheid regime and gave up on proposals to nationalize the banks and mines. As a result, Black South Africans gained equal rights, the Black middle class became more secure, and a few Black families with close ties to the new regime amassed great fortunes. But the old white elite and its corporations have largely retained control over the country's vast wealth.

For millions of Black South Africans, the neoliberal liberation has meant the elimination of jobs and the commodification of basic services. Economic restructuring has led to the collapse of industrial employment, the increasing precariousness of waged labor, and growing levels of permanent structural unemployment. Privatization has made essential services increasingly difficult to afford. And the official "land redistribution" program—guided by market-based "willing seller, willing buyer" principles—has led to the redistribution of only 8 percent of South African land. Hardest hit by these changes, of course, are the poor, Black communities that led the struggle against apartheid and are now being devastated by poverty and HIV/AIDS. The gulf between the wealthiest and poorest South Africans has grown so wide that postapartheid South Africa is now ranked as one of the three most unequal countries in the world.

Unlike Black South Africans, Palestinians have not achieved political freedom or legal equality. The Oslo negotiations established the Palestinian Authority (PA) as a limited self-governing body for Palestinians in a series of isolated enclosures in the West Bank and Gaza Strip. The PA was granted partial autonomy over civil affairs—such as education and health care—in exchange for working with Israel to police the Palestinian people and suppress resistance. The state of Israel retains full sovereign control over the entire territory and has continued to colonize Palestinian land while concentrating the Palestinian population into isolated and enclosed zones of abandonment and death.

From the start, Oslo has been a deeply neoliberal process. The Oslo negotiations were promoted by Israeli business elites concerned that political instability would impede their ability to attract foreign investors and multinational corporations. They were shaped by Shimon Peres's vision of a "New Middle East"—a regional free-trade zone that would open the markets of the Arab world to US and Israeli capital. Trade accords with neighboring countries allowed Israeli businesses to outsource production to low-wage industrial zones in Egypt and Jordan. And the economic policies of the PA, closely linked to those of Israel through the 1994 Paris Protocol, were shaped from the start by the World Bank and International Monetary Fund (IMF). The PA is also highly susceptible to donor pressure because its budget depends heavily on grants and loans from donor states. From 2000 to 2013, Salam Fayyad, a former IMF employee, was installed as PA minister of finance and later prime minister and tasked with implementing neoliberal projects. With support from the Palestinian elite, these projects have amplified the class divisions within Palestinian society.

Neoliberal restructuring has enabled Israel's policy of separation and enclosure by greatly reducing Israeli reliance on Palestinian labor. Israel has undergone a major transition, from a labor-intensive economy centered on production for the domestic market to a high-tech economy integrated into the circuits of global capitalism. This shift has undermined the basis of agricultural and industrial labor, eliminating the need for Palestinian workers and crippling both Palestinian and Israeli labor unions. Since the early 1990s, Israel has largely replaced Palestinian workers with hundreds of thousands of low-paid migrant workers. And Palestinian industries in the West Bank and Gaza Strip have been devastated by Israeli restrictions (and airstrikes), cheap imports, and outsourcing to Jordan and Egypt. As a result of these changes, Israeli—and some Palestinian—business elites have garnered tremendous wealth while the Palestinian enclaves have become sites of concentrated inequality. A small Palestinian elite with close ties to the PA has grown rich while the majority of Palestinians confront deepening poverty, land confiscation, and constant repression. Two of the main sources of income for Palestinian workers in the West Bank today are building Israeli settlements on confiscated Palestinian land or joining the PA security forces—trained by the United States and charged with ensuring Israeli security.

Postapartheid South Africa demonstrates the limitations of a liberation strategy that does not extend beyond the deracialization of the state apparatus. The South African left used to describe apartheid as a system of "racial capitalism" built to maintain not only white supremacy but also access to cheap Black labor for white-owned businesses. Unless racism and capitalism were confronted together, they insisted, postapartheid South Africa would remain deeply divided and unequal. This analysis emerged out of decades of scholarship and struggle and is widely shared among South African scholars today. The ANC preferred a two-stage revolutionary strategy that prioritized the struggle against racism and promised that the struggle against capitalism would come later. By the 1990s, this strategy had brought about a transition to democracy, but at the cost of institutionalizing neoliberal capitalism and protecting the wealth of the old white elite. In the words of the late Neville Alexander, "What we used to call the apartheid-capitalist system has simply given way to the postapartheid-capitalist system."[1]

Like most critical work on Palestine/Israel, the analysis of Israeli apartheid has largely overlooked the relationship between settler-colonialism and racial capitalism. Drawing on the UN definition of apartheid as a regime of racial discrimination and segregation, scholars and activists have focused on the forms of legal discrimination against Palestinian citizens of Israel, the dual legal system in the occupied territories, the colonization of Palestinian land, and the system of identity documents and permits used to classify and control Palestinian movement. In recent years, scholars have increasingly adopted political-economic approaches for the study of Palestine/Israel—highlighting the relationship between neoliberal restructuring and the Oslo process. Yet critical political economy has not yet been fully incorporated into the analysis of Israeli apartheid.

During an age of industrial expansion, South African factories, farms, and mines were absolutely dependent on Black workers. The Israeli strategy of separation and enclosure, on the other hand, has emerged during an age of neoliberal hegemony and involves the steady eradication of work for Palestinians. Some observers recognize the divergent relationship between capitalism and racism in apartheid-era South Africa and contemporary Palestine/Israel as simply a manifestation of contextual specificity in the operation of apartheid. But this is more than an academic question of similarities and differences. It goes to the heart of the crisis confronting Palestinians and South Africans today.

A familiar story throughout the world, the globalization of production made possible by neoliberal restructuring has generated surplus populations in both South Africa and Palestine/Israel: permanently unemployed, too poor to consume, and abandoned by the neoliberal state. In Palestine/Israel, neoliberalism has intensified a colonial dynamic already operating to turn Palestinians into a surplus population that can be enclosed, expelled, encouraged to kill one another, or simply slaughtered—as Israel has repeatedly made clear in Gaza. This raises important questions about the possibilities for forging movements to challenge a racial capitalist system that is increasingly producing surplus populations across the planet.

Over the last ten years, the Palestinian solidarity movement has made extraordinary gains, especially through BDS campaigns. Yet Palestinian movements on the ground face intense repression and fragmentation. At the same time, South Africa has witnessed widespread struggles against neoliberal capitalism—from service delivery protests to community-based social movements to independent labor unions. And throughout the world, people have risen up against neoliberal capitalism, corporate power, war, and racism. Global convergences of these social justice movements—such as the WCAR and the World Social Forum—have provided opportunities for Palestinians to forge connections with organizations and activists from South Africa and around the world. Understanding the ways that Palestine/Israel, like South Africa, is implicated in global processes of political-economic restructuring could contribute to the constitution of broader movements against global, neoliberal apartheid.

Chapter 6

# Apartheid as Solution

Bill Freund

In comparing Israel and South Africa, I would like to make a few preliminary comments that might preempt some otherwise justified criticisms. The first is the need to define *apartheid*, a word commonly bandied about to stop discussion. Apartheid then becomes some kind of horror vaguely used to cover many things happening during a fairly long period in South African history. Its foreign sound for English speakers is often taken up for the effect, deliberately intended, to give it a particularly sinister ring, unlike its once popular predecessor, *segregation*, used for a long time in South Africa even by those who called themselves liberals. *Segregation* was in fact deliberately copied from its usage in the American South. As Mahmood Mamdani points out—and I note that Mamdani is a figure with a deep sympathy for African nationalism—South African racial policies emanated out of the history of European colonialism in Africa and were very typical of policies in which all the European powers, including those with conventionally democratic governments, once engaged. These policies are no longer acceptable, but they certainly once were. Retaining and building on this edifice, in tandem with the emergence in the mid–twentieth century of a consumer society built on a significant industrialization project, was the unique path that made late twentieth-century South Africa anomalous. Once an antiapartheid struggle existed in earnest, the defense against it took the form at times of a dirty war, but

*Author's Note: I am very grateful to Daryl Glaser for reading this paper and suggesting revisions.*

that hardly explains a whole deeply rooted social, cultural, and economic system with a long past.

Consequently, exactly what one is comparing in Israel with what aspect of South African politics or society becomes important if one wants to go beyond movement hyperbole. For instance, Israel did much to assist South African militarization in the final decade and a half of apartheid, but this mostly reflected a convenient alliance between two countries with polecat status for some, rather than any deep inner logic. The Israelis were essentially strategic opportunists who had put themselves forth earlier as model anticolonial nationalists.[1]

Some years ago I read what I thought was a remarkably comprehensive and intelligent comparison of the two systems made by the British journalist Robert Fisk (one of the most trustworthy sources on what really goes on in and about Israel), syndicated in South Africa's *Mail and Guardian*. I could add little to his magisterial and detailed treatment. The essence of what Fisk had to say was a bifurcation between two situations. First of all, let us consider the situation now in what was 1948–1967 Israel. On the one hand, Israel has a liberal "virtual" constitution with civil rights elements quite unlike the old South Africa. For instance, the president of Israel recently went through the motions after the 2015 elections of a formal meeting with the third biggest political party, which represents almost all Arabs in Israel. On the other, security fears and chauvinistic attachment to an old-fashioned nation-state concept are equally striking and enshrined in some key legislation. Current prime minister Netanyahu's openly stated position, that an independent Palestine must never be allowed to have an independent military force and that no negotiations can take place without the Palestinians first recognizing that Israel is a "Jewish state," would be a good illustration of the values that percolate through Zionism. So would the outpouring of Jewish Israeli sentiment upon the January 2014 death of his unlovable and corrupt hardline predecessor Ariel Sharon, an event that for good reasons attracted few foreigners, not even US president Barack Obama.

Non-Jews can vote and sit in the Knesset. The Labor Party, when in power, even placed a few Arabs in junior cabinet positions, but rarely do they serve on the judiciary or in the diplomatic corps. Apart from certain groups who fought alongside the Zionists in the war for Israeli independence, they are not trusted enough to be eligible for conscription. Yet optimists suggest that in areas such as cultural performance, sports, and access to higher education, the secular and pro-citizen aspect has tended to strengthen in Israel over time, albeit unevenly, often with the support of the courts.

A fair account has to point out, moreover, that many predominantly Muslim states and others behave no better, indeed often far worse, toward their minorities. I am struck by the lack of excitement shown by Muslims in South Africa and elsewhere regarding the fates of Kashmir, the Copts in Egypt, or Muslims in Burma or Thailand, to cite some obvious examples of prejudice by or against Muslims, as compared to the great cause of Palestine. Israel is very far from the worst example of minority treatment or discrimination in our world, although it is also far from a model of fairness.

In Israel within these pre-1967 borders, the war for Israeli independence was marked by deliberate ethnic cleansing that drove most of the resident Palestinian population out of the territory won by the Jews, a territory that exceeded what they had been awarded by the new UN, and that in turn exceeded what they might be thought entitled to through a population count. Even the UN territory allocated to Jews on the map had Arabs as comprising close to half the population; this problem for Zionism was solved by the war. Very few Palestinian refugees were allowed to return to their homes. The essence of the Zionist project was to extrude Arabs and create a Jewish majority, not to exploit Arabs. In this way Israel was more like a typical settler colony such as Canada, Australia, or the thirteen colonies that came to make up the future United States of America, rather than the colonial situations in most of Africa.

There is consequently, as Fisk pointed out, a second terrain that needs to be discussed: the remaining territory that had previously belonged to the British Mandate Palestine, which had then been occupied by Egyptian and Jordanian troops and ruled as though it belonged to those two countries. Here, crowded together, were the largest number of refugees from 1948. In the Gaza Strip, especially, militancy is fueled by their poverty, and refugees are the majority population. In the 1967 War, these remnants of the Mandate Palestine were occupied in a mere few days by Israel, almost all of it still being today the occupied territories. From here, few of the inhabitants were expelled or fled. Yet here too, with the collusion of the authorities, much land has been alienated to Jewish settlers. Golda Meir was particularly strident as an Israeli leader in her rhetoric about the importance of "facts on the ground."[2] It seems a fair comment that the Israeli establishment initially hoped to use these territories as a bargaining chip to get what it wanted from Arabs in a one-sided treaty. However, since this has never happened, these territories, as Fisk observed, have become something like Bantustans, with no clear future. Visitors of many stripes find the situation of their population distressing, especially in the Gaza Strip, which houses more than one million people in an impoverished isolated city-state. This is no future Singapore.

Israel is not in a position to expel this population; its political elite has come to the view over time—reluctant for some—that some kind of Arab sovereignty will have to be granted if it can be done in a way that represents no threat to Israeli security. Here, as Fisk wrote, there are real similarities to the Bantustan policy that turned the old rural locations into pseudo-independent states. The Bantustans presented the one striking original policy feature of the 1948–1994 Afrikaner Nationalist government compared to its predecessors, and that, in my view, defines apartheid. In his last years, General Smuts, the leader of the rival United Party, admitted that segregation—or, otherwise, apartheid—just followed the lines along which he had been born, bred, and educated and to which he had no deep objection.

From two perspectives, I wish it were possible to find what is usually called a one-state solution to this conundrum. The first is my background in economic history and political economy. The whole of the old Palestine is a small territory, and the division into these two parts artificial and impractical. The Palestinian "capital" of Ramallah is spatially almost a suburb of Jerusalem, not a huge metropolis. The only excuse for the partition is that Jews and Arabs largely fail to embrace the idea of a union. The Israeli position in this regard is very clear—the maximum territory with the fewest Arabs is the desideratum—even though hardly more than three-fourths of the Israeli population within the pre-1967 boundaries is Jewish. The official Arab position is more ambiguous.

The second is that I do believe in the idea that South Africa crossed a huge historical threshold in getting rid of the Bantustans and taking a step toward becoming one nation for all its people—a task that still requires much work and that could ultimately fail, but that was the right thing to do in terms of building a stable, developed country in southern Africa.

It is not exactly a question of democracy. For whites the old apartheid South Africa was by no means a dictatorship, and, for Jews in Israel, democracy seems manifest. Indeed, if anything, Netanyahu panders to majority opinion. It is the national question—which is quite separate as an issue. It means overcoming the older definition of who constitutes the nation. Working toward a common South African society has, however, become so associated with democracy, with fairness, with a good national future, that the contrast could not be stronger. Visionaries and intellectuals on both sides in the Middle East conflict share these values, but, while they deserve a lot of credit, they don't win elections. Former opposition leader Tony Leon and former president F. W. de Klerk are among the not especially radical visiting South African whites who have made these points in the press.

Nation-states of the old stripe are surely not going to be the future of humanity. Zionism has its roots in the kind of nationalism usually initially associated with German ideologues who emphasized ancestry, origins, and cultural identity. By contrast the nationalism that became dominant in the political discourse of revolutionary France, of the British Empire, and of the United States held a much stronger sense of common ideals, of an ability to absorb immigrants and people of varying origins, even if the principles were sometimes honored only in the breach. Of course this second approach also has essentially Western roots.[3] Zionism also had a religious element insofar as the early Zionists insisted, after initial internal conflicts, that the territory where Jews could develop as a modern people and form in time a nation-state should be the land that was the site of the Old Testament. Otherwise, though, Zionism was in general militantly secular and internally shot through with ideas we associate with the left.[4]

Behind this lay and continues to lie a deep commitment on the part of most Israeli Jews to keep Israel a country where no gentile-run government could ever block Jewish immigration; could ever say there are too many clever Jews in the universities, the media, or the government; or could insist that jobs must be based, as South Africans like to put it, on the "demographics." This feeling was certainly intensified by the Holocaust, enshrined and cultivated as national motif in Israel, and still a governing one. Of course, this vision would be undermined by a one-state solution.

One should add that Israel, once egalitarian and relatively poor, has become affluent and very successful, one of the contemporary world's most triumphant development stories, respected in the business world everywhere. Its left-wing past is remembered and honored by few. It is estimated to have the highest research and development spending as a percentage of the economy of any country in the world, and, so far, the business community seems united in support of the government. This is in contrast to late apartheid South Africa, whose impressive but languishing big businesses turned against the regime and did much to engineer the 1990 truce and 1994 settlement.

Palestinian nationalism is easier to explain. It belongs to the powerful twentieth-century trajectory of anticolonial nationalism, of the link between human freedom and colonial independence. The presence of this incongruous so-called Jewish state in the very core of the Middle East seems like a tragic perversity. Sources friendly to the Palestinian cause maximize the number of Palestinians with the assumption that a free Palestine or a free one-state territory would attract all emigrants and refugees back and restore an Arab majority to the whole land—a questionable supposition. Nor, of course, can you turn the clock back to the status quo ante of 1947, almost seventy years ago. Whether the Arabs of the West Bank and Gaza would favor a one-state solution in which they would not be a majority, in which a large Jewish population would likely be on average far wealthier and more successful, is hard to say. Although, just as with the Jews, there are certainly men and women of goodwill who could settle for a Palestine eccentric to the Middle East.

I cannot see an easy answer to the question of what to do with the aspirations of Palestinians who fled in 1948 to return to what they see as their old legitimate homes. In South Africa, land taken by the state, usually for reasons of racial compaction after 1948, has been returned to Africans, although with very poor economic results. However, this is just a small proportion of the national territory. The number of whites forced to vacate such land must be close to zero. But in Israel there are hundreds of thousands of Jews, the descendants of the Holocaust survivors and immigrants from the Middle East who took over equivalent properties many decades ago, and these are now their homes. Even the less fortunate relate poorly to Arab claims and assertions of ownership.

Despite generous compensation, the howls of the few thousand Jewish settlers who were obliged to vacate the land around Gaza by Ariel Sharon were publicized as a great human rights challenge. Indeed this evacuation without negotiation or recognition of Palestinian rights, probably seen by Sharon as an undesirable but inevitable alternative, was no roaring success. The people of Gaza, and certainly the Hamas militants, hoped it spelled the beginning of Israeli defeat, not the start of a logical and acceptable partition, and have used their enclave despite the odds to launch missile attacks on their foes—or did so until massive retribution from the Israelis made a terrifying impact with the 2014 massacres as a second act.

As a result, it is important for us to recognize that the two-state solution, propounded by many who are very anxious about the wrongs of Palestinians, is the opposite of an antiapartheid solution. It is about establishing, whatever the boundaries, two totally separate countries with different national identities. As Yitzhak Rabin (the prime minister who signed the Oslo Accords and began talks with Yasser Arafat about a "peace of the brave" before a nationalist Jew assassinated him) said approvingly, what is wanted is not a marriage but a divorce.[5] This, too, is what international players have expected, at best.

Such a solution would enshrine the two nationalisms, neither of them more than grudgingly inclusive, at best on a fairer basis. A clear statement along these lines, going along with the longtime UN demand for Israel to withdraw back to the 1967 border, was judiciously put forward some years ago by the government of Saudi Arabia, a proposal rejected with contempt by the Israeli government. It could never give Israel what it wants in terms of security and territory. Nor could it create an Arab Palestine of much substance. The negotiations that get revived from time to time, and that the media inform us are somewhat "hopeful," seem largely a farce, a stage act performed for a foreign audience that sustains Israel but officially claims to sympathize with aspirations of Palestinian statehood.

The current situation has very few silver linings within dark clouds. One is the presence in 2015, for the first time, of so many Arab parliamentarians in Israel. Aligned with the more reasonable Jewish Israelis, they surely have the best potential for organizing a government capable of making serious concessions and a real peace, moving the country down a very different path. Maybe this will come about someday if this trend gathers enough strength.

The other change is the way the boorish Netanyahu has alienated an American government. The United States has made the troubled Middle Eastern state one of its very closest allies, a relationship marked by complex and intimate military and intelligence ties. However, this alliance is becoming less stable. One wonders if Netanyahu went too far in allowing the truth about the Israeli—as opposed to the fictitious Iranian—bomb to become public knowledge instead of a more or less state secret in America. Netanyahu obviously sees himself making a bold play, anticipating a victory of the right-wing Republican Party in the upcoming US election, and he may well win that gamble. However, Israel without US support, *with* US pressure to force negotiations based on substantial real concessions no matter how painful, would be in a very different situation, and perhaps we can see that on a more or less distant horizon. The demographics of the United States are themselves gradually changing in ways that will not help the American right. Supporting a Likud-type government in Israel is certainly counter to US interests, and Israel under the likes of a Netanyahu is anything but a source of stability in the Middle East. The Israeli Labor Party in particular obviously picked up the message from influential Jewish Democrats and the Obama administration as to what could be in the cards. With serious US pressure, the attitude of Labor and, no doubt, of key businessmen of Israel, so dependent on international markets and investments, would surely have to move further. This could change the odds and tip the balance to more plausible scenarios of change.

When I started to study South Africa in the 1960s, a well-known title by American Newell Stultz featured the Transkei as South Africa's proffered "half-loaf" to Blacks. Of course, the loaf was much less than half. It is not clear that any significant group of Israeli or Palestinian participants really wants a Transkei-type solution, even with an international godfather and recognition of Palestinian independence, and it is hard to be optimistic about a solution that is also one in the end of separation, of half-loaves or less. Can we get the combatants to settle down to a fairer sort of apartheid? Would a Palestinian government act as an Israeli gendarme force suppressing ultras who wanted to continue the struggle by whatever means? And even the most benevolent of Israeli governments would surely long continue to have serious security concerns. Somehow a system would need to be created where everyone's security depended on mutual commitment. This is the reason I think the apartheid analogy, however morally satisfying to many activists, does not really come to grips with this complex problem. Much as I would be very happy to hear of any kind of peaceful solution in the Middle Eastern conflict, we are very far from a dismantling of the Middle Eastern equivalent of apartheid even as an ideal held by participants in the conflict. From the point of view of a solution, the analogy is not so easy to sustain.

# Chapter 7

# The Historian and Apartheid

## T. J. Tallie

The Israeli apartheid analogy is a complex one, particularly for me as an African-American historian whose work focuses on histories of race, gender, and conflict in South Africa. In many ways, the structure of apartheid as a governmental system and overlapping series of exclusionary laws and policies does indeed resemble that of contemporary Israel, as figures like Desmond Tutu have made clear time and again.[1] Historically, the partnership between Israel and the apartheid government in South Africa was a contested but close one, made stronger by both governments' view that they were bastions of Western, anticommunist order in a region surrounded by hostile native peoples. *Die Burger*, a newspaper in the Cape Province (now Western Cape) that frequently served as a mouthpiece for apartheid's National Party (NP), invoked this connection most starkly in May 1968:

> Israel and South Africa have a common lot. Both are engaged in a struggle for existence, and both are in constant clash with the decisive majorities in the United Nations. Both are reliable foci of strength within the region, which would, without them, fall into anti-Western anarchy. It is in South Africa's interest that Israel is successful in containing her enemies, who are among our own most vicious enemies.... The anti-Western powers have driven Israel and South Africa into a community of interests which had better be utilized than denied.[2]

Indeed, the structural parallels of apartheid and Zionism in Israel are strikingly visible in multiple forms, from ruthless expulsions of peoples to the claims of newly arrivant peoples to authentic indigeneity, religious justifications, and hypermilitization.

The similarities between the two state systems led South African exile Alfred Tokollo Moleah, then a professor in Pan-African studies at Temple University in Pennsylvania, to write a scathing indictment of both Israel and South Africa in 1979, in which he called both countries

> the manifestation of a shared ideology, a common worldview. Both Israel and South Africa feel that they have a religious call-ing; both see themselves as Western outposts in a sea of barba-rism. They both see their states and the political programs as the unfolding of a divine drama. . . . When a divine injunction rests on privilege, floats on oil, is gilted as well as festooned with dia-monds, and is girded by uranium, chrome and platinum group metals, you then have a most explosive mixture.[3]

Yet, as a historian, I do feel compelled to point out that the compari-son is not without its flaws. The word *apartheid* itself and its origins have much to do with a specific regional, temporal, and cultural context within southern Africa. Using the word *apartheid* as an analogy is a decisive mo-bilization of the term in order to link Israel's policies with a now entirely discredited regime of exclusion and oppression in South Africa. To make the analogy provides rhetorical power, but it also can flatten considerable historic differences between both regions.

While Israeli limitation of "legitimate" Palestinian political spaces to the West Bank and Gaza is in some ways reminiscent of the infamous Ban-tustans of South Africa in the 1970s, the two are not identical. Although the Israeli state and the NP's assumption of government in South Africa share the same year of origin (1948), their preceding histories are not the same. Apartheid's origins are rooted substantially in the particularities of settler-colonialism in southern Africa, in the mutual antagonisms between English- and Afrikaans-speaking white minority populations, and the histories of oppressive rule these two populations tried to establish over numerically superior African populations between the seventeenth and twentieth centuries. Apartheid as a political and cultural project sought to create a modern, industrial nation-state that specifically served only the white minority population. The creation of the state of Israel and its rela-tionship to the Palestinian population is different historically, albeit no less problematic. The initial creation of a Jewish state in a region where Jewish people were not the majority population also contains within it the inherent problems of minority rule and the use of oppression to maintain this order. Significant claims of historic origin notwithstanding, the majority of Israel's Jewish population has arrived in the region within the last century.

Yet, the analogy remains significant as both countries' governmental systems, from the point of view of the colonized, are oppressive minority regimes. Both regimes make recourse to broader nationalism or disingenuous claims to universal democracy to allow full citizenship and access to power only to a significant minority of the population. The majority of the population in both countries, then, has been locked outside of institutional access to power and resources even as the minority regime justifies itself through claims of democracy. It is therefore understandable why critics of Israel's continued oppressive regime wish to use the label *apartheid* in order to link it to the universally discredited South African government.

In thinking through these comparisons, I am reminded of the extrajudicial killing of Black Consciousness Movement leader and antiapartheid activist Steve Biko in 1977 by South African police forces. When Jimmy Kruger, minister of justice and the police under prime minister John Vorster, first spoke of Biko's death at an NP meeting in the Transvaal, he commented abruptly, "Dit laat my koud" (It leaves me cold).[4] Kruger's comment feels an apt exemplar of the institutionalized brutality and quotidian indifference in the face of suffering that marked life under the apartheid regime. It is a form of calculus that decides which lives are grievable and which are not to be lamented in the name of a regime's survival.

The Kruger quote inevitably came to mind as I sat riveted to online news coverage of the unrelenting Israeli assault on Gaza in the summer of 2014, particularly after the deaths of four children on a beach in Gaza (itself an echo of an earlier killing of a Palestinian family on the beach in 2006).[5] While the Israeli military declared that it was a "tragic outcome," there is a certain measure of coldness to the killing of civilians in what now seems an indiscriminate choice of targets. It remains very apparent that while Palestinian deaths are lamentable, they are deemed necessary, collateral damage for an operation aimed at securing a "protective edge" for an oppressive settler regime.

But again, I am reminded that this rhetoric is neither new nor unique to the South African or Israeli contexts. As Chickasaw scholar Jodi Byrd has addressed, my own country, the United States, is built upon a history of the ungrievable Indian, a necropolitics that decides that, while unfortunate, the death and clearing of indigenous peoples is a necessity for securing the settler state.[6] Settler societies, ones in which colonists come to stay, occupying the land and in a dark irony claiming that land as their own to the exclusion of the earlier inhabitants, share many similarities. As anthropologist Patrick Wolfe has argued, settler-colonialism is a structure rather than an event.[7] It constantly shapes the daily, lived realities of the people within the settler state (be it the United States, Israel, South Africa, Australia, Canada, or other similar countries). Those in the population of settlers come to view their expansion as "inevitable," "natural," and "right." The constant, oppressive violence that structured the lived reality of earlier inhabitants is regrettable yet "necessary." As an American I must reflect on how often our history is taught as the regrettable violence of occupying indigenous lands and the unfortunate destruction of earlier occupants in order to expand an empire of liberty: one that increasingly brings new groups of people into an ever-widening circle of freedom. (Indeed, this freedom becomes a terrible, powerful, and unrefusable gift for subjected peoples, as theorist Mimi Thi Nguyen has argued so well.[8])

This intersection is where I find myself as an African American scholar of South African history viewing the Israeli–Palestinian conflict. I am intellectually struck by the similarities of settler logics in Israeli repressive measures against Palestinians—as well as the simultaneous fear and resentment of peoples who are themselves locked in cycles of repression and violent occupation—to those I have spent much of my career reading about in colonial South Africa and, more aptly, in its apartheid iteration. Yet I remain profoundly aware of the privilege provided by distance from both South Africa and Israel and by the naturalization of our own settler violences here. As a non-native person of color, I understand very well the constant and disproportionate violence meted out to nonwhite peoples within the United States. And these moments of repression are still shaped by a complicated relationship to a settler nation-state: the very claims I make to belong to a body politic, to push against oppression, are often done through recourse to an American identity that exists only through the oppression and marginalization of indigenous North Americans.

I do think that I have an obligation to continue to articulate the similarities between institutional Israeli settler repression and that codified in twentieth-century South Africa. While apartheid is a historic and culturally specific political system with a specific frame of reference, many of its political, social, and psychological impacts seem very similar to the Israeli context. Yet, I feel that as an American historian I am equally called to a systematic and searching reflection on my own political and social contexts as an academic and as a researcher. My observation of these phenomena is not neutral and it, too, is shaped by my own experiences of settler violence.

I believe that a critical assessment of Israeli apartheid that does not also involve self-reflection upon American anti-indigenous genocide and historic anti-Black segregation runs the risk of being myopic and self-serving. It all too easily reinscribes the unfortunate American trait of advocating for political justice in other locations while obfuscating historical oppressions in which we are imbricated. This is not simply a call for navel-gazing, self-flagellating scholarship in the place of incisive and productive comparative work. But I do think that as a historian I am required to remember my own contexts in writing as much as the place I seek to write about.

Indeed, the connections between settler regimes and oppressive violence run very deep between Israel and the United States. The brutal killing in August 2014 of Michael Brown, an unarmed Black teenager, in the streets of Ferguson, Missouri, shocked many with the revelations of systemic state brutality against people of color. Yet, the St. Louis Police Department, like many departments across the country, has been marked by a profound militarization in tactics, one that treats civilians as ever-constant threats, as expendable lives to be removed. It is not surprising, then, to learn that Joseph Mokwa, the former chief of the St. Louis Police Department, traveled to Israel in 2008 as part of a law-enforcement exchange program designed to teach police advanced counterterrorism methods.[9] While the United States, Israel, and apartheid-era South Africa all have significantly different historical origins, the rhetoric of settler rule and hypermilitarized repression is shared between them. Indeed, as the case in St. Louis demonstrates, these regimes shared (and continue to share) information, building their logics of oppression and violence in relation to each other. Due to this shared logic of oppression, analogy is a useful tool of critique and response. It allows us to see how certain systems are oppressive and how they relate to and inform others.

Nowhere is this more apparent than the response of besieged Palestinians in the immediate wake of Michael Brown's death and the chilling militarized occupation of Ferguson, Missouri. From Gaza and beyond, Palestinians released a statement of solidarity with protesters in Missouri, proclaiming:

> We recognize the disregard and disrespect for black bodies and black life endemic to the supremacist system that rules the land with wanton brutality. Your struggles through the ages have been an inspiration to us as we fight our own battles for basic human dignities. We continue to find inspiration and strength from your struggles through the ages and your revolutionary leaders, like Malcolm X, Huey Newton, Kwame Ture, Angela Davis, Fred Hampton, Bobby Seale and others.[10]

Analogies can cut both ways. Just as the Israel/apartheid analogy exposes similar structural disadvantages for populations, so too can the struggles of African Americans within white supremacist institutions in the United States inspire and shape Palestinians' fight against what they view as an ever-constant Israeli occupation. So too, can these analogies reverberate in ostensibly postapartheid South Africa, itself confronting the two-year anniversary of brutal police violence against striking miners at Marikana. The prevailing logic of these state actions presumes that civilians exist as omnipresent threats to be eliminated, lives to be cheaply disposed for state power. As the South African political scientist Richard Pithouse observed in August 2014, "The impunity of the Israeli state, like the impunity of the American state, like the impunity with which our own state increasingly uses murder, and legitimates the use of murder as a tool of social control, must be smashed. The militarization of social questions must be smashed everywhere."[11] While profoundly imperfect, analogies offer a point of reference, of common understanding, to challenge extant oppressive systems from South Africa to Israel to the United States.

## Chapter 8

# Teach for Your Life

### Teresa Barnes

T he United States is periodically gripped by episodes of intense para-
noia in which emotional appeals from politicians to protect "our way of
life" resonate loudly with heightened anxieties of ordinary people about
this or that. The results are a potent combination of narrow-minded,
fear-mongering rhetorical excess and actual physical purges. US historians
will point to other episodes as well, but I have in mind mainly resonances
between 2015 and the McCarthy period.

The United States in 2015 also resembles apartheid-era South Africa.
It is painful to make this comparison, because it implies bedfellow status
for president Barack Obama and South African one-time prime minister
Hendrik Verwoerd, the "architect of apartheid." But in both places we see
racial segregation as the virtual default position. In both we see self-cen-
sorship brought on by an unprecedented level of state surveillance. In both
we see a common worship of militarism and the military (listen to audience cheers during showings of the movie *American Sniper*). In both we
see the constant glorification of the state and adulation of its militaristic
symbolism. In both we see a common proliferation of secretive and shad-
owy state organizations that routinely undertake executions without any
accountability whatsoever—secrecy that is, in any case, unnecessary, since
the bored and anesthetized public only yawns dismissively at word of yet
another assassination by bomb or drone.

Both countries have proudly pointed to their adherence to "the rule
of law." In South Africa in the 1980s, the cross-border raids of the apartheid state killed people in Lesotho, Mozambique, Swaziland, Botswana,

Zambia, Angola, Namibia, and Zimbabwe. America is killing people to-day even farther afield from its own borders, in Yemen, Iraq, Syria, Af-ghanistan, and Pakistan. South Africa's domestic and foreign wars were waged to make the country and the region safe for white supremacy. In the United States today, while the racial component is not to be denied (how could it be in an era when the killers of Trayvon Martin, Rekia Boyd, Tamir Rice, Michael Brown, Shelly Frey, Eric Garner, Alberta Spruil, Aiyana Stanley-Jones, and so many others go scot-free?), the state is ulti-mately seeking to protect class supremacy and the ability of the 1 percent to continue to rape, pillage, and plunder the actual and ecological pension plans of the 99 percent.

As other chapters in this volume show, Israel is another link between present-day United States and apartheid South Africa. These were three of the "great" settler-colonial societies of the late twentieth century. The leaders of Israel and apartheid South Africa overcame their mutual dislike (as Zionists and neo-Nazis) to become firm, if secret, allies by the 1970s. South Africa became the largest client of the Israeli arms industry, and South Africa's nuclear bomb capabilities were partially culled from Israeli technology. Israel made huge business deals in white South Africa and in the Bantustans, the fake "countries" for Africans that the apartheid state set up inside its own borders. Similarly, the current US financial, business, and military support for Israel cannot be underestimated. As we enter an-other burlesque for the 2016 US presidential elections, for example, that's perhaps the one and only thing that every single major party candidate, right or left, will agree on.

Universities are the most prominent social institutions that could raise voices against this insanity. There is no other social reservoir of peo-ple who supposedly are trained to ask difficult, unpopular, theoretically informed, and popularly accessible questions. The "critical thinking skills" that we traditionally invoke as the goal of our teaching really only add up to a willingness to ask "why" when no one wants to give reasons and to ask "how" when no one wants to provide logistical details. Critical thinking is not rocket science—just an abiding instinct to search out and expose the gaps in rhetorical armor and the weak links in chains of logic.

The axe of a police state thus falls hard on universities. It fell hard on universities in South Africa, where dissenting voices were silenced through bans, exile, and assassination. The majority of South Africa's academics submissively acquiesced to mediocrity and racist cant, producing scholarship and teaching that sought to inculcate herd thinking in generations of students. They were, sadly, successful, and South Africa is paying the price today for decades of substandard education and the false consciousness that it generated.

The signs are very troubling that the current US academy is running aground on the same rocks, but with even less controversy. Where are challenging, unpopular voices speaking now in the US academy? Where is ethical research deeply committed to social justice being conducted? Where is the critical debate? Where are the administrators standing up to donors and funding agencies to defend the intellectual independence of their academics? Only in shrinking little pockets of our institutions, that's where. In the larger spaces of our universities, where most of our colleagues reside, the situation is, to be honest, abysmal. We see meaningless, unethical, and frankly ignorant question-asking passing for and being funded as, legitimate research. Public assets—physical and intellectual—are privatized at a galloping rate. Massively overpaid managers and administrators have less understanding of the rights and responsibilities of academic freedom than your Uncle Jake. The public circuses of college athletics provide formulaic thrills; young bodies are forced to produce results at inhumanely elevated standards; the marching bands toot on. As both public and private higher education push tuition fees past the levels of credulity, the enrollments of students of color, especially those coming from family backgrounds in "the precariat," have fallen to dangerously low levels.

Although US universities have fallen on hard moral times as the academic spaces of critical engagement shrink, campus-based developments can still sometimes throw otherwise shadowy national trends and dynamics into high relief. Thus, the boycott, divestment, and sanctions (BDS) movement against Zionist Israel is most visible on US campuses, as it publicizes and tries to undermine the academic, financial, business, and military ties between the United States and Israel in the interest of historical justice for those who have been trampled by the Yankee and Zionist versions of apartheid.

At my own university, the University of Illinois Urbana–Champaign (UIUC), all these forces came into high relief in 2014 with the purging of professor Steven Salaita. A literature scholar and a member of the global Palestinian diaspora, Salaita was offered and accepted a tenured post in the

UIUC American Indian Studies (AIS) program as it sought to strengthen its intellectual reach in transnational studies of indigeneity. Not coincidentally, an AIS faculty member, professor Robert Warrior, has cited a visit to Palestinian villages as an undergraduate and graduate study under Edward Said as formative intellectual influences.[1] Over the past decade, AIS has been a small but mighty presence on our campus, fighting (among other things) the racist backlash among students, staff, alumni, and the local community to the reluctantly taken official decision to "retire" the university mascot, a caricature of Native American people locally known as "The Chief." In agreeing to join AIS, Professor Salaita had duly resigned his position at Virginia Tech University and prepared for the move to central Illinois. His Virginia home had been sold and the moving van was literally in the driveway when he received a call from UIUC chancellor Phyllis Wise. She informed him that she was invoking a little-known, fine-print provision of UIUC academic job offers. The university's board of directors has final approval of all academic contracts, and Chancellor Wise informed Professor Salaita that she had decided not to forward his employment contract to the board. Without its final approval his employment could not go through—and he was thus unemployed.

It has been shown that Chancellor Wise had been pressured into this decision by a pro-Zionist campaign that was mounted against Professor Salaita in the wake of his own series of messages on social media that passionately criticized the brutal Israeli crackdown in the Gaza Strip in 2014. Despite the fact that his presence and opinions in the world of social media were outside the classroom and the campus, and had nothing to do with his academic performance (he has no fewer than six books to his name) or his teaching (he had received stellar teaching evaluations at Virginia Tech), Chancellor Wise declared that she was acting to "protect" UIUC students who, she claimed, would now doubtless feel uncomfortable in his classrooms.[2]

As of this writing, Professor Salaita is suing UIUC for denying his rights of free speech and firing him without any kind of due process or appeal. Chancellor Wise has stated that she wished she had consulted with more people on campus before she made her decision, but she and the university's other top administrators have stuck by the decision to purge him from UIUC employment. Almost 20,000 people signed a change.org petition that demanded Professor Salaita's reinstatement, and 1,200 academics around the world declared that they would have no further dealings with the University of Illinois until his job was restored. The three campuses of the University of Illinois have at least 2,000 full-time academics; 350 of them signed a petition to protest the firing. Fifteen departments on the Urbana campus independently passed motions of no confidence in the university administration; Chancellor Wise was called a hypocrite to her face at a raucous campus meeting, when she declared that she believed deeply in academic freedom. A handful of students tried to occupy her office. A small, doggedly resolute coordinating committee supporting re-instatement sponsored rallies, talks, and panels on academic freedom; the Department of Gender and Women's Studies sponsored three boisterous teach-ins on academic freedom, Black Lives Matter, and "race, indigeneity, and environmental justice." The UIUC senate's Committee on Academic Freedom carefully noted that, in its opinion, "We do not believe that Dr. Salaita's political speech renders him unsuitable for office [at UIUC]" and recommended that the entire matter be reconsidered.[3] Meanwhile, shad-owy outside campaigns of whisper and innuendo were mounted against colleagues who supported Professor Salaita here. Horrible death threats have been sent to defenders of academic freedom on our campus. An ac-ademic boycott was called on the university, and, in June 2015, the uni-versity was censured by the American Association of University Professors (AAUP) over the Salaita Affair.[4] The academic year 2014–2015 was annus horribilis at UIUC.

The Salaita Affair has eerie parallels with aspects of the infamous 1968 Mafeje Affair at the University of Cape Town (UCT) in South Africa. After the passage of apartheid legislation in 1959, South Africa's universities were strictly segregated by race and ethnicity. Separate facilities were eventually built for all conceivable groups such that, when apartheid finally officially ended in 1994, the country had no fewer than thirty-two institutions of higher education, from universities through technical colleges and teachers' colleges. There were complete sets of these institutions for English-speak-ing whites, Afrikaans-speaking whites, each major African ethnicity (Zulu, Tswana, Xhosa, and so forth), Indians, and so-called Coloureds. Back in 1968, it was illegal for the "white" universities to employ academics of color. The UCT Anthropology Department, however, offered an academic po-sition to Dr. Archie Mafeje, a trained and qualified Black anthropologist who had earned BA and MA degrees from UCT (gained before 1959) and a PhD from Cambridge. However, when the apartheid state got wind of the fact that UCT was about to appoint "a Bantu" to teach at a white university, it threatened UCT with dire consequences for its funding support if it proceeded with the appointment. UCT's governing council caved in and rescinded Mafeje's job offer. When this news broke on campus, a famous protest ensued. Eager to join their international counterparts on the 1968 barricades, students and a few academics occupied the UCT administration building for nine days. The council did not change its mind, however, and Professor Mafeje never did receive the position for which he was so completely qualified. He went on to both a distinguished career in Pan-African anthropology and, reportedly, a lifetime of bitterness at his treatment at the hands of the craven UCT council and administration.

Mafeje and Salaita have several things in common. Both were vocal representatives of indigeneity. Both were highly qualified and well-regarded academics, who were offered positions through legitimate academic channels but were denied those positions by administrators who cracked under pressure from forces outside their respective institutions.

It should be noted that very few South African academics showed the courage of their convictions when apartheid was imposed on South African higher education. One was Maurice Pope, a classicist who was the UCT dean of humanities in 1968. He resigned in protest when UCT reneged on Mafeje's job offer.[5] British by birth, it was perhaps less difficult for Pope to find work in his native country, as he did by joining the faculty at Oxford. Nonetheless, it was brave of him to resign from UCT. Similarly, when the apartheid axe fell on the University of Fort Hare in 1959, only one academic resigned rather than teach the gutter education the state was imposing. Other academics certainly left Fort Hare, but it was because their contracts had not been renewed by the apartheid state. Professor Z. K. Matthews—who, despite his Anglo surname was a Black African—was the only Fort Hare academic who publicly resigned his position, knowing that it meant he would lose not only his job but also a lifetime of accumulated retirement benefits.[6] In choosing to refuse complicity with the educational crimes of the apartheid state, Pope and Matthews joined a select band: the handful of Christian professors in Germany who resigned in protest over Nazi purges of Jewish academics in the 1930s, for example.[7]

Part of my own research agenda concerns the dynamics of complicity and collaboration among South African academics in the apartheid era.[8] We know that there were a few brave resisters, but there were many more who kept their heads down in silence—or who openly supported, justified, and applauded the inequalities of apartheid. Although we need much more research on the specific histories and politics of knowledge production in South Africa, it is safe to say that apartheid received majority support from students, academics, and administrators on South African university and college campuses.

In the wake of the purging of Professor Salaita, life continues at UIUC. The term papers and multiple-choice quizzes keep rolling in. This generation of American undergraduates was born in the mid-1990s. I think of them as "the *Lion King* generation": they were parked in front of videos of that 1994 Disney classic instead of having babysitters. They know every twitch of its tale, every frame, every nanosecond of its music. They have a Disneyfied, simplistic grasp of good and bad, male and female, implanted in their very bones. Want to alienate a roomful of US undergraduates? Ask them to critically analyze *The Lion King*. It's like asking them to beat their grandparents to death. The vast majority of these students have not an inkling of the analyses of the United States that can be found in the pages of W. E. B. Du Bois or Howard Zinn. They have little or no idea about life, attitudes, and history in the rest of the world, only sensing vaguely, through the dense fog produced by the bread and circuses of popular culture, that the world is a blank slate on which America is destined to write in big red, white, and blue letters. Pedagogically, the era of "no child left behind" (like so many apartheid-era policies, a chilling name for a policy designed to accomplish the diametric opposite) education has prepared US university students to follow instructions and to complete narrowly conceived and rigidly assessed tasks at high speed. Like apartheid-era South Africans, our students haven't been trained to ask "why?" when no one wants to give reasons and to ask "how?" when no one wants to provide logistical details.

And this is why I hope it is acceptable for US academics who learned to ask questions in more combative, more open, more solidarity-minded eras to show the courage of their convictions by continuing to teach about the history, sociology, literature, geography, music, and gendered dynamics of social justice, always explaining to our students why and how we do what we do. Maybe this is only a self-and-bank-account-serving argument, but I don't think it would be productive to boycott our classes or quit our jobs. Not that anyone is actually doing those things—and besides, if more US states follow the example of governor Scott Walker and Wisconsin, state-appointed committees (the university councils, boards of trustees, boards of regents) will soon be able to purge us whenever they want any-way.[9] While we still can, we have to teach.

I think about the recent vote in the state of Utah to bring back the firing squad to conduct public executions.[10] Five people will then have to aim at and shoot a target pinned over the heart of a hooded, shackled human being. We have to keep teaching in the hope that some of our students will become people who will think to put down their guns and ask "why" this is permissible and "how" it is making the world a better place.

As academics we are teaching for our lives in countries like the United States and Israel that lie along a bloody axis of the historical dispossession and impoverishment of indigenous people, people of color, poor folks. Like the white South Africans of the twentieth century, we now live in an atmosphere of privilege on the one hand, and, on the other, as witnesses to the scenes of intense, daily violent outrages committed in our names. Like them, we can live in glass houses, throw stones, and succumb to injustice with our heads down and in silence. Or, knowing what the consequences can be, we can keep trying—to trudge on together, to keep speaking the truths that we see, and to do better.

Chapter 9

# Along the Edges of Comparison

Marissa J. Moorman

Raphael Singer, Israel's ambassador to Angola, in an editorial in the August 8, 2014, issue of the Angolan newsweekly *Novo Jornal*, warned that a new form of anti-Semitism was on the rise. Violating (or even discrediting the principle of) the Israeli state's right to exist is anti-Semitism's latest avatar. Eduardo Galeano's article "Of Palestine, There is Almost Nothing Left," originally published in 2012 in *Sin Permiso* (Without Permission) and reprinted in *Novo Jornal's* August 1 cultural section, was one such example, Singer said. The African continent, Ambassador Singer hoped, would not accept such nonsense. It hadn't done so historically. Cast in the most general terms, this appeal to Africa disguises a specific Israeli/Angolan bond. The relationship had two distinct phases. Hostile at first, it began with Angola's independence and emplotment in the global Cold War. After the Cold War, it shifted to a friendly and lucrative partnership.

Israeli–Angolan relations surface publicly now and then. But they have a distinctly subterranean sensibility. Rafael Marques de Morais's book *Diamantes de Sangue: Corrupção e Tortura em Angola (Blood Diamonds: Corruption and Torture in Angola)* exposes the precise nature of the relationship in some detail.[1] Official accounts emphasize a different hue. On Angola's website the Israeli Embassy highlights "Green Earth" (Terra Verde), which amounts to bilateral cooperation in agriculture: Israeli expertise promises to make Angola's fields glitter again. Yet at the UN, Angola votes in favor of the Palestinian cause, over and over again. What explains this contradiction?

What is this little *cafecolo* (Angolan term for the thumb pocket in blue jeans) of geopolitics? How has it been sewn into the larger global order?

We cannot make sense of this by drawing a straight line from one place, person, empire, or geopolitical juggernaut to the present. This jagged line of cozy economic relationships between Israel and Angola and finger-wagging political rhetoric is twenty-first-century tender. Polished to a high gloss in the last decade, such relations originated in the muck of the late twentieth century: Angola's civil war, the Cold War, and the morass apartheid wrought in the southern African region. It involves the United States and South Africa. At the beginning is an alliance of white settler states (the United States, South Africa, and Israel) that pursued shared interest in the region, supporting southern African rebel groups (such as the Union for Total Independence of Angola [UNITA] in Angola and Mozambican National Resistance [RENAMO] in Mozambique) in the socialist republics of Portugal's former colonies. After the Cold War and the official end of apartheid, the connections linking South Africa, Israel, and Angola became less state-driven, more convoluted, but no less destructive. The takeaway: the ends of epochs (Cold War, apartheid, colonialism) provide reorganization more than rupture, different messiness, not a clean slate.

A little more history to understand the current tangle of Angolan–Israeli relations is in order. Angola's independence was declared on November 11, 1975, by the MPLA (Popular Movement for the Liberation of Angola) with the help of Cuban troops armed with Soviet military hardware and holding off Zairean (now Congo) and FNLA (Front for the National Liberation of Angola) forces (buoyed with CIA funding) to the north, and having fought back South African and UNITA troops to the south. The new Angolan flag and civil war unfurled together. Israeli and South African complots hovered at the border.

Scholars have noted the similarities of the Israeli and South African apartheid systems: delimitation of land, population control, passbooks and special IDs, archipelagos of ethnicity, labor migration, militarized states, torture, and terror. But this listing and lining up always hits its limit. Comparison eschews isomorphism: the smallest bit of difference provides a wedge for naysayers. But it courts it, too: the adage "compare apples to apples and oranges to oranges" demands a baseline of sameness. Quibbling over that essence is the hobgoblin of comparison. It hides deeper processes of relation. Micol Seigel, in "Beyond Compare: Comparative Method after the Transnational Turn," glosses it like this:

Comparison requires the observer to name two or more units whose similarities and differences she or he will then describe. This setup discourages attention to exchange between the two, the very exchange postcolonial insight understands as the stuff of subject-formation. Foucault's insights into power suggest that a view of two parallel objects that never meet proves inadequate to the explication of this dynamic relation. Comparisons obscure the workings of power.[2]

In the ledger gap, between the lists, hangs a web of connections. Following Seigel, what happens if we sketch exchange and cooperation between Israel and South Africa, as they sit at Angola's border? A world opens up, one that eventually produces relations between Angola and Israel.

Sociologist Jan Nederveen Pieterse reminds us that Israeli military brass helped plan the 1975 South African invasion of Angola.[3] Pieterse notes that this strategy had a parallel in the Israeli strategy of driving the Palestine Liberation Organization (PLO) out of Lebanon and in the US strategy against the Nicaraguan Sandinistas, blamed for the insurgency in El Salvador: Israeli military supplies proved critical in skirting congressional bans on the sale of arms in Central America just as South African military hardware avoided the constraints on US arms imposed by the Clark Amendment in Angola. Perhaps more significant, the invasion of Angola drew on counterterrorism strategy developed in the West Bank and Gaza. Cooperation in the form of counterinsurgency and rebel support in the southern African region activated transnational tentacles that spanned the Middle East, Southern Africa, and Central America.

Those tentacles opened in the interest of three white settler states in the name of the Cold War. Israel, like South Africa, did not act as a simple proxy for US interests any more than Cuba acted at the behest of the Soviet Union (as Piero Gleijeses, and others, amply demonstrate). When Angola's civil war lost its Cold War allies after 1988 (yes, 1988, not 1989), we should not be surprised that Israel and the Angolan MPLA-ruled state, once on opposite sides of the Cold War, would eventually find each other. Interest superseded ideology.

But first, Angola's civil war had to incarnate another continental stereotype: resource war (this was key to the shift in the relationship from Israel-South Africa-UNITA to Israel-MPLA). In this stage of the war, UNITA controlled the diamond-producing regions in northeastern Angola, allowing it to purchase weapons on the international market. In 1993, former South African Defense Force officer Fred Rindel helped UNITA leader Jonas Savimbi establish selling mechanisms to a DeBeers subsidiary with offices in Antwerp and Tel Aviv.[4] The Angolan state fattened the Angolan Armed Forces (FAA) on a rising tide of oil production. Between 1994 and 1998, a period Angolans referred to as "neither peace, nor war," FAA and UNITA generals exchanged fuel for diamonds in a strange state of peaceable co-exploitation of the diamond rich Lundas region.

By 1999, the FAA managed to drive UNITA troops from the region and the Angolan state began to take over the diamond trade. It authorized Ascorp (Angola Selling Corporation) in 2000 to a legal monopoly on Angola diamond marketing. Ascorp stakeholders include the Angolan state subsidiary SODIAM (51 percent), Welox of Israel (of the Leviev Group—24.5 percent), and TAIS of Belgium (24.5 percent). TAIS was originally held by Isabel dos Santos, daughter of Angolan president José Eduardo dos Santos, but she transferred her shares to her mother Tatiana Kukanova (now Tatiana Regan) in 2004. She is her mother's sole heir.[5]

Lev Leviev is an Israeli businessman born in Uzbekistan who resides in London. He is the world's largest cutter and polisher of diamonds. He is Vladimir Putin's friend. He owns key New York City properties. Among his holdings is Africa-Israel, a company with an investment profile in other mining ventures on the continent and in settlements on the West Bank. Yes, that's right: settlements on the West Bank. *Electronic Intifada* and Adalah-NY reported success by divestment movement protesters against this company in 2009 and 2010. Deep ironies and human rights abuses aside, these investments violate Angolan law. Angolan public officials, like the generals who are major stakeholders in the diamond mining companies, cannot, by law, do business with state-run companies.

More official, less problematic relations also pertain. In late 2001 and early 2002, Israeli intelligence lent assistance to the FAA, then in hot pursuit of Jonas Savimbi. While official and public relations focused on greenhouse veggies and agricultural expertise, an Israeli drone cruised the skies of eastern Angola tracking UNITA troops and attempting to pinpoint Savimbi's whereabouts. After a few months of careful recon and skirmishes driving him into open terrain, Savimbi made a rare call from his satellite phone. The jig was up. The FAA attacked and killed him in February 2002, bringing twenty-seven years of civil war to a close by April of that same year.

Meanwhile, in the Lundas provinces, a new kind of war zone developed. Ascorp, intended to create a single buyer and seller for Angolan diamonds, to abolish "blood diamonds," has done the contrary. Residents of the Lundas, rich in resources beyond diamonds, can only mine. According to de Morais, Law 17/94 turned their region into a reservation zone. The state can confiscate anything from any person or enterprise, in the name of the public good, for the mining companies. Large swaths of land have been expropriated from local owners. The population is forced into mining and denied the possibility of producing a livelihood from agriculture. In Lunda North, where alluvial mining predominates, the security firm Teleservice, owned by top-level FAA generals, rules with impunity. They recruit forced labor to mow the company lawn and wash their uniforms. In 2010–2011 a spate of murders and ritual organ removals of the victims hit the area. Female genital organs, removed and sold, some believe, guarantee mining prosperity. One murderer was caught on his way to sell female genitals to a diamond salesman for $6,000.[6] The terror in the area, as recounted by de Morais, evokes scenes reminiscent of Leopold II's murderous red rubber regime in the Congo. Diamonds apparently support a local regime in the Lundas worse than Gaza, in an area larger than Portugal. Angolan generals profit. Israeli businessman Lev Leviev profits. And with profits from the alluvial miners in Lunda Norte and the industrialized mine at Catoca in Lunda Sul, together with companies like Alrosa, they've broken the DeBeers monopoly.

Israel will countenance Angolan support for Palestine at the UN because Israeli businesses prosper in Angola. But what work does that do for Angola? Angola recognized Palestine as a state, and Arafat visited Angola regularly. In the 1980s Angola's radio call, "From Luanda, Angola: the firm trench of the revolution in Africa!" keened a rally cry to fight imperialism around the globe. Those connections weren't just official. Angolans strategically employ socialist rhetoric on their uber-capitalist rulers, who still have a cog and machete on the nation's flag, in a party (the MPLA) where protocol still finds cadres referring to each other as "comrade."

Global links inflect in other ways too. Reginaldo Silva, an Angolan journalist, blogger, and Facebooker of renown, recently opined that he was pretty sure that the term *gazar* (meaning to decimate as in the July 2014 attacks on Gaza) might become slang on Luanda's streets, where world news events often work their way into local language. But such moves aren't just integrative of whatever is out there. Dilapidated buildings named "Sarajevo" and "Baghdad" make local a global topology of war that both repels and attracts Angolans.

The connections between Israel and Angola operate in ambiguous historical terrain, no matter how glaring the profit of their current bond and its bind with justice. Subtending this new, friendly, lucrative relation is Angola's socialist international and anti-imperial past. Today, the MPLA-ruled state cultivates symbols from that past to produce a sense of continuity and historical legacy. Some powerfully placed old-school cadres still believe in the right to self-determination and sovereignty. Political rhetoric (for example, electoral advertising, Kilamba housing project promotions, and urban renewal campaigns) mobilizes this tension between old and new values. In international relations it is no different, it just gets played out across a border of profit for Israel/Angola and righteousness for Palestine/Angola. But Angolans may yet "gazar" state discourses. While liberation solidarities burnished twentieth-century ideals in the work of anti- and postcolonial scholars and activists, we might also see some possibility here in the fallout of the late twentieth and early twenty-first centuries. Even as states and elites share their terror tactics and hone their investment strategies through exchange at the cost of their own populations, so too do young activists and new flights of consciousness take off from older lines of thinking and practice.

Chapter 10

# Academic Freedom and Academic Boycotts

Shireen Hassim

Academic freedom is an important right and one worth struggling for. The degree to which it exists in any society is often a barometer of the extent to which other freedoms are allowed to thrive. Universities have a particular role to play in defending academic freedom and not only because of the importance of this principle in supporting teaching and research: advancing the space for free thought within universities can widen the space for free expression in society as a whole. And as we are making comparisons in this debate between Israel and South Africa, it is worth recalling that under apartheid, white liberal university administrations (themselves pressured by students and faculty) sought university autonomy from the state. In the process, these universities became spaces in which antiapartheid activists were relatively more able to organize and mobilize. Ultimately, however, the dependence of these universities on state funding limited the extent to which even the liberal universities were able to allow open access to all. For most of the twentieth century, Black students entered those universities as little more than tokens of liberalism.

Context matters. In societies deeply divided by conflict, such as South Africa during the era of apartheid, the abstract idea of universities as open and autonomous constantly comes up against the constraints of unfreedom. When access to education is fundamentally limited by restrictions on movement, by conditions of public violence against some categories of persons, and by proscriptions on free association whether in private relationships or political affiliation, academic freedom on its own is a difficult value to sustain. Moreover, in such conditions, elevating it above other rights and freedoms could be seen as an elitist luxury. Those of us committed to justice need to consider what ends we are serving in defending this ideal at all costs under conditions of repression. To be sure, more academic freedom is always better than less. But placing this goal above all others may have unintended consequences. In South Africa, the apartheid state insisted that there was academic freedom for Black people in the "Black" universities. It pointed to "separate but equal" facilities for Black students and argued that the state operated within the framework of the law. This was patently false, of course, and academic boycotts (and, to a much greater extent, sports boycotts) were very important weapons in exposing the falsehood of these claims.

Many arguments against academic boycotts have, in my view, both overstated the impact of academic boycotts on academic freedom (particularly on the flow of ideas in an age of social media) and simply failed to address the conditions in which Palestinian scholars work. In effect, they end up focusing on the adverse effects for some Israeli academics while ignoring the daily realities of conditions of work (and life) for Palestinians students and faculty. They avoid the challenge of building a stronger, justice oriented discourse on the Israel/Palestine issue—one that would indeed benefit from the engagement of intellectuals concerned with freedom. The unqualified defense of academic freedom, and the rejection of any tactic that might be understood as curtailing the full (but for some rather than all) expression of this freedom, constrains the possibility of collective action by the academic profession in contexts where other freedoms are violated on a daily basis.

If we were to put aside, for the moment, debates on the perfect conditions for adopting principles, reading the academic boycott as a political tactic introduces a set of considerations: What does this tactic seek to achieve, within what array of tactics is it based, and how effective is it likely to be? In making these judgments, careful attention needs to be paid to the debates and voices from within the society in which change is being sought. This is not because the voices "from below" or "from within" are necessarily always correct, but because they may have the best strategic understanding of the costs and benefits of different tactics. There are indeed strong voices within Israel calling for an academic boycott, and they are supported by a large cohort of Palestinian academics in the region and in exile. That is not so different from the situation under apartheid, when the call for a boycott was strongly supported by major academic staff associations. Although many liberals did oppose the academic boycott, by the late 1980s they were very much in the minority, in large part because the notion of academic autonomy could not be sustained as state repression intensified.

As I understand it, the call for a selective academic boycott seeks to isolate the Israeli state as part of a strategy of sanctions and divestment. It calls on Israeli academics to take a public stand against the occupation and against the violation of the human rights of Palestinians. It is a nonviolent strategy and, on these grounds, has considerable merit in a situation in which violence on both sides has escalated to frightening proportions. Any strategy that offers alternatives to suicide bombings and targeted assassinations, to daily abuse and bombings, needs at the very least to be taken very seriously. How effective would it be? This would depend on a number of factors, including whether or not Israeli academics as individuals and especially as members of their professional associations are moved to examine the nature of their relationship to the state and its policies.

Also important is whether there is sufficient international solidarity for a boycott to effectively pressure Israeli academic institutions. It is noteworthy that, in the absence of an academic boycott, no Israeli university administration or professional association has to date protested against the treatment of Palestinian academics and students. Ultimately, the effectiveness of a boycott depends on whether the Israeli state itself feels pressure and thus engages more actively in advancing a political solution. Whether or not this is likely to happen requires a deeper knowledge of the Israeli situation than I have. These are issues to be engaged, not to be pushed off the table by a principled, liberal-absolutist opposition to academic boycotts.

The references to South Africa in many arguments for and against the boycott invite some comment from the South African academics participating in the debate. Was the boycott successful in South Africa? Of course there were some costs. Gatekeepers did emerge (but as frequently as not were challenged); some academics who actively opposed apartheid had invitations to international conferences withdrawn; it was not always possible to target the supporters of the apartheid regime; and South African academics' understanding of global issues was certainly weakened. It is the nature of such weapons to be double-edged. But, as part of a battery of sanctions, the academic boycott undoubtedly had an impact on both the apartheid state and on white academics and university administrations. The boycott, together with the more successful sports boycott and economic divestment campaigns, helped to strengthen the struggle of Black people for justice.

The Afrikaner elite, very proud of its European roots and of the legacy of Jan Smuts as a global representative in the postwar system, and convinced that there would be support for its policies abroad, was rudely shaken. University administrations could no longer hide behind an excuse of neutrality, but had to issue statements on their opposition to apartheid and introduce programs of redress. Academic associations (some more than others) examined the nature and conditions of research in their disciplines and faculty unions became part of broader struggles for justice rather than bodies protecting narrow professional interests. Universities became sites of intense debate, and, indeed, intellectuals became critically involved in debates about the nature of current and future South African societies.

Would the BDS strategy succeed in advancing justice in Israel/Palestine? That is not a question that is easily settled. As an academic and a social justice activist, however, it is an ethical choice that appears to me increasingly urgent.

---

*Ed. Note: This piece was originally written for a 2006 conference organized by the American Association of University Professors that was canceled due to pro-Israel action by influential donors. The full discussion can be found at www.aaup.org/file/Papers-From-A-Planned-Conference-on-Boycotts.pdf.*

Chapter 11

# Toward a Queer Palestine

Kelly Gillespie

I'm fighting for the abolition of apartheid, and I fight for the right of freedom of sexual orientation. These are inextricably linked with each other. I cannot be free as a black man if I am not free as a gay man.
–Simon Nkoli, speech at the first Gay Pride in Johannesburg, 1990

One of the most ambiguous maneuvers in the politics of Palestine/Israel has been Israel's deployment of gay rights as a way of proving its credentials as a democracy. In the darkest days of South African apartheid, it was unimaginable that homosexuals could be used in this way: steered into frame as the happy face of the regime, the sign of democracy. In South Africa, the nationalisms of apartheid and the antiapartheid movement were coterminous with homophobic and transphobic violence. Sexuality that wasn't resolutely heterosexual was persecuted, forcing non-normative sexualities into silence and underground. In contrast, we are today faced with a regime that hoists the rainbow flag up next to the Israeli flag, a conflation that has bewildered and angered queers around the world.

Friendly young women from Israel's public affairs departments are sent to speak at global universities about how well Israel treats its LGBT citizens. Pink tourism is courted to showcase Tel Aviv as one of the world's best gay destinations. Campaigns are run to show how open-minded the Israeli Defense Forces (IDF) is on matters of sexual orientation. "Where in the Middle East Can *Gay Officers* Serve Their Country? Only in Israel!" reads one poster. On another, "The Best Army in the Middle East Does Not Discriminate Against Gay Men and Women. Real Liberals Love Israel."

Pinkwashing, as it has come to be known, is the strategic use of "gay rights" to create the veneer of democracy over a conservative political project. It is the deployment of the progressive history of "gay rights" as a resource in the maintenance of other systems of coercion and inequality. This strategy has only been able to take hold as, over the past twenty-odd years, the legislation of LGBT rights has come to be a crucial liberal democratic marker of a good society. Israel has been using this historical fact as a way to insert itself into the international community as a "good state," effecting the appearance of being a progressive country even as the occupation of Palestine sustains ongoing violations of Palestinian life. Jasbir Puar has named this political assemblage "homonationalism," a peculiar equation that extends the privileges of citizenship to homosexuals as it withdraws them from others. It is not an equation that has "gay rights" as a threshold to other progressive inclusions but rather employs LGBT inclusion as a deliberate means of sustaining other forms of discrimination and exclusion, usually racist and imperialist.

This relegation of "gay rights" to the function of handmaiden of racist nationalism strips the history of struggle for sexual freedom of its radical trajectories and banalizes its claim on freedom. Perhaps this shouldn't have felt like such a rude appropriation. After all, gay marriage, the celebration of the "pink dollar," and the increasing assimilation of sexual minorities into the status quo of racial capitalism has been a rather depressing feature of "gay rights" for quite some time. And yet pinkwashing has been sufficiently cunning that it has angered queers around the world and produced an international resistance that has seen more and more LGBTIAQ activists turn their attention to Israel, refuting the perversion of the history of our struggle, and declaring in no uncertain terms, "Not in Our Name."

LGBTIAQ, and in particular queer, activism against Israel's Zionist occupation has produced an important and somewhat unlikely political alliance between queers and Palestine. Queers have not only been working to extend the boycott, divestment, and sanctions campaign against Israel, but we have also been working to support—and to bring to international attention—LGBTIAQ activists and organizations in Palestine. Pride marches in many cities across the world will now have small and radical anti-Zionist/anti-occupation mobilizations within them, offering a solidarity that both refuses the homonationalism of the Israeli state project and also makes a more general point about the necessity of principled intersectional struggle.

One important node in this movement has been Queers Against Israeli Apartheid (QuAIA), a Toronto-based mobilization that operated between 1988 and 1995 to campaign against pinkwashing and in solidarity with Palestine. One of the key organizers of QuAIA also founded the Simon Nkoli Anti-Apartheid Committee in the 1980s to fight the South African apartheid regime. QuAIA understood its work against Israel to be a continuation of the internationalist solidarity that fueled its work against apartheid in South Africa. Over the course of its seven-year history, QuAIA has had to fight a powerful Zionist lobby in Toronto for the right to march against Israel within the context of the annual Pride Toronto. In 1992, they were almost prevented from marching because a complaint had been made to the city by Zionists who did not want the term *apartheid* to be used in relation to Israel. In the month before Pride, the Toronto City Council carried the following motion:

> City Council reaffirm its recognition of Pride Toronto as a significant cultural event that strongly promotes the ideals of tolerance and diversity, but condemn the use of the term "Israeli apartheid" which undermines these values and also diminishes the suffering experienced by individuals during the apartheid regime in South Africa.[1]

In solidarity with the work of QuAIA, and outraged by this tactical maneuver to close down political space by reserving the term *apartheid* strictly for South Africa, queers from South Africa wrote a letter to the Toronto City Council, demanding a retraction of their motion:

> While we appreciate the efforts to recognize the extreme nature of systematic violations of human rights that occurred in South Africa under the name of apartheid, we by no means support efforts to prevent the term "apartheid" being used to describe similar violations elsewhere. For the Toronto City Council to assume the right to argue for such prevention in the name of South Africans is to ignore the many South Africans who themselves have described the current Israeli state as an "apartheid" state. Leading South Africans such as Archbishop Emeritus Desmond Tutu, Deputy President Kgalema Motlanthe, Human

Rights leader Zackie Achmat and anti-apartheid icon Winnie
Mandela are but a few of those to have directly compared the
experience of South African apartheid to the experience of
Palestinians under the Israeli occupation. . . . We object most
strongly to our history being used as a mechanism to minimize
the suffering of Palestinians, and to prevent the speaking out
against systematic oppression in other contexts.

The letter quoted South African antiapartheid activist Simon Nkoli
as emblematic of forging an expansive vision of the politics of antiapartheid. Nkoli was exemplary in his insistence on expanding the definition of
freedom and linking struggles, especially in the way he brought together
antiracist and antihomophobic struggles under one political mandate. The
letter cited Nkoli to insist that Pride at its best is a venue for the understanding that "oppression needs to be fought in all its manifestations if freedom
from any one form of oppression is to be achieved." Nkoli's fight for gay
rights within the antiapartheid movement in South Africa, and his fight
against white supremacy within the gay rights movement, made him one of
the very first to bring these political energies together, publicly, in South Africa in the 1980s. His bravery in coming out to his comrades in prison while
serving time for political activities emboldened others in the antiapartheid
movement to begin imagining how to intersect political trajectories that
until then had seemed incompatible. Similarly, his presence in nascent gay
rights movements challenged the white male hegemony that operated in
many of those spaces and forced open political space and possibility.

It was the difficult work that was done by Nkoli, Edwin Cameron,
Zackie Achmat, and a number of others, in beginning to articulate an
antiheterosexist politics within the antiapartheid movement, that—
slowly, delicately, and always wary of a still resolutely homophobic
environment—created conditions for the African National Congress to
accept sexual orientation as having a viable claim on political inclusion
in the new dispensation. Through the presence of gays and lesbians in
the antiapartheid struggle, and their careful and precarious insertion of
sexuality into the debates in the beginning of the 1990s, South Africa
became the first country in the world to include sexual orientation in
the Bill of Rights in its constitution. There is no doubt that the legal protection afforded LGBTIAQ people in postapartheid South Africa has
everything to do with the presence of self-identified gays and lesbians

within the structures of the antiapartheid movement, who were willing to work at the interstices of different kinds of struggle, insisting that their future should accommodate a broad and inclusive definition of freedom.

There are many queers in the struggle for a free Palestine. The LGBTIAQ movement against pinkwashing and homonationalism continues to be a significant contribution to the critique of the Zionist occupation. One can only hope that our solidarity in this struggle might secure a capacious place for progressive sexual politics at the end of the occupation, and even, perhaps, in the midst of its rule. One can but hope that the solidarities that are being forged in the struggle against the Israeli regime will open political space for imagining a future Palestine where freedom is an expansive project reflecting an antiracist, anti-imperialist sexual politics. And one can hope that the struggle against the occupation can, in turn, create a refusal of any version of sexual politics that, like Israel's nefarious use of gay rights to support its racist regime, relies on the continued subjugation of others for its existence.

Chapter 12

# Cultural Weapons Against Apartheid
## Art, Artists, Cultural Boycotts

M. Neelika Jayawardane

In 1986, during a decade that witnessed some of the most violent clashes between the apartheid police and Black South Africans, an exhibition of photo-essays by a multiracial group of twenty South African photographers, sponsored by the Second Carnegie Commission on Poverty and Development, was exhibited at The International Center of Photography in New York.[1] The exhibition, titled "South Africa: The Cordoned Heart," was the first time that most Americans had seen the grueling poverty contrasted with the excesses handed to a handful of those privileged under apartheid. It gave South African documentary photographers a chance to show what life was like behind the battles shown in spectacular news stories. Americans got a firsthand view of the violence of the poverty with which South Africans lived: the images record people being attacked by police forces, the effects of forced removals, of traveling long hours in search of employment, and the indignities of being treated like second-class citizens with no rights to the land on which they had once lived. In the midst of all these violations, American audiences also got to observe South Africans organizing, meeting, unionizing, and—fists defiantly in the air—commemorating losses and celebrating gains.[2]

However, in *People* magazine's "Picks and Pans" review of the publication that accompanied the exhibition, the reviewers offered a more skeptical view of the photography. They remarked: "The book provides a painfully intimate look at a society that can often, to Americans, seem hopelessly remote. And even assuming the worst—that these pictures were taken and edited with the aim of misleading the outside world about the extent of poverty among South African Blacks—the book makes a credible case."[3] This ambivalent review in a pop culture–focused magazine reflected a condition obvious to any activist or politically conscious person living in the United States: Americans are often woefully unaware of the political and social struggles of those beyond their shores, especially if American lives are not directly affected by those struggles. Despite the fact that the UN had been actively condemning racial discrimination in South Africa since the 1940s, with a record of activity evident "in the sixty-four resolutions passed by the General Assembly between 1946 and 1981," the US government remained unmoved by these appeals until the late 1980s, voting in favor of South Africa multiple times in international bodies and supporting the regime in other fashions.[4] Still, many Americans—having seen and learned about the brutality of the apartheid state—took part in disinvestment rallies, camping out on their picturesque university lawns to protest university endowments that had portfolios that included corporations continuing to do business in South Africa.

Almost two decades later, in May 2003, the "first museum exhibition in the United States devoted to the contemporary art of Palestine" opened at the Station Museum in Houston, Texas.[5] The artists participating in "Made in Palestine" included those living in the West Bank, Gaza, and parts of Israel, as well as artists living in the diaspora. In the preface to the publication that accompanied the exhibition, Tarif Abboushi introduced the artwork as statements about the lack of liberty, freedom of movement, and home: "If the essence of art is freedom of expression, then framed in the context of its national legacy of *al Nakba*, Palestinian art is in essence an expression of freedom denied."[6] Abboushi identified the origins of Zionism as a "late nineteenth century European political movement established to infuse the religion of Judaism with a nationalistic ideology." This ideology, wherein the establishment of a homeland "for a people without a home" was a central tenet, required the willful denial of the existence of indigenous Muslim and Christian Palestinians in the proposed homeland.[7] The "Made in Palestine" exhibition, intended to highlight the continued existence of those denied people, included visual works of fine art, documentary films such as *Jenin* (Mohammad Bakri), *Nightfall* (Mohamed Soueid), and *Green Bird* (Liana Badr), as well as poetry by Mahmoud Darwish, Natalie Handal, and Fadwa Tukan.

The exhibition covered the modern history of the Palestinian people from "the catastrophe" of the *Nakba* in 1948 to the present, with twenty-three artists "revealing with clarity" their struggle against erasure.[8] Their works evoked the memory of the destruction of villages by Israeli army tanks, forced relocation of Palestinians into camps or those driven into exile, and the obliteration of olive and orange groves. The works also portray later projects of erasure engineered by Israeli occupation, including photographs of the Apartheid Wall and depictions of routine harassment at "ubiquitous military checkpoints" that have made mobility and traveling to and from places of employment as intolerable and dehumanizing as possible for Palestinians.[9] Works also alluded to resistance: whether the boxes of stones with which Palestinian children defend themselves against the Israeli military's rubber-tipped bullets or the lines of poetry for which writers have been imprisoned. But the "tour de force in the exhibition," wrote James Harithas in his introduction, was a "mural-sized work by Mustafa al-Hallaj that summarized the history of the Palestinian people from the ancient myths to their present tragic struggle."[10] The Zionist state has been overwhelmingly successful at disseminating two myths: one, about an empty desert devoid of people; and, two, about the Jewish people's historical and God-given right to this "empty" land. Al-Hallaj's work, which commemorates a long memory of existence, being, surviving, thriving, and producing, neatly countered that propaganda.

Activists and academics around the world have long drawn parallels between apartheid South Africa and Israel. In many ways, both Palestine and apartheid South Africa became metaphors of imperial occupation, colonial injustices, forced removals, and the everyday violence of settler groups, as well as the resistance of those whose homelands were occupied. This creates a particularly sharp dilemma for artists. Although artists from both locations understand the significance of inserting themselves into their respective nation's narratives, many support organized movements to boycott "normalizing" cultural projects. Normalizing cultural projects are those that attempt to draw artists from the colonized and colonizing groups together to display a united front without taking into account the enormity of historical and day-to-day violence experienced by people who live in occupied landscapes *or* the privileges inherited by occupiers. The website of the Palestinian Campaign for the Academic and Cultural Boycott of Israel (PACBI) explains that cultural projects that portray the oppressor community and the oppressed community as symmetric, or on a par morally, are counterproductive because they normalize violent occupations as experiences of suffering experienced by both parties equally.[11]

Projects such as "South Africa: The Cordoned Heart" and "Made in Palestine" are all the more significant for the fact that the organizers understood the dilemmas that South African and Palestinian artists face: publicly voicing their distance from "normalizing" efforts remains as important as contributing their voices in efforts against erasure. Yet Palestinian artists and writers—like South African artists grappling with the cultural boycott in support of the antiapartheid movement—are also faced with the dilemma of what to do when "suffering [is] taking place all around, when one's history and present reality are represented in a distorted manner, when you feel you have no voice and others are speaking for you, misrepresenting your reality."[12] Given these conditions, how might Palestinian artists and writers produce work that represents their experiences without further erasing themselves from conversations essential to their survival?

§

Despite the popular belief that artists remain critical of dominant narratives, many have been instrumental to fashioning national identities and the ideologies of nation-states. Artists reflect the face of their community and its values, even though they may simultaneously question those values. If a nation can be thought of as disparate communities brought together by an imagined sense of shared identity, cultural practitioners become especially important to how nations shape their understanding of self and belonging. As any nation fashions a desirable or ideal identity for itself, it employs cultural production to help define boundaries of who the national "self" is, to exclude undesirable elements within, and to differentiate that self from neighbors. In situations of conflict and war—when land, history, and culture are contested—art is deployed as an argument for a people's right to belong (or the right to encroach on another's land). Artists are liable to being co-opted to create "heritage," to signal togetherness after a long battle, to confirm solidarity between ordinary people despite political differences. Thinking in these ways about the symbolic value of art, we begin to comprehend the significance of cultural production and the ways in which art can be harnessed as capital to coin legitimacy for nations, powerful leaders, and power itself.

As in apartheid South Africa, Palestine contends with the all-encompassing reality of occupation. In oral, visual, and literary narratives, the contested landscapes of both countries were (and are) depicted as objects of an insatiable desire, at once calling out to occupiers' hearts and—contradictorily—rejecting occupiers' attempts to tame and "settle" the landscape. In South Africa's case, the settler myth of superiority is woven through historical and present narratives, despite the fact that much of the agricultural success was created by the labor of enslaved or indentured workers, or—as is the current status quo—those who have little ability to negotiate for better conditions. In addition, a fruitful body of fantasy sprang up to deny the very existence of the indigenous populations, thereby strengthening occupiers' claims to an "empty landscape" devoid of people. This mythology of an empty landscape was reinforced by the "fathers" of landscape painting in South Africa, J. H. Pierneef and Jan Ernst Abraham Volschenk, whose representations "epitomize the height of this colonial tradition [. . .] present[ing] the South African landscape as visions of pure, idyllic nature, and more significantly a land with no trace of history and empty of inhabitants."[13]

A large body of visual art and literary narratives produced by South Africa's settler community—"documenting" everything from occupiers' experiences of being visited by celestial messengers who delivered holy words of encouragement to settlers' day-to-day labor of turning barren land to agricultural paradise—legitimized occupiers' "right" to the landscape. It was important for South Africa's colonists, most of whom subscribed to Protestant traditions, that they were constantly engaged in labor. Indigenous people who resisted forced labor were painted as "idle and brutish."[14] Their "incorrigible indolence" was repetitively mentioned in order to construct the industrious settler's superior right to southern Africa.[15] The settler, to borrow a phrase from another context, "made the desert bloom." At the same time, the settler was plagued by doubts about Africa turning "out not to be a Garden but an anti-garden [. . .] ruled over by the serpent where wilderness takes root once again in men's hearts."[16]

The central problem for South African settlers was that Black laborers carried out farm work and city construction. But the presence of Black laborers unsettled settler "claims to 'occupation by right.'"[17] Paintings of landscapes, farms, and even cityscapes thus rarely represented Black laborers—or depicted them as happy serfs going about daily work in a picturesque manner—since showing that "others" labored on one's land was to admit that one did not "earn" a right to it.[18]

Palestine is not only written into the cultural imaginary of the geopolitical West, but molded—through everything from travelers' narratives to political documents—in ways that make its landscape fit with the mythologies carried by European and American visitors. Githa Hariharan argues, "Palestine has been invented time and again," wherein the "inventions have been exercises in imposing a sacred landscape onto a real one."[19] Countless authors produced accounts of Palestine, using the Bible as their common guidebook. Writes Hariharan: "Writers like Thackeray, Twain and Melville to journal-keeping lady travelers and evangelicals" wrote their accounts of the Holy Land. So profound was their connection to the "pictures they had seen in the illustrated Bibles of their childhood" that upon seeing the actual landscape they "experience[ed] an overwhelming sense of connection, of 'coming home'" and marveled at the "way in which Biblical places and persons came to life before [their] eyes."[20]

When it did not live up to their expectations, Hariharan contends: "reality was not necessarily a deterrent."[21] Instead, they turned their disappointments into an explanation using leaps of imagination. Where the sacred sites were "undoubtedly" defaced or destroyed, they were "restored" to the glory depicted in picture-book versions of the Bible. Because visitors and settlers were drawn by the strength of constructed mirages, Hariharan concludes: "Palestine lived—as it still does—a life of its own in the settler-colonial imagination."[22] Like South Africa, Palestine was depicted as an "empty land" devoid of people or one "laid to waste" by wars, neglect, and depopulation.[23] Not only did these visitors willfully ignore the existence of the people who already lived in Palestine, but they also argued that the "fertile land described in the Bible had 'vanished into desert and desolation' and, in the mid–eighteenth century, Palestine did not have enough people to till its soil."[24] Not even the "nascent medium of photography and the advent of archeology influenced how the Holy Land was seen," argues Hariharan. Even as "photographs of Biblical sites replaced

fanciful illustrations based on artists' sketches," these images instead "produce[d] distorted views" that visitors wished to see: a Palestine forever
stuck in a mythical history.[25]

Like South African artists before them, Palestinians must contend
with this overwhelming body of art and literature as they produce coun-
terhistories, record memories of trauma and loss, and create new cartogra-
phies of belonging in landscapes emptied of their presence. Ironically, for
many Palestinians depicting themselves and their homeland is an exercise
of the imagination: they must conjure up disappeared cityscapes and villages, and reconstruct erased histories, in order to regain entry into landscapes now barred.

§

At the heart of any movement to boycott, divest, and impose sanctions
is the conviction that it is a way of ending complicity. Omar Badsha, a
renowned South African photographer and trade unionist, notes that the
boycott of South Africa

> persuaded people not to go to shows that were segregated—for
> people not to perform in segregated venues. We in the under-
> ground networks . . . encouraged progressive groups and indi-
> viduals to exhibit and perform abroad. We also welcomed many
> progressive artists to visit so as to experience the evil that was
> apartheid. We never used violence to get our point across—yes
> there were instances where people used violence but we con-
> demned it.[26]

The refusal to share one's aesthetic products with those who create
inhumane living conditions sends a powerful message—a message as powerful as an economic boycott. Cultural boycotts recognize that art and
artists are imbricated in structures of power and thus the violence that settler-colonial ideologies produce.

The close relationship between the South African and Palestinian
movements has often been acknowledged. On its website, PABCI declares its shared history with that of the antiapartheid movement, stating
that it was "inspired by the historic role played by people of conscience
in the international community of scholars and intellectuals who have

shouldered the moral responsibility to fight injustice, as exemplified in their struggle to abolish apartheid in South Africa through diverse forms of boycott."[27] Both movements sought/seek to create discomfort by encouraging (and sometimes shaming) artists, writers, and academics to boycott the "rogue" nation. They aim to make those who live within those nations aware of the fundamental problem of their collective silence, of their ability to do "business as usual," and of their ability to live comfortable, intellectually and aesthetically productive lives. Both movements are invested in highlighting the problem of normalization within the rogue state, where the dominant group becomes so accustomed to imagining that the "oppressor's reality is the only 'normal' reality... and that the oppression is a fact of life that must be coped with."[28] According to Palestinian activist Omar Barghouti, South Africa's condemnation of Israel as an apartheid regime at the 2001 UN antiracism conference in Durban was a "main trigger" for the launch of the BDS call by Palestinian civil society in 2005.[29]

The movements have also faced the same criticisms. As BDS activists note, a "key argument put forth by the South African regime and its apologists around the world against the antiapartheid cultural and sports boycott—that boycotts violate the freedom of expression and cultural exchange."[30] Few have refuted this argument more brilliantly than Enuga Sreenivasulu Reddy, the director of the UN Center Against Apartheid. In a statement issued in 1984, Reddy explained that misleading reports "have appeared recently about a United Nations 'blacklist' of entertainers and other cultural personalities visiting South Africa."[31] In his detailed response, Reddy addressed critics' claims point by point. He made it clear that any lists produced "are not lists for persecution, but essentially lists for persuasion."[32] However, the committee realized that "Through bribery and propaganda, South Africa was able to attract several entertainers from abroad—especially because of the problems of employment of entertainers."[33] They had collected "a list of people who have performed in South Africa because of ignorance of the situation or the lure of money or unconcern over racism," hoping to persuade them "to stop entertaining apartheid, to stop profiting from apartheid money and to stop serving the propaganda purposes of the apartheid regime."[34] Reddy then noted with characteristic irony: "It is rather strange, to say the least, that the South African regime which denies all freedoms . . .

to the African majority . . . should become a defender of the freedom of artists and sportsmen of the world."[35]

Reddy's words, Barghouti notes, reveal the cynical politics of statements calling for artists to "transcend political division, unifying people in their common humanity."[36] Those who make such idealistic arguments about artists' magical ability to exist outside of their circumstances, Barghouti concludes, "forget, it seems, that masters and slaves do not quite share anything in common, least of all any notion of humanity" and sidestep the fact that many regimes that demand freedom of expression have no compunctions about stepping on others' freedom of expression.[37]

§

Despite the similarities, the ways in which the antiapartheid movement fashioned and mobilized the boycott movement and the ways that the PACBI functions have some key differences.[38] First, the Palestinian boycott, from the very beginning, targets institutions, not individuals. South African activists began by issuing blanket statements and drawing up lists of individuals. Barghouti points out that, in contrast, "the BDS movement, of which PACBI is a part, being a civil society movement, does not subscribe to drawing up lists to decide who is a good Israeli and who is not based on some arbitrary political criteria."[39] The focus is on the boycott of cultural institutions, he explains, because "those institutions, far from being more progressive than the average in Israel, are a main pillar of the Israeli structure of colonial and apartheid oppression."[40] Second, in apartheid South Africa, audiences were segregated. A Black South African would not be permitted in spaces designated as "whites only" spaces. The only way around those laws was to designate actors, performers, and artists as waiters or cleaning staff for the purposes of getting them entry into these spaces, especially in the evening hours. In Israel, audiences are not segregated. However, there is widespread animosity and suspicion towards Palestinian and/or Muslim Israelis, so though they are not legally segregated, the climate of fear and prejudice orchestrates multiple forms of cultural exclusion.

Sama Alshaibi, a U.S.-based Iraqi-Palestinian artist, explains that another key difference that exists between apartheid South Africa and occupied Palestine is in the belief that the conflict is "complicated" by Jewish people's experience of the Holocaust: "One key difference between South African and Palestinian situations is that here in Palestine, people (outsider do-gooder types) tend to think there are 'two stories' to this conflict, and they both have claim, and therefore it's a 'complicated' situation."[41] There is a tendency to excuse the occupation of Palestine as a plan intended to create "safe" space for Jewish people, whereas in South Africa's case the global public tended to view apartheid as an unacceptable violation. Because of this perception, there is a "rush to have exhibitions in which both Palestinians and Israeli artists are represented."[42] As Barghouti argues, the desire to see "two sides" leads to the demand that Palestinians must "overcome the gap or hatred between us." Ultimately, he points out, that demand leads to a "whitewashing of the oppressor–oppressed relationship and the power structures between perpetrators and victims."[43] Rhetoric that attempts to create such emotional equality, he emphasizes, "is dishonest, both intellectually and morally. For instance, "mothers in South Africa during apartheid 'empathising' over common grief but not taking a position against apartheid and not doing anything to dismantle it were also considered 'normalisers.'"[44]

Through normalization, or efforts to equate their conditions with that of Palestinians, "Israel attempts to re-brand itself, or present itself as normal—even "enlightened"—through an intricate array of relations and activities encompassing hi-tech, cultural, legal, LGBT and other realms."[45] According to Barghouti, in order not to be a part of normalizing propaganda, public projects need to fulfill two conditions:

> The Israeli side must recognize comprehensive Palestinian rights under international law as a minimum; and the project itself has to be a form of what one young Palestinian activist coined "co-resistance," not "co-existence." In a situation of oppression no normal public relations can exist between the oppressed and the oppressor except in the context of co-resisting oppression— that's the only place we can have a normal relationship.[46]

However, despite artists' and activists' efforts to make normalization visible, funders almost always specify that they prefer "collaborative" work. As Alshaibi explains, art institutions promote normalization through encouraging "alliances" between groups of people who inevitably experience oppression very differently:

[Collaboration is] almost always [part of] propos[als] from outsiders or Israeli institutions. Israeli artists love it and would jump at the chance. Israel would even fund it. [Palestinians] don't do it because besides [normalizing the occupation] we are broadcasting that [. . .] as artists, we are promoting some artificial, warm fuzzy feeling of peace, when there is none. [It used to be that] Palestinians [did] not participate if Israeli artists were present in international shows, but we have changed since then, realizing we were not getting our narrative and part of the story out. So now we do that, so as long as other international artists are involved, and there is no mythical peace-fakeness attached to it. Palestinian artists living in Israel with Israeli citizenship were historically caught between a rock and a hard place. Also, artists from the Arab region (not even Palestinian) are constantly being asked to show in Israel (because Palestinians won't). Do you know that word "Jew" is interchangeable with Israeli? Well the same goes for "Arab" [interchangeable with Palestinian] . . . so it's a big deal for progressive left leaning Israelis to show "Arab" (non-Palestinian) artists. Anything that gives them legitimacy, or to make us appear less "open" to debate . . . well that is all great when you are occupying our country [while] doing nothing . . . almost nothing in your own country (Israel) to alleviate the pain of what Palestinians are living [through and] enduring. There is no risk for Israeli artists doing this kind of work . . . [but] for Palestinians, it's everything.⁴⁷

Alshaibi points out that the additional fear of being thought of as a collaborator or a spy for Israel, who gets personal favors "for turning over information"—whether that information is true or false—"about your relatives, friends, and colleagues," deters Palestinians artists from exhibiting their work in projects connected to Israel in any way.⁴⁸

The state of Israel also has more insidious and effective ways of controlling which cultural institutions and whose individual voices are represented. According to Barghouti, "a hidden aspect of the Brand Israel effort [is] a contract that obliges artists and writers, as 'service providers' who receive state funding, to conform with, and indeed promote, state policies. Basically, the contract buys the artists' and writers' consciences, making a mockery of the 'freedom of expression' mantra."⁴⁹ Because of these obvious efforts to use artists as propaganda, Palestinian artists boycott art exhibitions intended to promote "togetherness." Yet, boycotting these projects also means a loss of opportunities for Palestinian artists, whose voices are already marginalized. Barghouti's "long view" of the purpose of a boycott helps us understand the reasons behind such sacrifices. He argues, "The oppressed lose nothing when people of conscience boycott institutions that are persistently complicit in the system of oppression; in fact, they gain enormously from the ultimate weakening of this complicity that results from an effective and sustained boycott."[50]

§

Boycotts of cultural events create shame and discomfort for those who continue to do business with an oppressive state. Both are essential tactics of persuasion. However, while it may open up productive responses, shame can also produce stultified individuals who, lacking alternative pathways, often feel powerless to change themselves or their situations. They justify their actions, rely on authority figures to ritually absolve them of guilt, and compartmentalize so that the acts they regard as "shameful" are separated from their "honorable" lives. Shame is often useful to those in authority because individuals rely on authority figures to absolve them of guilt and shame; those persons are then beholden to religious leaders or authority figures for temporary release and permission to reenter the community of "acceptable" and morally sound people. However, the release one obtains in this system based on shame, guilt, and exclusion is always temporary. Often, a person who operates on shame will repeat their actions, usually in great secrecy, return to authority figures for absolution and release from guilt, and depend completely on those authority figures to signal their reinclusion within love and community.

Nations that employ their citizens to carry out human rights violations of targeted Others operate in not dissimilar ways. To begin with, they, too, depend heavily on shame and guilt to create a sense of obligation and self-sacrifice to the nation, and similarly rely on secrecy and absolution from higher authorities. Nations will ensure that there are mechanisms in place to contain knowledge about the effects of wreaking havoc on Others and to cover up unethical and violent activities of state actors, especially those of decision-makers in the upper echelons of power. Absolution and release is offered to lower-level actors tasked with carrying out atrocities through the use of patriotic ceremonies highlighting the significance of those actors' self-sacrifice and duty to the well-being of the nation; in turn, those who are included within the nation's self-definition are exhorted to feel obligated to state actors and to partake in celebrating those actors' actions—of which self-sacrifice and duty are highlighted. When all these mechanisms fail, we turn to those in authority once again, hoping that they will provide scapegoats. However, most of us do not want any real contemplation of our individual and collective roles, nor do we demand substantial changes that will challenge the fundamental ways in which our nation operates.

Given that we are encouraged to respond to our nation's actions in ways that aid violent, imperial projects, how should we deal with our reactions? If shame is the "go to" emotion most of us feel when we discover that our nation has engaged in unethical actions that we cannot reconcile with our vision of who we are, we inevitably seek to avoid dealing with the issues and hide the causes. Clearly, shame does not work on those who have been taught that the Other exists outside their obligation to civil behavior. As such, the state of Israel does not feel morally obligated to behave civilly toward Palestinians or its own Muslim and other non-Jewish populations, as it expects the international community to act toward Jewish people. That is because, to begin with, an agreement about what constitutes "civil" behavior is necessary to motivate people to behave within ethical frameworks; and in order for us to behave "civilly" toward each other, it is necessary for us to be able to see others as people who—despite their differences from us—still fall somewhere within our definition of self. Colonial enterprises operate by ensuring that those whose land and resources are being conquered are engineered as extreme others who exist far outside the imperial nation's definition of self. While some subjects of nations are comfortable with a broad and expansive definition of the self, imperial projects test such generous impulses. Given conditions of pressure, misinformation, and propaganda, extending civility to those who are typically regarded as Other often proves to be difficult, if not impossible.

For these reasons, calling on a population's feelings of shame to get them to confront their nation's violent treatment of an Other may not be a productive methodology. However, there may be another, less spectacular way to erode comfortable habits of avoidance and justification. Imperial nations that justify their colonial projects and their violence toward an Other also seek to belong within circles of power; they wish for international discourses of civility to include them, and for their subjects to be seen as part of the realm of the "civilized." Their subjects display their inclusion within flows of power and discourses of civility by participating in activities and pleasures available to subjects of other nations already recognized as powerful. However, denying access to the cultural participation—the accouterments of aesthetic pleasure, learning, and contemplation—creates a sense of lack and, with that lack, a constant unease about oneself and how one stands in the world.

Discomfort, then, rather than shame, is a more generative emotional response. As Barghouti states, discomfort produces "psychological pressure" to the point that the negative stimulus becomes "intolerable" for individuals, communities, and nations; discomfort, for the occupier, is the "price to be paid for their state's crimes and denial of human rights against the Palestinians and for their deafening silence and prevalent complicity."[51] That discomfort, creating a lack of normalcy in the occupier's day-to-day life, may "win people over . . . through sustained moral pressure and persuasion that follows it."[52] That heightened level of discomfort, reminding us of our own otherness, and of the far greater pain endured by occupied and subjugated people, may be a more powerful tool for redirecting a nation than we realize.

Chapter 13

# Apartheid's Black Apologists

Robin D. G. Kelley

In 2011, the Vanguard Leadership Group (VLG)—a self-proclaimed "student group" made up of a few graduates from Historically Black Colleges and Universities (HBCs)—published an advertisement accusing Students for Justice in Palestine (SJP) of spreading "misinformation" that Israel practiced apartheid. Calling the comparison with South Africa an "illegitimate analogy," the ad claimed that anyone familiar with "the truth about Israel's record on human rights" would find the analogy "patently false" since the "Arab minority in Israel enjoys full citizenship with voting rights and representation in the government."[1]

I learned of the VLG ad just days before traveling to the West Bank with a delegation organized by the US Campaign for the Academic and Cultural Boycott of Israel (USACBI) in January 2012. Its vigorous defense of Israel as an ideal nonracial democracy differed radically from what I observed simply standing on the rooftop of a crumbling housing complex inside Bethlehem's Aida refugee camp. The illegal Apartheid Wall dominates the landscape. Rising above the twenty-foot wall is the notorious Bethlehem checkpoint, where Palestinians entering Jerusalem are subject to frequent interrogation, harassment, and abuse. Beyond the wall, atop a low-sloping rise, sits the illegal Jewish settlement of Gilo. In the valley adjacent to the camp are the remains of what was once a thriving Palestinian village but now consists of a handful of ramshackle family homes. The children who live there attend the camp's UN-run school just a few hundred yards away, but the wall has turned a ten-minute walk into a two-hour ordeal.

Throughout the West Bank, from Hebron to Nablus to Ramallah and the countryside in between, our delegation saw piles of rubble where Palestinian homes had been demolished and their olive trees uprooted by the Israeli Defense Forces (IDF). We walked through the souk in Hebron, which was littered with bricks and garbage and human feces thrown at Palestinian merchants by messianic settlers. We negotiated the narrow, muddy pathways separating overcrowded, multistoried shacks in the refugee camps, built in the shadows of West Bank settlements with their gargantuan poured concrete buildings. We heard refugees' stories of dispossession, different generations pushed out of their homes, their bank accounts, personal effects, even libraries seized without compensation—actions rendered legal by Israel's Absentees' Property Law (1950). We saw pristine settler swimming pools filled to the rim, just a stone's throw from Palestinian communities where water is scarce. We spoke with Palestinian "citizens" of Israel and learned very quickly that the precious rights they reportedly enjoy are a myth. They, too, have no rights to lands, houses, bank accounts, or other property they had owned prior to 1948.

Most are obliged to live in exclusively "Arab" villages that have been prohibited from expanding, attend severely underfunded schools, are denied government employment, and are prohibited from living with their spouse if she or he is a Palestinian from the occupied territories.[2] They are routinely arrested for participating in protests critical of the state. Indeed, as I write these words, hundreds of Palestinians—many of whom are students—are being held in Israeli prisons for political activity or for reasons unknown based on "secret evidence." Israel can detain Palestinians for up to six months without charge or trial, with no limits on renewal. Administrative detention, as it is called, is based on three laws: Military Order 1651, which empowers the army to issue orders to detain civilians in the West Bank; the Unlawful Combatants Law, which applies to Gaza residents; and the Emergency Powers Detention Law, used against Israeli citizens. These laws violate Article 9 of the International Covenant on Civil and Political Rights, which prohibits arbitrary detention, requires that detainees be told why they are being held, and stipulates that every person has the right of habeas corpus.[3]

Under the right-wing Likud Party, Israel has passed laws that directly infringe on the freedom of speech and academic freedom of Arab and Jewish citizens, including the so-called boycott law,[4] which allows citizens to file a civil suit against anyone in Israel who calls for a boycott against the state or Israeli settlers in the West Bank—whether or not any damages can be proved. Palestinian members of the Knesset have been indicted and/or had their parliamentary privileges revoked for legitimate political activities and speech. Hanin Zoabi, the first and only Palestinian woman elected to the Knesset, was severely censured for participating in the Freedom Flotilla to Gaza and for advocating that Israel become a secular democratic state for all of its citizens. Consequently, the Knesset voted to revoke her diplomatic passport, her right to participate in Knesset discussions and to vote in parliamentary committees, and other parliamentary privileges. During the war on Gaza in 2014, she was suspended from the Knesset subject to a criminal investigation for suspicion of inciting others to violence and insulting two police officers.[5] In 2011, the Knesset even passed a law forbidding the commemoration of the *Nakba*. The *Nakba* ("catastrophe" in Arabic) refers to the violent expulsion of some 750,000 Palestinians from 380 villages during the 1947–1948 War and the barring of the refugee population from the right to return or reclaim lost land, homes, personal property, and bank accounts. The law permits the minister of finance to reduce government funding to any institution (including schools and universities, civic organizations, and local governments) that commemorates either independence day or the anniversary of the establishment of the state of Israel as a day of mourning ("*Nakba* day") or mentions the *Nakba* in school textbooks.[6]

Contemporary Palestine is not South Africa of a quarter-century ago, and employing an analogy is not to suggest that conditions in both places are identical. But in looking for one-to-one correspondence with South Africa's system of racial subjugation, many critics of the occupation have balked at the apartheid label, arguing that the situation in Palestine is not an elaborate system of racial segregation but rather a set of necessary steps to protect the security of Israel. Indeed, countless progressives and leftists have dismissed the apartheid label as inaccurate, inappropriate, and insulting. This stems in part from a rather narrow, if not dubious, interpretation of apartheid. Apartheid did more than strip Black South Africans of voting and civil rights. The regime dispossessed Africans of their land and, through legislative and military acts, razed entire communities and transferred the population to government townships and Bantustans. It was a system of racial classification and population control that limited the movement of Africans in towns and cities, denied them social and economic privileges based on race, and prohibited marriage and sexual relations across the color line. Under the authority of the Suppression of Communism Act (1950) and similar legislation, South Africa under the National Party outlawed organizations that challenged the right of an apartheid state—in other words, a state based on racial or ethnic hierarchy—to exist, and used state violence and detention to suppress opposition. The Bantu Education Act (1953) created a draconian, state-run education system based on the principle of racial segregation and imposed a national curriculum for Africans, allegedly suited to their status as a permanent cheap labor force—all under the guise of preserving "traditional" cultures. Science and anything but the most remedial math were prohibited, and the social science curriculum promoted white supremacy and nonwhite inferiority.[7]

That Israel and its colonial occupation meet the UN's definition of an apartheid state is beyond dispute.[8] Therefore, given the history of African American opposition to apartheid and all forms of racial oppression—here and abroad—how do we understand the rise of groups like VLG or the AIPAC-backed organization, Christians United for Israel (CUFI), founded by the controversial Reverend John Hagee? VLG and CUFI recruit Black students, elected officials, and religious leaders to serve as moral shields for Israel's policies of subjugation, settlement, segregation, and dispossession. Is this a new phenomenon—evidence of AIPAC's successful pivot toward people of color? Or signs of the expanding influence of evangelicals and their Christian Zionist leanings? And how are Black lobbyists for Israel able to invoke the memory of Dr. King in the service of settler-colonialism and genocidal war in the West Bank and Gaza? Michael Stevens, CUFI's coordinator of African American outreach, described Dr. King as "a strong African-American Zionist."[9]

Of course, in the Black imaginary, Jerusalem is not Johannesburg. Black Christians have been making their own pilgrimages to the Holy Land for decades, revering Israel as a living embodiment of God's Chosen People. Black identification with Zionism predates the formation of Israel as a modern state. For over two centuries, the biblical book of Exodus, the story of the flight of the Jews out of Egypt and the establishment of Israel, emerged as the principal political and moral compass for African Americans. Exodus provided Black people with not only a narrative of emancipation and renewal but also a language to critique America's racist state, since the biblical Israel represented a new beginning.[10] As Keith Feldman aptly put it, for most Black leaders and intellectuals, "Palestine was legible only through the lens of Jewish Zionism. Jewish Zionism provided a functional analogy to think diasporic Black political consciousness rooted in an imaginative articulation of ancient scriptural reference and modern nationalist ideology."[11] Marcus Garvey and his Universal Negro Improvement Association not only identified with the modern Zionist movement—comparing their struggle for an African homeland with the quest for a Jewish homeland in Palestine—but he also patterned his Universal African Legion after the Jewish Legion. He benefited from the patronage of major Jewish (Zionist) financiers such as the American William Ritter and Jamaican residents Abraham Judah and Lewis Ashenheim.[12] In 1925, cultural critic and philosopher Alain Locke placed the "New Negro movement" alongside the struggle for a Jewish homeland in Palestine and other nationalist rebellions in China, Ireland, Russia, and Egypt, which he described as "those nascent movements of folk-expression and self-determination which are playing a creative part in the world to-day. . . . [W]e are witnessing the resurgence of a people."[13]Most Black leaders and the Black press welcomed Israel's founding in 1948. There was virtually no mention of Arab dispossession, of the *Nakba* or the terror tactics of the Haganah. Instead, they identified with the founding of Israel because they recognized European Jewry as an oppressed and dispossessed people who survived near-extermination, determined to build a nation. In a speech backing the partition plan, A. Philip Randolph said that he could not conceive of a more "heroic and challenging struggle for human rights, justice, and freedom" than the creation of a Jewish homeland. "Because Negroes are themselves a victim of hate and persecution, oppression and outrage," he argued, "they should be the first to be willing to stand up and be counted on the side of the struggle of the Jew to achieve partition of Palestine and an international police force to maintain peace under the United Nations to give reality to the interest of Negroes in this fight for the right of the Jews to set up a commonwealth in Palestine."[14] The National Association for the Advancement of Colored People (NAACP) passed a resolution in 1948 stating that "the valiant struggle of the people of Israel for independence serves as an inspiration to all persecuted people throughout the world."[15] W. E. B. Du Bois had long championed a Jewish state and took no heed of Ralph Bunche's failed efforts to promote a binational alternative to partition. Several years before Israel's founding, Du Bois lamented, "The only thing that has stopped the extraordinary expansion of the Jews in Palestine has been the Arab population and the attempt on the part of English and Arabs to keep Palestine from becoming a complete Jewish state."[16]

During the 1947–1948 War, the Black press generally portrayed Arabs as brutal, bloodthirsty aggressors and the Jews as heroic defenders of the nation and purveyors of civilization. In an article praising the creation of Jewish vocational schools in the new state of Israel, Charles A. Davis points out that military training may become the priority with "Arab armies menacing their foothold in the Holy Land."[17] In March 1948, the *Atlanta Daily World* carried the following image of Arab "snipers" juxtaposed against Jewish men standing guard under the caption, "Violence in the Holy Land."[18]

A few months later, the same publication reported on a lecture delivered by Reverend Isaiah Domas, a prominent member of the faculty at Atlanta University (an HBC). An eminent racial liberal, Domas compared Jewish Tel Aviv, with its beautiful, well-kept homes and streets, opera house, modern buildings, playgrounds, with the Arab town of Jaffa, "in which the streets are littered with refuse, buildings are destitute of white wash, and the population diseased." He accused Arabs of harboring pro-Nazi sympathies and praised the Jews for being the only civilized and progressive force in the region: "The Jews in Palestine are building a society which recognizes and emphasizes the fundamental dignity and significance of the individual, and [in] such a society it is impossible for a narrow self-limiting nationalism to flourish."[19] It was an ironic prediction in light of contemporary Israel, where a "self-limiting" ethnic nationalism continues to prevail and flourish.[20] Ironically, the creation of Israel indirectly served as a vehicle to advance racial democracy and Black citizenship demands in the United States. African Americans took pride in the fact that Black police officers and servicemen made up one-fifth of the UN peacekeeping force sent to enforce the truce and oversee the partition. The unit represented the first completely nonsegregated armed force in which African Americans could serve.[21] And the fact that the distinguished Black intellectual Ralph Bunche had been appointed to broker the partition agreement held enormous symbolic significance. Recognizing his celebrity status, Bunche tried to use the Black press to offer an alternative to the uncritical promotion of a Jewish state. In a February 1948 interview with the *Pittsburgh Courier*, Bunche framed the issues not in terms of a homeland for Jews but a colonial problem. As he put it, "Two peoples, Arabs and Jews, both of whom have been governed under what is essentially a colonial regime, are to realize their national aspirations and are to be given independence."[22] The editors of the *Amsterdam News* partly agreed, though they applied Bunche's framework solely to the Jews. "No nation or people anywhere can afford to be indifferent to the future of Israel and that of oppressed minorities and colonial peoples throughout the world. This newspaper salutes Israel and hopes that the Flag with the Star of David will bring peace, security and full democracy not only to the nationals of the new Jewish state, but to the peoples of the Middle East."[23]

Of course, a few Black writers expressed concern over the displacement of the Arab population in Palestine. *Chicago Defender* columnist Robert Durr, for example, questioned whether there could ever be peace in the region so long as the United States and Britain refused to protect Arab rights and promoted unlimited Jewish immigration. He quoted Eve Edris, an Egyptian delegate to the Asian Relations Conference, who worried that continued Jewish immigration would reduce "the local inhabitants to a minority condemned to extinction. Which people of the world would tolerate such an injustice?"[24]

But Zionism's most strident Black critic in 1948 was the iconoclastic writer George Schuyler. He used his column in the *Pittsburgh Courier* to criticize the expulsion of the Arabs. "The same people who properly condemned and fought against German, Italian and Japanese imperialism and its ruthless aggression against other peoples, now rise to the vociferous defense of Zionist imperialism which makes the same excuse of the need for 'living space' and tries to secure it at the expense of the Arabs with military force financed and recruited from abroad." Schuyler dismissed characterizations of Arabs as "'backward,' ignorant, illiterate and incapable of properly developing the land" as thinly veiled justifications for a Jewish state, reminding his readers that this was the same reasoning the Nazis used to justify their invasion of Czechoslovakia, Poland, and Russia, and that European colonial powers used "in taking other people's lands." He closed by excoriating the NAACP for praising the "'liberation' of Palestine when elsewhere it defends aggression's victims."[25] Needless to say, Schuyler was deluged with letters accusing him of anti-Semitism and downright lunacy.

A month later, Schuyler's own paper ran an unsigned editorial rebuking his claims without naming him. Blaming the British and American governments for colluding with Arab elites to block the creation of a Jewish state, the article repeated the received wisdom that Jews would bring democracy and prosperity to the backward Arabs. A Jewish state "will disturb these Arabs, will cause them to lift their heads and begin to look around. They might even yearn for democracy and prosperity themselves." Such yearning may lead to the violent overthrow of Arab despots, and "with blood as the purchase price," the results will be irreversible. The editorial went on to apply this "blood" principle to the Jewish struggle for independence and its violent seizure of Palestinian lands. What Arabs called the great catastrophe, *al-Nakba*, the *Pittsburgh Courier* editorial hailed as a heroic act of self-determination and a lesson for African Americans seeking justice. "There is a grim moral for Negroes in all this. If the Jewish state in Palestine survives (and we hope it does) Jews will have paid in such a way that no one can dispute their ownership. The possession of nothing won through favor is ever as secure as that which is bought with blood."[26]

In other words, most Black intellectuals, activists, and political leaders who had defended Zionism and the war that led to the creation of Israel were not dupes, nor were they acting out of some obligatory commitment to a Black–Jewish alliance. Rather, with the exception of figures such as George S. Schuyler, it was virtually impossible for them to see Israel as a colonial project, specifically as a settler-colonial state founded on the subjugation of indigenous people (Palestinians—Muslim and Christian; Bedouin; Mizrahi Jews; and imported racialized labor) *but with the backing of international law.* Why? Part of the answer lay in the unique historical context for Israel's founding, as well as the power of its founding myths. There is the convergence of Israel's Zionist roots—a nationalist ideology generated partly in opposition to racist/ethnic/religious oppression, but also motivated by an imperative to bring modernization to a so-called backward Arab world—and the post-Ottoman colonial domination of the region by Britain and France. Ultimately, this convergence put Jewish settlers in conflict with British imperialism. The nationalist and anticolonial character of Israel's war of independence camouflaged its own colonial project.[27]

Second, the Holocaust was critical, not just for the obvious reasons that the genocide generated global indignation and sympathy for the plight of Jews and justified Zionist arguments for a homeland, but because, as

Aimé Césaire argued in *Discourse on Colonialism* (1950—before Hannah Arendt), the Holocaust itself was a manifestation of colonial violence. Therefore, in 1948, Israel comes into being as a nation identified as victims of colonial/racist violence, forged through armed insurrection against British imperialism. It is a narrative that renders invisible the core violence of ethnic cleansing, resulting in the destruction of some 380 Palestinian towns and villages and displacing more than 700,000 Palestinians. The myth of Israel's heroic war of liberation against the British convinced even the most anticolonial intellectuals to link Israel's independence with African independence and Third World liberation. And, at some point, even Israel's ruling Labor Party pursued alliances with newly independent African nations under the guise that they, too, were part of the Non-Aligned Movement.[28]

Of course, the Non-Aligned Movement did not invite Israel to participate in its founding meeting in Bandung, Indonesia, in 1955, and events soon thereafter reinforced this decision while generating the first significant rift in the African American–Israel alliance. As the *Nakba* fanned the flames of Arab nationalism, a revolution in Egypt brought Colonel Gamal Abdel Nasser to power in 1952 and radically changed the political landscape, especially as Nasser positioned himself as the world's most visible exponent of Pan-Arab solidarity and Third World unity. Egypt took a leading role in Bandung, and Nasser followed up with his own Afro-Asian People's Solidarity Conference in Cairo, which drew support from prominent African American leaders. But the event that made Nasser a hero in the Third World and transformed Israel's image from an anticolonial David into an imperialist Goliath was Nasser's decision in 1956 to nationalize the French- and British-owned Suez Canal Company, after Britain and the United States withdrew financial assistance to build the Aswan High Dam. In retaliation, Britain, France, and Israel militarily invaded Egypt until pressure from the United States and the Soviet Union forced them to withdraw.[29] Among the Black left, in particular, Israel's occupation of the Suez Canal generated a contentious debate. Jewish Communists, encouraged by the Soviets to drop their critique of Zionism, adopted the slogan "Arms for Israel." In contrast, W. E. B. Du Bois, who had moved closer to the Communists, condemned the action as a manifestation of Western imperialism—a far cry from his staunch defense of Israel eight years earlier. Leading Black Communists like Benjamin Davis (elected councilman from Harlem on the CPUSA ticket) and Ed Strong backed

Egypt. For this they were accused of anti-Semitism. Davis and Strong shot back, criticizing the *Daily Worker's* editorial policy on Israel and accusing Jewish liberals of pressuring Black newspaper editors to defend Israel's position. Davis insisted that Nasser enjoyed the support of the majority of African Americans, citing the "strong pro-Egyptian influence among the Negro masses expressed in part . . . by the increasing growth of Moslem influence and organization in Negro communities. . . . I venture to say that Negroes are anything but neutral in this matter. . . and they're right."[30] Letters to the *Daily Worker* concurred with Davis. In one such letter, the writer called on "progressives" to "ask themselves, why is it that Israel is today so completely isolated from the Bandung powers, the colonial peoples, Negro Americans and the Socialist bloc."[31]

There was even more at stake for Palestinians. As part of the war on Egypt, Israel invaded and occupied southern Gaza, where Israeli soldiers committed a number of atrocities against Palestinian refugees and other civilians. On November 3, 1956, IDF troops summarily executed some 275 men in Khan Yunis and in a neighboring refugee camp, and nine days later repeated the act in Rafah, killing about 200 unarmed Palestinian men. On October 29, Israeli border police massacred 49 Palestinians near the village of Kafr Qasim on their way home from work. Official reports claimed they had violated a curfew, though the villagers were never informed that a curfew was in place.[32] Eight years later, Malcolm X traveled to the Gaza Strip during his two-month stay in Egypt and visited the refugee camp at Khan Yunis. Learning of the 1956 massacre and meeting survivors had a profound impact on him. Although he often swung back and forth between exhorting Black people to emulate the Jews and criticizing Israel, his experience in Gaza inspired his now widely circulated and oft-quoted essay, "Zionist Logic" which appeared in the *Egyptian Gazette*, September 17, 1964. Malcolm concluded that Zionism represented a "new form of colonialism," disguised behind biblical claims and philanthropic rhetoric but still based on the subjugation and dispossession of indigenous people and backed by US "dollarism." Echoing Schuyler, he asked:

> Did the Zionists have the legal or moral right to invade Arab Palestine, uproot its Arab citizens from their homes and seize all Arab property for themselves just based on the "religious" claim that their forefathers lived there thousands of years ago? Only a thousand years ago the Moors lived in Spain. Would this

give the Moors of today the legal and moral right to invade the
Iberian Peninsula, drive out its Spanish citizens, and then set
up a new Moroccan nation . . . where Spain used to be, as the
European Zionists have done to our Arab brothers and sisters
in Palestine?[33]

Before 1967, most liberals, progressives, and leftists would not have
agreed with Malcolm X or any critic who portrayed Israel as a colonial
regime. Throughout the early 1960s, Israel's leaders publicly condemned
racism, offered aid to developing African countries, and projected itself
as a model democracy—if not a semisocialist society. In 1961, when South
Africa's prime minister, Hendrik Verwoerd, tried to deflect international
criticism of his country by describing Israel as "an apartheid state" ("The
Jews took Israel from the Arabs after the Arabs had lived there for a thousand years"[34]), Israel's leaders were quick to distance themselves from Verwoerd. Indeed, in 1963, then foreign minister Golda Meir told the UN
General Assembly that Israelis "naturally oppose policies of apartheid,
colonialism and racial or religious discrimination wherever they exist."[35]

The Arab–Israeli War of 1967 changed everything. It not only enabled
a sharper African American critique of Zionism and the possibilities of
solidarity with the Palestine Liberation Organization (PLO), but it produced a sense of betrayal from liberal Zionists who equated criticism of
Israel with anti-Semitism. Writer Cynthia Ozick expressed this sense of
betrayal over two decades ago in an afterword to her essay, "Literary Blacks
and Jews." She attributed the breakup of the vaunted "Black-Jewish alliance" to African Americans' "uninformed assaults on Israel" and "a willed
misunderstanding of Middle Eastern events since 1967."[36] Ozick offers no
evidence that Black critics of Israel's occupation of Gaza, the West Bank,
East Jerusalem, and the Golan Heights deliberately misrepresented the
events of 1967, but evidence was never the issue. Liberal Zionists detested
any characterizations of Israel as a colonial regime and yet this is exactly
what an increasingly radical, internationalist, and vocal core of Black activists concluded. And their condemnation of Black criticism of Israel was
swift and unapologetic. When the Black Caucus of Chicago's New Politics
Convention of 1967 proposed a resolution condemning the "imperialist
Zionist war," it was met with such vehement opposition that it was subsequently withdrawn. The Black Panther Party followed suit, not only
denouncing Israel's land grab but also pledging its support for the PLO.[37]

The event that drew the most ire from liberal Zionists, many of whom had been veteran supporters of the civil rights movement, was the publication of "Third World Round-up: The Palestine Problem: Test Your Knowledge," in the Student Nonviolent Coordinating Committee (SNCC) newsletter. It portrayed the Six-Day War as a war of dispossession, Israel as a colonial state backed by US imperialism, and Palestinians as victims of racial subjugation. In short, Black identification with Zionism as a striving for land and self-determination gave way to a radical critique of Zionism as a form of settler-colonialism akin to American racism and South African apartheid.[38]

The fallout generated by SNCC's article was significant. "Responsible" Black leaders were called upon to denounce SNCC leaders H. Rap Brown and Stokely Carmichael as anti-Semitic and to pledge their fealty to Israel. It was in this atmosphere that Dr. Martin Luther King, Jr., was expected to publicly rebuke anti-Zionist "Black militants," and in which he made his oft-quoted statement: [We must stand with all of our might to protect [Israel's] right to exist, its territorial integrity. I see Israel, and never mind saying it, as one of the great outposts of democracy in the world." Pick up most literature from AIPAC or Stand With Us or CUFI and you will likely see this quote emblazoned in bold letters but bereft of any context. King's words come from a long, public interview conducted by Rabbi Everett Gendler at the sixty-eighth annual convention of the Rabbinical Society on March 25, 1968—ten days before King's assassination and ten months after the Six-Day War.[39] It is worth returning to in full because it exposes some fissures between King and the Rabbinical Society and reveals King's position vis-à-vis Israel as both more complex and more naïve than is generally acknowledged.

First, Israel was a minor topic. About 80 percent of the dialogue concentrated on King's critics, the "extremist element" in the Black community, allegations of Black anti-Semitism, the question of Black Power, and the future of the civil rights movement. Gendler worried that the civil rights movement might not remain moderate; King retorted that he was never really "moderate" but militantly nonviolent. Second, Gendler peppered King with what can only be described as leading questions:

> What steps have been undertaken and what success has been noted in convincing anti-Semitic and anti-Israel Negroes, such as Rap Brown, Stokely Carmichael, and McKissick, to desist from their anti-Israel activity?

> What effective measures will the collective Negro com-
> munity take against the vicious anti-Semitism, against the
> militance and the rabble-rousing of the Browns, Carmi-
> chaels, and Powells?
>
> What would you say if you were talking to a Negro in-
> tellectual, an editor of a national magazine, and were told,
> as I have been, that he supported the Arabs against Israel
> because color is all important in this world? In the editor's
> opinion, the Arabs are colored Asians and the Israelis are
> white Europeans. Would you point out that more than half
> of the Israelis are Asian Jews with the same pigmentation
> as Arabs, or would you suggest that an American Negro
> should not form judgments on the basis of color?[40]

Such questions made it difficult for King to maneuver, since they pre-
sumed Gendler's rendering of events and attitudes were accurate. Yet, King
pushed back, rejecting the claim that anti-Semitism was rampant in the
Black movement: "First let me say that there is absolutely no anti-Semitism
in the black community in the historic sense of anti-Semitism." Echoing
James Baldwin, King argued that what appeared to be anti-Semitic attitudes among Northern urban African Americans were actually conflicts
stemming from economic inequality and exploitation. Attributing the
business practices of individual Jews to religion or culture is classic anti-Semitism, King acknowledged, but he also challenged the audience "to
condemn injustice wherever it exists. We found injustices in the black community. We find that some black people, when they get into business, if
you don't set them straight, can be rascals. And we condemn them. I think
when we find examples of exploitation, it must be admitted. That must
be done in the Jewish community too."[41] In other words, King not only
insisted on condemning all forms of injustice but also refused to allow the
charge of anti-Semitism to silence legitimate criticism—of Jews or of Israel.

His remarks about Israel and the Middle East are even more striking. Short of condemning war altogether, he called for "peace" above all
else. For Israel "peace . . . means security," though he never specified what
security meant in this context. He praised Israel as "one of the great outposts of democracy in the world," but added a qualifier when he spoke of
how "desert land *almost* can be transformed into an oasis of brotherhood
and democracy." Finally, he addressed what he thought peace meant for
the Arabs/Palestinians. "Peace for the Arabs means the kind of economic

security that they so desperately need. These nations, as you know, are part of that third world of hunger, of disease, of illiteracy. I think that as long as these conditions exist there will be tensions, there will be the endless quest to find scapegoats."[42] The statement reveals a surprising ignorance of the history as well as the consequences of the 1967 War. He repeats the mantra that Palestinians suffered from hunger, disease, and illiteracy because they were poor and assigned to a Third World existence, not because they were dispossessed of their land and property and subjected to a security state that limits their mobility, employment, housing and general welfare. King's solution? A "Marshall Plan for the Middle East, where we lift those who are at the bottom of the economic ladder and bring them into the mainstream of economic security."[43] We can only speculate on how King's position might have changed had he lived, but, given the opportunity to study the situation in the same way he had studied Vietnam, he would doubtless have been less sanguine about Israel's democratic promise or the prospect of international aid as a strategy to dislodge a colonial relationship. To be sure, his unequivocal opposition to violence, colonialism, racism, and militarism would have made him an incisive critic of Israel's current policies. He certainly would have stood in opposition to the VLG, CUFI, and the litany of lobbyists who invoke King as they do Israel's bidding.

While groups like the VLG have some claim on the long tradition of Black Zionism I've briefly outlined here, they also represent a fundamental break from an era when Israel's future was seen as bound up with the future of Black America and a global struggle for racial justice. But the VLG evolved into an arm of AIPAC to deflect criticism of Israel as an apartheid state. VLG members have participated in AIPAC-sponsored tours of Israel and developed their talking points through its Saban Leadership Training seminars. AIPAC not only honored VLG founders Darius Jones and Jarrod Jordan, both graduates of Clark Atlanta University, with its Jon Barkan Israel Advocacy Award in 2009, it named the VLG AIPAC Advocate of the Year for its attack on SJP. Darius Jones continued to speak for the VLG, even after AIPAC hired him as its Southeast Regional Outreach Director.[44] Indeed, AIPAC is so desperate for Black allies that it overlooked or ignored the VLG leaders' anti-Semitic comments. Jarrod Jordan, for example, compared the SJP's decision to hold its 2011 national conference at Columbia University "to the Ku Klux Klan holding a conference at Morehouse College in Atlanta, a total affront to Jewish culture and identity."[45] In other words, Morehouse is an HBC; ergo, Columbia University is a historically *Jewish* institution in a historically Jewish city! Reeking of Jesse Jackson's "hymietown" slur, Jordan not only ignores Columbia's anti-Semitic past and paints "Jewish culture and identity" as a monolith, but he equates a student solidarity movement with the Klan—an organization whose anti-Semitism rivaled its anti-Black racism.

And then there is the curious case of Darius Jones, who, just two years before his involvement with AIPAC, wrote a blog called *9Ether News* that reads like a cross between Herbert Spencer and *Mein Kampf*. On October 4, 2006, Jones wrote: "Our race would be wise to learn from nature. We would be even better served to harmonize with its evolutionary designs. Clearly, survival of the fittest is the moral of the story. However, we continually ignore what is patently obvious. . . . Social dynamics move more in accordance with biological prerogatives than humanistic ideals."[46] Jones presumably views Israel/Palestine in Social Darwinian terms. Israel prevailed because Palestinians could not compete.

Ironically, while the VLG, CUFI, and their allies all lay claim to Dr. King's legacy, two of the finest examples of King's vision of nonviolent resistance are the boycott, divestment, and sanctions (BDS) movement and the long struggle to end apartheid in South Africa. These movements, after all, are inextricably intertwined. In fact, the global solidarity movement that helped topple apartheid in South Africa inspired more than a hundred Palestinian civil society organizations to issue the original call for BDS in 2005.[47] Although the African National Congress (ANC) launched a limited armed struggle against the apartheid regime, it was massive nonviolent civil disobedience that generated a crisis for the regime. And like virtually every nonviolent movement, disruptions exposed the real source of violence: the state. When the ANC, Black trade unions, and later the United Democratic Front boycotted elections, Bantu schools, and buses and organized stay-at-homes, they were met by vicious state and vigilante violence. In the case of South Africa, not unlike the Montgomery bus boycott, the success of local and even national boycotts depended on internationalizing the struggle. Ultimately, it was the retaliatory violence, the complicity of the state, the silence of liberals, the blatant violation of human rights, and the media projection of such violations that generated international solidarity and proved most disruptive to business as usual.

And the combination of international support and moral authority em-
powered activists to persevere against great odds.

The international boycott was not responsible for the defeat of apartheid, but it did mark a turning point in the movement. Indeed, the case of
South Africa may be the best example we have of how a principled international boycott can help change the conditions of struggle on the ground.
Archbishop Desmond Tutu drew inspiration from Nelson Mandela's
warning against reading "reconciliation and fairness as meaning parity between justice and injustice" in defending his own support for BDS, in general, and the academic and cultural boycott of Israel, in particular: "It can
never be business as usual. Israeli Universities are an intimate part of the
Israeli regime, by active choice. . . . Palestinians have chosen, like we did,
the nonviolent tools of boycott, divestment, and sanctions."[48] Postapartheid South Africa continued to walk the talk. Besides being home to one
of the largest BDS campaigns on the planet, the ANC-ruled government
has backed the Israel boycott when it decided to ban products made in
illegal Jewish settlements in the West Bank. South Africa also withdrew its
ambassador from Israel to protest the IDF's violent raid on the MV *Mavi
Marmara* (part of the Free Gaza Flotilla) off the Gaza Coast in May 2011.

Finally, the lessons Palestinians have taken from South Africa's long
struggle against apartheid are more than tactical or strategic. For all of
its limitations, the ANC's effort to replace apartheid with an authentic,
nonracial democracy generated a vision of citizenship that was not based
on race or religion. For Palestinians this is an old idea (the notion of a
bi-national state) given new life (the demand for one democratic state).
As writer/activist Ali Abunimah reminds us, Nelson Mandela accepted
Afrikaner claims on a South African identity, and in so doing

> was able to accept his enemy's narrative without compromising
> on the demand that Afrikaners relinquish their exclusive claim
> on power. Mandela urged South Africans to embrace any Af-
> rikaner who abandoned apartheid, and thus Afrikaners gained
> a legitimacy in the eyes of other South Africans that they were
> unable to wrest through centuries of domination. It is an incred-
> ibly simple and powerful maneuver, yet one that so far has been
> beyond the ability of most Israelis and Palestinians.[49]

In the end, apartheid died on the sharp edge of principles, struggle, and solidarity, not forgiveness, apologetics, and compromise. South

Africa is certainly not the country envisioned in the Freedom Charter, and the kind of neoliberal politics that has sadly prevailed has also found its proponents among Palestinian elites. But what remains deeply embedded in civil society—both in South Africa and Palestine—is a legacy of principled movement, driven by a vision of democracy free of domination or exclusion.

## Chapter 14

# Checkpoints and Counterpoints
## Edward Said and the Question of Apartheid

Suren Pillay

> If we are all to live—this is our imperative—we must capture the
> imagination not just of our people, but of our oppressors.
> —Edward Said, 2001

I n 1991, as a young undergraduate student at the University of the Western Cape (UWC) in Cape Town, I first heard Edward Said speak live.
Said was invited to South Africa to deliver a public lecture at the University of Cape Town, but he also came to give a talk at the English Department at UWC.[1] South Africa was at the midpoint of its formal negotiated settlement. He returned later in 2000 to give another talk, as guest
of the minister of education, Kader Asmal, to a conference planning the
new education system. Edward Said was invited to return, always. He was
sought out because he meant something to a number of South Africans,
just as he has meant something to so many diverse audiences and consti-
uencies around the world: activists who found in him an anticolonial and
anti-imperialist comrade, or intellectuals in the universities, who found
in him a way to talk anew about literature in a world where people had
been thrown about by colonialism and capitalism. A world where literature, art, music, and film had to be practiced within the ebbs and flows
of movement, flux, and exile rather than as stasis or in compartments.

But what I wish to speculate on here is the question of what South Africa might mean for a Palestinian exile.

To ask the question more broadly, it might be this: "What does South Africa mean for a critical movement of solidarity with Palestinian aspirations for national sovereignty?" What South Africa *means* for Palestine is a question that connects all the contributors to this volume, since it is South Africa as the name of a crime against humanity that concerns us here. We are concerned with the colonial occupation of Palestine by an occupying force that coheres around Zionism to produce a state called Israel and with the ongoing violence that ensues from this relation between colonizer and colonized. Rather than as embodied by Edward Said, what I wish to do is think about Israel and apartheid along the grain of ways in which some of Said's hopes and anxieties politically resonated in and drew on South Africa.

The analogy of apartheid and Israel is a powerful one. It puts an internationally accepted crime against humanity alongside one that struggles to be accepted as a legitimate struggle from powerful Western states. Palestine is always, it seems, a struggle that has to be legitimated, always under question, always under doubt and suspicion despite what international law says. It is as if the colonial tropes of Arabs mobilized in the nineteenth century, which Said discusses in the powerful essay, "Zionism from the Standpoint of its Victims," continue to bedevil Palestinian claims to victimhood.[2] The colonial consensus on the figure of the Arab who is wily, untrustworthy, and prone to lies and exaggeration continues to bring into question the occupation's violence, despite these being written about, witnessed, catalogued, filmed, photographed, enacted in the candid light of day. Unlike the struggle against apartheid, which was more easily taken up as a legitimate struggle against an illegitimate regime, the struggle against Israel's colonial occupation is often, we are told, a story that must be narrated with balance. There always has to be two sides to this story, the implication being that the violence of the occupying force is justifiable, its security concerns legitimate, its assassinations necessary, its walls understandable. It was very difficult to defend apartheid in this way, even by the defenders of white racial supremacy in South Africa. The legitimate discourse that they could do it by the end of the twentieth century was as a common cause against the evils of communism, rather than as an outright defence of the right of a racial minority to rule over a majority. And then, with the end of the Cold War, that argument itself was no longer available.

It is therefore quite obvious to those of us who share our solidarities with the Palestinians that twinning apartheid to Israel successfully in an international campaign has the potential to render the occupation less defensible, less palatable, less ambiguously wrong and unjust. The more we show that Israel increasingly resembles, and, in fact exceeds, apartheid rule in its violent management of space, territory, and security, the more we succeed in bringing about its isolation.

And yet, as the momentum of this campaign of isolation grows, I have continually returned to a comment by Edward Said that has stuck with me: "If we are all to live—this is our imperative—we must capture the imagination not just of our people, but of our oppressors."

I often thought about that line when I was doing my doctoral research on the killing of a group of Black South African activists by an apartheid hit squad during the state of emergency in the mid-1980s. It encouraged me to start my research not with the outrage we all share that attends victims of political violence. It was an outrage I myself inhabited vividly since I had been an activist in the banned student movements of late 1980s Cape Town and I recall the very necessity to make known, to make heard, and to make legitimate the victim's side, to cede no ground to the justifications of oppressive state power. In my research I decided, however, that I would be interested in the perpetrator's narrative. What worldview, ideology, cultural, and political milieu could make violence like this thinkable, could render a group of young Black men enemies who needed to be eliminated? While I arrived at these questions quite late, the imagination of the oppressor was indeed something that the political leadership of sections of the antiapartheid movement did think about and, in the end, provided a turning point of sorts.

Edward Said lamented in a number of writings and interviews how very little the Palestinians understood American politics or Israeli politics:

> Thus Israel itself has tended to appear as an entirely negative entity, something constructed for us for no other reason than either to keep Arabs out or to subjugate them. The internal solidity and cohesion of Israel, of Israeli's as a people and as a society, have for the most part, therefore eluded understanding of Arabs generally. Thus to the walls constructed by Zionism have been added walls constructed by a dogmatic almost theological brand of Arabism.[3]

Said's impatience with this lack of attention to understanding American and Israeli domestic historical-political dynamics was, I think, a strategic political question shaped by the enduring ethic that drove both his political work as well as his intellectual writings, if they can be disentangled. Contrapuntal thinking, as he called it, was after all more than a way to read texts in context—it was a potential way of being in common in the world.

One of the most powerful features of his path-breaking book *Orientalism* (1978) was to describe imperialism in a way that distinguished it from a swath of left thinking that explained colonialism and imperialism through the logics of economic interest.[4] Shifting from the primacy of *homo economicus*, *Orientalism* was a book that drew our attention to the work of the imagination, an imagination that he had, through his own Anglophile colonial history, been absorbed by as a young man. Said's professional erudition was primarily in the philological tradition of studying the classic texts of the Western canon. These were the texts he mainly taught in his classes at Columbia—he never actually taught Arab literature as such. The West was an imagination he inhabited ambiguously, though, and even more so after the 1967 Arab–Israeli War. It signaled a turning point, an eruption into his consciousness of being Arab, and a transformation of his reading of these texts with the fresh eyes of an incisive critical consciousness. My point here is to stress the centrality of the work of the imagination in his world, and in the world at large, as a temporal, geographical, and historical immanence. He offered us a way to think of the worldliness of texts, of arts, and of aesthetics. Drawing on Foucault, he traced their effects in the world and turned to Gramsci to navigate how it these became hegemonic. Said drew our attention to the work of the imagination because colonial and imperial rule had to be thought, imagined, lived in, desired. Its justificatory discourse, as Partha Chatterjee calls it, worked through knowledge: the novel, the chronicle, the colonial administrator's report, the police commissioner's log book, the magistrate's administration of justice, the court translator's translations, the journalist, the botanist, the scientist, and so on.[5]

Now, if we are to make the case, as is becoming the doxa of the solidarity movement, of Israel *as* apartheid, I think there are a few implications to think through with regard to the work of the imagination and its political effects and countereffects. Does thinking of Israel as a form of apartheid help us to do the work Said was imploring us to do—to understand the imagination of our oppressors, in this case Zionism and its support within the United States? And does it, in a related and politically necessary way, help us to do the work of "capturing the imagination" of our oppressors?

As a graduate student I was drafted to help organize a conference at Columbia University that brought a group of South Africans to engage with Israelis and Palestinians. Said was ill but had committed doggedly to give the keynote address, which he delivered at the end of workshop. He was particularly drawn to the idea of the conference, as he told me, because it brought a group of *white* South African critics of apartheid into conversation with anti-Zionist, revisionist, and critical Zionists. The idea being that the white South Africans might encourage Jewish Israelis toward stepping out of the mindset that imprisons that polity in a seemingly unified terror authored by the imperatives of national security. As he would point out:

> I don't think we've spent enough time trying to involve segments of the Israeli public in our struggle. The ANC from the very beginning announced that it would include whites in its ranks. We've never done that. Even now, sympathetic Israelis are not welcome as equal participants in Palestinian institutions on the West Bank and Gaza. They're never invited. That doesn't mean that there isn't a form of normalization going on between Israeli academics and Palestinian academics . . . Its not the same thing however as being involved in a militant common front for liberation.[6]

When I read Said's quote, "If we are to live . . ." based on everything else he has said about the entwined fates of Jews and Arabs, I take that "we" to refer to those who live in the land called Palestine/Israel:

> Palestinians will cling to the past; they will cling to the land. And they simply are not going to go away. So, my sense of realism is such that the only way this problem is going to be settled, as in South Africa, is to face the reality squarely on the basis of co-existence and equality, with a hope of truth and reconciliation in the South African style. You have to say that these are equal peoples and they have to live together as communities, each with its own sense of self. I think that's the way to go. . . . Separate states, separate populations on a tiny land, drenched in the history of two peoples who have been living with and fighting each other for the last one hundred, it is simply unrealistic.[7]

The similarity between Israel and South Africa is that both are settler colonies and, in settler colonies of the modern period, the settlers do not leave.[8] In some cases, as in North America and Latin America, many natives were exterminated, dissolved, or diluted. In South Africa the settlers realized that despite conquest, the natives could not be liquidated physically. Apartheid tried, however, to erase the native population politically, by rendering that population foreigners and migrants, subjects of Bantustan homelands. It was the violence in the attempts to administer this that animated the resistance and popular revolt. When the white elites eventually realized that South Africa could never really mean white South Africa, and when the antiapartheid movements in South Africa realized that any future would mean living with our white settlers, it occasioned a gradual, sometimes conflicted, but fundamental shift in political thinking and in strategy and tactics. It was then that the dominant liberation movement "captured the imagination" of our oppressors, or at least significant enough sections of it.

After 1976 the apartheid regime increasingly had to rely on a repressive apparatus to win the battles it was losing politically. Every ingenious and convoluted effort it was making to co-opt support, to win political favor in the southern African region, to restructure local government, and to engineer constitutional amendments was shown for what these were—as many efforts to preserve white settler rule. They were rendered illegitimate by the revolt of the Black population and the solidarity of others. The more its political sophistry failed, the more the apartheid regime turned, in Stuart Hall's felicitous phrase, to "policing the crisis."[9] This created an increasingly uneasy white population, less enthusiastic about defending legal racial discrimination and yet also overwhelmingly expressing greater and greater support for repressive techniques to maintain minority rule. This contradiction was explained incisively as a fear in the Afrikaner journalist Rian Malan's memoir, *My Traitor's Heart*: taking the foot off the neck of someone you have kept under your boot for so long and so violently could only release a vengeance of genocidal proportions on yourself.[10]

The Palestinian issue can now be characterized as a hundred-year war of sorts. At its heart in the modern period was the project of sections of the European Jewish community to create a homeland for Jews. Zionism emerged from the same mindset that gave rise to various other nationalist projects in Europe in the wake of the collapse of the Habsburg and

Romanov empires. This particular form of nationalism took ethnos and nation to be collapsible entities. It was framed in the period when to think of the nation was also to think of a homogenous cultural-linguistic community with certain unique characteristics or essential features.[11]

Tony Judt, the late historian, pointed out that the problem was that the Zionist project "arrived too late."[12] It had imported a characteristically late nineteenth-century separatist project into a world that had moved on: a world of individuated rights, open frontiers, and international law. That homeland, seen as even more necessary after the ghastly Nazi genocidal violence, was to be in what was then Ottoman Palestine, which came under British mandate with the collapse of the Ottoman Empire. The homeland would be a place where Jews could be assured of their safety. It is of course a richly instructive and tragic irony then that there are few places where one is more unsafe as a Jew today than in Israel.

We may also think of Palestinian nationalism as the victim of bad timing. As a nationalist movement, it was relatively unsuccessful in realizing its aims during the heyday of decolonization. It endured through the Bandung period of nonalignment, Pan-Arab nationalism, and the Manichean division of the Cold War—all of which exerted their own forces of repulsion and attraction in international alliance politics. Palestinian nationalism remains unfulfilled, whereas other nations, like South Africa, Northern Ireland, and East Timor, have found some form of realization, giving the conflict its intractable dimension today. In a post–Cold War world, Palestinian nationalism is situated within another appalling dichotomy, which is being framed as religious and cultural. Palestinian nationalism now suffers a disputatious association with Islamic fundamentalism, as part of an extended family of terror defined as "Islamic." It makes demands in a world where the identity of being Muslim carries with it for some an increasingly pejorative connotation where these things seem to matter most: the Euro-American world.

My point in recalling this is that there is a structure of nationalism that was animated by the project of Zionism as well as by the revolt against it. Said was well aware of this dynamic and worked within it while being critical of it. It was an indispensable phase, leading toward a certain kind of future less defined by identity politics. But one had to have the right to the identity in order to exercise the sovereign right to *choose* to give it up, and how and in what way to do that, without erasing the distinctiveness of histories of filiation. Colonial occupation precisely withholds sovereignty and by extension invalidates the right to choose one's identity. In a discussion of the figure of the exile through the writings of those he admired (Nietzsche, Lukacs, Auerbach, and Adorno), Said paused on a remarkable quote by Hugo of St. Victor that was cited by the exiled Erich Auerbach. Hugo noted poignantly that "the tender soul has fixed his love on one spot in the world; the strong man has extended his love to all places; the perfect man has extinguished his." But as Said went on to emphasize—lest we see in that a rejection of an attachment to place that a colonized and exiled subject holds on to—for Hugo the "the 'strong' or 'perfect man' achieves independence and detachment by working through attachments, not rejecting them."[13]

There are two ways in which we can mobilize the association of apartheid and Israel. We need not choose one way to make the analogy of Israel and apartheid, but we do need to think strategically about which association we want to champion most vociferously, at this point, at this time. My caution would be that to emphasize only the first dimension of the analogy without the other will be politically egregious to the cause of resolving the conflict in a just manner. The first is the one that works to draw an association in order to render morally scandalous, politically putrid, and legally sanctionable the desires and effects of Israeli occupation. There is little doubt that much of that argument increasingly holds up. That is, it captures a form of administration and colonial rule that maintains the right of a minority to be the dominant power in a geography where it *is* a cultural minority. It is an analogy of resemblances in and across the realms of bureaucracy and space/territory: walls, passes, separations of roads, discriminations of quotidian life, and its own racial taxonomies. I would say this is the analogy of apartheid and Israel.

A second way in which we can associate apartheid and Israel is the analogy of apartheid with Zionism. It is the comparison that resonates more forcefully with Said's injunction to understand the imagination of our oppressors in order to capture their imaginations. In other words, it is strategic and subversive because it works to undo hegemonies, to unsettle consensus, to ferment and further the existing fissures, fractures, and doubts *within* Israeli society, particularly the doubts about the equation of being and living as a Jew and living in a Zionist state. From the second vantage point, what is useful about the analogy with apartheid might be less about the features that are like apartheid at its worst (and they are palpably there). Perhaps it is the acceptance that, like in South Africa, a Jewish population and a Palestinian population are not going anywhere else. Ending apartheid actually means living together in what Said called a "state of citizenship."

There is a way in which Said found in his other passion, that of music, a way to imagine this kind of living together, glimpsed in his work with the Israeli pianist and conductor, Daniel Barenboim. It was a collaboration that gave practice to counterpoint, a musical concept that he put to political work in the world. In the words of John Rahn:

> It is hard to write a beautiful song. It is harder to write several individually beautiful songs that, when sung simultaneously, sound as a more beautiful polyphonic whole. The internal structures that create each of the voices separately must contribute to the emergent structure of the polyphony, which in turn must reinforce and comment on the structures of the individual voices. The way that is accomplished in detail is . . . "counterpoint."[14]

Judt was then a bit misplaced to suggest that the problem with Zionism was that it emerged when we had given up group solidarities for individual rights. If anything, it is quite apparent that group solidarities and cultural filiations and affiliations continue to animate politics in the most impassioned and hopeful, but also tragic and violent, ways. The challenge then, thinking from within Said's oeuvre, is how to arrive at a state of counterpoint, how to arrive at a conjuncture where Jews can feel safe in a state of shared citizenship with Palestinians. The question then of Palestine is a question of our times, from immigrant Europe to postapartheid South Africa learning to live with immigrants from elsewhere in Africa and the world. It is the question of how we step out of the script of colonial rule that politicized culture everywhere, first by ordering hierarchies of cultures through racial science and, second, by naturalizing the right of some, as their manifest destiny, to rule over others. Culture came to define us all politically and thereby determined our fates in the world. Undoing that means asking how we depoliticize culture and create political communities that can fold difference into their very being, creating communities in which one group's existence is not at the expense of the Other. The difficult question that Said's encounter with South Africa raises for me is less then about whether Israel today resembles apartheid. It is more about the

ways in which the resolution to the conflict might best resemble the resolution to the citizenship question in South Africa: where the oppressor's
imagination and the oppressed can find a consensus that the land belongs
to all who live in it.

A campaign of solidarity has to ask itself very frank and strategic questions as to whether we understand the mind of the defenders of Zionism
and whether we are formulating answers to the question of Palestine that
increasingly persuade Jews that Zionism is not in the best interest of a Jewish way of life. This might sound too idealistic and improbable from the
bleak view inside the concrete facts on the ground. Yet that is precisely
why Said's thinking and being in the world continues to embody a politics
and ethics of such importance—his was a secularism of transcendence.
The answer to the question of Palestine will have to be like the answer to
the end of apartheid. It will have to transcend the impasses of hardened
fears. It will have to connect fear of annihilation with the counterpoint of
life lived in a future, together.

Chapter 15

# The South African Moment

## Mahmood Mamdani

$\mathbf{B}$oycott, divestment, and sanctions (BDS) activists who wish to learn from the South African struggle need to place the South African boycott in a larger context, the antiapartheid struggle. There was no military victory against apartheid. The end of apartheid was a negotiated settlement. Boycott and collaboration were two ends of a single spectrum. In the middle lay different forms of critical engagement. The boycott was one instrument among many. To view the boycott in isolation would be misleading. To see the boycott in a larger context is to understand the politics that informed the boycott. Thus my question: What was the decisive moment in the development of the antiapartheid struggle in South Africa? What was the South African moment?

My argument will be the following. The South African moment involved a triple shift. First was a shift from demanding an end to apartheid to providing an alternative to apartheid. Second was a shift from representing the oppressed, the Black people of South Africa, the majority, to representing the whole people. The third was the turn from resisting within the terms set by apartheid to redefining the very terms of how South Africa should be governed.

The South African moment took shape over time, in response to a set of challenges faced by the antiapartheid struggle.

I will begin with the birth of the armed struggle in the aftermath of the Sharpeville massacre of 1960. The stated objective of the armed guerrilla was to liberate the unarmed population. The professional revolutionary was patterned after Lenin's injunctions in *What Is to Be Done?* He and she were part of a vanguard whose mission was to lead and liberate the people. In Maoist imagery, guerrillas were to be like fish in water—the fish would be active, the water supportive.

As the armed struggle unfolded as a project, the results were by and large negative. The more activists moved into exile, the more the population was pacified. Capital took command: the sixties were a time of rapid economic development, a time when huge amounts of foreign capital moved into South Africa. Economic historians speak of the sixties as the second major significant period in the industrial transformation of South Africa, the first being the 1930s. Unlike the 1930s, which was marked by the Great Depression, the fillip to industrialization in the 1960s came from an expanding wave of foreign investment. From the point of view of the people, however, the 1960s were a decade of relative silence, the silence of the graveyard.

That silence was shattered by two volleys. The first was the Durban general strike of 1973. The second was the wave of township protests provoked by the police shooting of protesting students in Soweto, on June 16, 1976. I will discuss Soweto first, and then come to Durban as the counterpoint. The significance of Soweto was threefold. First, Soweto shifted the initiative from professional revolutionaries in exile to community-based activists. Second, it shifted the focus from armed struggle to direct action. The youth of Soweto had no more than stones to throw at gun-toting police. In both these, Soweto evokes the first intifada in Palestine. But Soweto also signaled an ideological shift, a shift in popular political perspective, a shift so vast that one may speak of it as a sea change.

Before Soweto, the resistance in South Africa developed within the framework set by apartheid. To understand this framework, one needs to look at the apartheid mode of governance. Apartheid divided the whole population into races: Africans, Indians, Coloureds (a "mixed race" group), whites—many so-called population groups. In response, each population group organized separately, as a race: Africans as the African National Congress (ANC); Indians as the Natal Indian Congress, first organized by Gandhi; Coloureds as the Coloured Peoples Congress; and whites as the Congress of Democrats. The Congress Alliance was an umbrella alliance of these separate racially based resistance groups—and the Congress of South African Trade Unions, which was not organized along racial lines. This is how the mode of governance of apartheid became naturalized as the mode of resistance against it.

There were two major breaches in this mindset. The first was the Freedom Charter, adopted by the Congress Alliance in 1955, and its ringing declaration: "South Africa belongs to all those who live in it." Though a declaration by one elite to disaffected sections of another elite, this declaration marked the birth of nonracialism. As such, it turned out to be of huge ideological significance.

The second breach, just as fundamental, if not more so, was the work of Steve Biko and the Black Consciousness Movement. This was an alliance of ordinary people, mainly students, from below. In contrast, the Freedom Charter created the basis of an alliance at the top. Its effect was to incorporate individual whites into the antiapartheid movement. Yet, its importance cannot be underrated.

South Africa claimed to be the only democracy south of the Sahara—just as Israel claims to be the only democracy in the region. Both were racially defined, and Israel still is: it was a democracy for only Jews in Israel, and only whites in South Africa. In both cases, democracy turned into a fig leaf hiding racial privilege. It is in this context that the ANC put forward a meaningful notion of democracy—not a democracy of only one racial group, not even of the majority against the minority, but a democracy for all. Soon, individual white antiapartheid activists began to join the ANC.

I am tempted to ask: How many anti-Zionist organizations in historic Palestine have opened their doors to Israeli Jews opposed to a Jewish state? Not only as ordinary members but also as leaders? I ask because I do not know the answer. If the answer is not any or hardly any, why not?

The historical significance of Black Consciousness (BC) was that it constructed a unity from below, a unity of all the oppressed: Africans, Indians, Coloureds. Apartheid power had fragmented the subject population into so many groups, recorded separately in the census: Africans, Indians, Coloureds. The great historical achievement of BC was to pull the rug from under apartheid. Black, said Steve Biko, is not a color, Black is an experience—if you are oppressed, you are Black!

Is there a lesson here for the anti-Zionist struggle?

The Palestinian predicament is not the same as that of South Africans under apartheid; it is worse. Only a small minority of South Africans were driven out of their country; the majority of Palestinians live outside historic Palestine. When a Palestine Liberation Organization (PLO) delegation visited Tanzania in the 1960s and went to pay a courtesy call on President Nyerere, he told them: "We lost our independence, you lost your country!"

One cannot but be struck by the extraordinary resilience of the Palestinian people in the face of overwhelming odds. We live at a time when political violence has been conflated with criminal violence, when all forms of resistance are being redefined as terror, when repression is embraced as a war on terror. The major exception to this global trend is Palestine. It is a tribute to the tenacity of the Palestinian people, led by those in Gaza, and the political work done by the Palestinian resistance, including the BDS movement, that Israel and the United States have been unable to tar popular resistance in historic Palestine with the brush of terrorism. More than ever, the world is convinced that the cause of the Palestinian people is just.

What, then, is the major hindrance to a forward movement? Is it the military power of the United States and Israel? It would be a mistake to think so.

The problem is twofold. It is certainly a problem that the United States and Israel are not yet convinced that a military solution to the Palestinian resistance is out of question, but it is a *secondary* problem. The *primary* problem is that the Israeli people, the majority Jewish population within the state of Israel, is not yet convinced it has an option other than Zionism. The Zionist message to the Jewish population of Israel is this: Zionism is your only guarantee against another Holocaust. Your only defense against a second Holocaust is the state of Israel. The real challenge the Palestinian resistance faces is political, not military.

Let me return to apartheid South Africa to clarify that challenge. Consider two facts. The party of apartheid, the National Party, came to power through elections in 1948 and was returned to power with greater numbers throughout the 1950s. The dissolution of political and juridical apartheid also involved a Whites Only referendum—whereby a majority of the white population authorized its government to negotiate with representatives of the Black majority. The referendum went alongside a debate in both the Black and the white population. In the Black population, the rejectionist view was advanced by the Pan Africanist Congress in its mobilization, though not in its official pronouncements: *one settler, one bullet*! The white rejectionists belonged to a number of organizations, from the Conservative Party to the separatist Afrikaner Weerstandsbeweging. Their point of view was best reflected in a popular book by Rian Malan, *My Traitor's Heart*.

Malan was a descendent of a former South African state president. As a reporter for the Jo'berg *Star*, Malan covered the crime beat in the Black townships of Jo'berg. He wrote a book about what the apartheid press called "black-on-black crime." One chapter narrated the story of the Hammer Man—a big Black man who wielded a heavy hammer with which he smashed the skull of his victim. The violence was largely gratuitous, out of proportion to the benefit he got from it. The story had a subscript: If they can do this to one another, what will they do to us if given half a chance?

Rian Malan failed to convince the majority of whites in South Africa. Why? Because important sections of the liberation movements had moved to thinking in holistic terms. They told anyone who would listen—and there were plenty—that the struggle was not against settlers, but against settler power. Without a state that legally underwrites settler privileges, settlers would turn into just ordinary immigrants.

The South African moment was when important sections of the liberation camp redefined the enemy as not settlers but the settler state, not whites but white power. By doing so, they provided whites with an alternative—not a democracy for whites only, but a nonracial democracy.

In 1993, when the head of the South African Communist Party, Chris Hani, was assassinated in a suburb of Jo'berg, hundreds of thousands gathered at his funeral to pay him homage, and to listen to Mandela, police said they were not sure they could control the crowds. The National Union of Mineworkers said they could and they did. That day, Mandela addressed the whole country, not just the mourners at the stadium in Soweto. The day after, though de Klerk was still the president of South Africa, Mandela was its undisputed leader.

I gave my inaugural lecture at the University of Cape Town in 1998. I asked: When does a settler become a native? My answer was, "Never." Native, I argued, is the creation of the settler state. The native is invented as the other of the settler. If the settler is defined by history, the native is said to be defined by geography. If the settler makes his and her own history, the native is said to be the unthinking captive of an unchanging custom. My conclusion was that the settler and the native go together. They are joined by a relationship. Neither can exist in isolation: should you destroy one, the other would cease to exist.

Liberation in South Africa was the result of a combination of factors: war in the region, direct action within the country, and a changing balance of power globally. War in Angola was the epicenter of the war in the region: South African Defense Forces were defeated by Cubans and Movimento Popular de Libertação de Angola at Cuito Cuanavale in 1987–88. This development precipitated the independence of Namibia. South Africa's regional isolation was complete and the limits of its military power were clear. Direct action developed in waves: from Durban 1973 and Soweto 1976 to insurrection in the townships and the international campaign for divestment and boycott in the 1980s. Internationally, there was a marked change with the end of the Cold War—once the Cold War ended, there was no morally or politically compelling reason to support apartheid. All three developments were important, but the decisive development was internal. This will be my last point.

Direct action began in the 1960s and developed in the 1970s and 1980s. It was a response to what was evident to all, that the armed struggle was a propaganda weapon at best and an empty boast at worst. The beginning was in the late sixties. It came with a split in the liberal white student organization, the National Union of South African Students (NUSAS), which had admitted Black members. Led by Steve Biko, the Black section formed a separate organization, the South African Students' Organization (SASO). And out of SASO grew the Black Consciousness Movement.

Both wings of the antiapartheid student movement, white and Black, reached out to mobilize wider sections of society against apartheid. Black consciousness students moved to the township, and white students to organize migrant workers in hostels on the fringe of townships.

Out of this two-pronged initiative developed two wings of the labor movement, one based in migrant hostels, the other in the community (the township), the former drawing its intellectual vision from white students, the latter from Black students in townships. The first to be organized, in 1979, was the Federation of South African Trade Unions (FOSATU). Its core was unions organized following the spontaneous strike wave by Black workers in Durban and Pinetown in 1973. The constitution emphasized nonracialism, workers' control of trade unions, and worker independence from party politics. In contrast, the Congress of South African Trade Unions (COSATU), organized in 1985, made the alliance with the ANC and the South African Communist Party a central part of its strategy.

Though relatively few in numbers, white students were of strategic significance. They were key organizers of FOSATU. Later, they joined the

Communist Party, and then the ANC. When the time came, they provided effective channels of communication to the white population.

## Conclusion

The antiapartheid struggle educated white South Africa: that apartheid's claim that there would be no white security without white power was a hoax. Indeed, the reverse was true: their security required that whites give up the monopoly of power. The Palestinian challenge is to persuade the Jewish population of Israel and the world that—just as in South Africa—the long-term security of a Jewish homeland in historic Palestine requires the dismantling of the Jewish state. The South African lesson for Palestine and Israel is that historic Palestine can be a homeland for Jews, but not only for Jews. Put differently, Jews can have a homeland in historic Palestine, but not a state.

My second conclusion is that legal and political apartheid ended in 1994. But 1994 was also the year of two events that outlined two very different destinies for Africa. It was the year of the end of apartheid in South Africa and the genocide in Rwanda. Both took place in the first half of 1994. Ten years earlier, if you had told African intellectuals and activists that a decade hence there would be reconciliation in one of these countries and a genocide in another, the vast majority would have failed to identify the countries correctly—why? Because in 1984, the South African army had occupied most key Black townships and Rwanda was the site of an attempted reconciliation. In ten years, everything had changed—testifying to one fact: nothing is inevitable in political life!

---

*Ed. Note: This text is based on remarks as discussant for a talk given by Omar Barghouti of the BDS campaign, at Columbia University, New York City, December 2, 2014.*

Chapter 16

# Reflections in a Mirror
## From South Africa to Palestine/Israel and Back Again

Heidi Grunebaum

W hen I was invited to write about the documentary film I created with Mark J. Kaplan, *The Village under the Forest* (2013), I was going to explore what it means to be implicated in state atrocity and historical catastrophe in apartheid South Africa and Israel/Palestine. I wanted to write about psychic landscapes of complicity and how these unfold in our film from a non-Israeli Jewish South African perspective. In light of Israel's 2014 genocidal onslaught against Palestinian civilians in Gaza, however, to write about the politics of the apartheid analogy in a way that places the subject of complicity, the "implicated subject," at the center of discussion seems both obscene and all the more urgent; at once a double bind, a poisoned chalice, and a space of almost impossible thought.[1] But perhaps it is precisely these difficulties that also lie at the heart of the political effects of measurement, judgment, and the weighing of state and human-inflicted experiences of suffering. And perhaps these are challenges that must be also be encountered when writing about the politics of analogies between historical and human-made catastrophes more generally. It is these challenges arising out of the possible effects of the logic of analogy and how we approached them with our film that I would like to contemplate in what follows.

*The Village Under the Forest* set out to explore the question of what it could mean to be implicated in obliterating the traces of life, of people, of history, and of place in historic Palestine. To do this, the film excavates

161

how forests planted by the Jewish National Fund (JNF) to "make the wilderness bloom" in Israel were cultivated on top of the ruins of many Palestinian villages that were depopulated and destroyed during the 1948 *Nakba*, or catastrophe. The ruins of one of these villages, Lubya, lie beneath a JNF forest named South Africa Forest. Prompted by a questioning of what it means to have been complicit with apartheid in South Africa, the film explores the historically intertwined processes by which the village and the forest have been made and unmade from a non-Israeli Jewish perspective. Using a personal narrative voice, a role that I also play as narrator of the film, it grapples with the question of moral responsibility in light of the erasure of the village.

In the film, the question unfurls across the span of three decades that are marked on either side of time's passage between two different visits to the JNF's South Africa Forest. In the crossing from South Africa to Palestine/Israel and back again, the film opens a space in which to ask what debts of history might be encountered through the crossing. Between the narrator's first visit to the JNF forest and her return after learning about the ruins of Lubya beneath a vast area of pine trees, the film excavates the unmaking and making of the two counterposed spaces: Lubya and the JNF forest and the conscription of non-Israeli Jews in this process.

Until 1948, Lubya had been home, life, and livelihood to an estimated 2,730 people.[2] A robust culture of memory has ensured that the life-worlds associated with the destroyed Palestinian villages from 1948 live on in books, oral histories, commemorations, photographs, personal archives, and digital and community archives, as well as in the arts and intellectual production of Palestinians and their descendants. Mahmoud Issa—social historian, descendant of Lubyans, historical consultant for and interlocutor of the film—has published a social history of the village.[3] In it he enumerates how Lubya had been one of the largest villages in the Tiberias district with an area of almost 40 square kilometers. Lubya's "placeness" was contained in the life of its houses (about a thousand), its lively cultural clubs, mosque, coffee house, travelers' inn, school, nine shrines, almost forty wells, cemetery, and structures for grain, livestock, and agriculture. A place bustling with the accumulated stuff of centuries of life in the Galilee: love and politics, debate and scholarship, pilgrimage, travel and hospitality, trade and agriculture, gossip and grievance, and a fierce anticolonial sensibility. Situated close to both Tiberias and Nazareth, Lubya was home and homeland for the few thousand who counted the village as their place in the world whilst encountering the effects of political and economic change through the early decades of the twentieth century.

Lubya was conquered in mid-July 1948 following three military attacks by units of the Haganah, the pre-state military formation. It was forcibly depopulated and physically destroyed, along with about five hundred other Palestinian villages, towns, and urban areas, during the so-called War of Independence in Israeli nationalist histories or, for Palestinians, the *Nakba*. Civilians from Lubya joined the estimated 750,000 Palestinians who were forced out of the new state as refugees scattered across the West Bank, Gaza, and countries in the region and other parts of the world, forced into the ongoing existential twilight of exile, statelessness, and otherness. Some Lubyans, along with Palestinians from a number of other villages, became internally displaced inside the 1949 armistice line. Many continued to live in the nearby village of Deir Hanna. After the establishment of the state, an administrative matrix of laws and military orders prohibited displaced "internal" refugees from returning to their lands or homes. Unlike Jewish Israeli citizens, internally displaced Palestinians were subject to military rule until 1966. In 1950, the Knesset passed the Absentees' Property Law, inventing the term that would come to describe displaced Palestinians inside Israel, an act of legal naming whose irony is stunning. The law was also used by the state to appropriate depopulated lands and villages, which were then nominally purchased by the JNF through a Custodian of Absentee Property.

In a drive to "Judaize" the land and the landscape of the new state of Israel, official maps were redrawn and Arabic place names were Hebraicised.[4] Based on a Talmudic reference to an ancient school of Jewish learning said to have been located in the area, Lubya was renamed Lavi. Two Jewish settlements were established, the first, Kibbutz Lavi, in 1949. An Israeli military museum and memorial dedicated to the military unit that conquered Lubya and other Palestinian villages in the Galilee was also built on Lubya's lands—and that was one of the places I visited as a young Jewish South African in 1983, during my participation in a South African equivalent to the American Birthright program called Tochniet Akiva. South Africa Forest was planted over the ruins of Lubya in the mid-1960s. In the years following the depopulation and destruction of the Palestinian villages, the JNF planted eighty-six pine forests and leisure parks on top of the remains of *Nakba* villages. When I began the research for the film, in 2009, I recalled my visit to the forest in the 1980s. Palestinians had been erased, rendered "absent" from Israel's narratives of place, history, belonging, and nationalism that I was taught and with which so many non-Israeli Jews identified—we were baldly informed that "Palestinians do not exist." At that time, I had not yet the capacity to imagine that "my" trees were erasing the presence of people who had lived there and been forcibly removed. In addition, in the 1980s, Israel offered itself to me as a way out of the moral dilemmas of being white in apartheid South Africa, a promise to which I clung for many years.

## Looking in the Mirror

Israeli similarities with apartheid South Africa are multiple. When considered together with dates, laws, forced displacements, spatial erasures, pedagogies of violence, and the making of histories that justify ethnonationalist claims, the systemic resonances are even uncanny. So too are the psychic landscapes of implicated subjects in which the distinction between knowing and not knowing may be blurred by systemic silence and silencing, the systematic indoctrination of fear and ethnic chauvinism, and the cognitive disavowal of complicity. These affective states are conditioned and enlisted by an exclusionary state recruiting compliance both as a kind of "active passivity" and through the militarization of collective self-identity and public discourse. Similarities extend to the militarization of social discourse, civic identities, and public spaces, and to the existential fears engendered in the constant production of a dangerous and terrifying "enemy." They stretch to the familiar rhyming of denial, justification, excuse, moral accommodation, wilful ignorance, "partitioned" thinking/feeling, and the totalizing apocalyptic logic of state systems reproduced in their political rhetoric and social discourses. And they extend to the ways that complicity and consent are socially marshaled and institutionally policed through fear, censorship, shunning, exclusion, and the branding of those who challenge the systems as "traitors" to "their people."

Mark Kaplan and I faced two major challenges when developing the film treatment and script. The first was how we would interweave the making and the unmaking of the forest/village space within the same visual and narrative framework. The second was how South Africa should figure in the film and what kind of place it would be given in the narrative.

We sought a different way of telling such a politically and emotionally freighted story set within the charged space of Palestine/Israel. We wanted to avoid a morally didactic narrative and sought, rather, to raise questions different from those framed by the reductive binaries of "two sides" that characterize representations of "the conflict"; different questions that might chart a way toward thinking about outcome differently. In this, we wanted the film to raise moral dilemmas rather than to prescribe solutions. We tried to make a film that could open a space to think. We sought to avoid dogmatism, didactics, and finger-pointing to enable the complexity of a personal meditation on complicity to resonate more widely with the experiences and emotional responses of many other non-Israeli Jews.

To do this, we needed to avoid an individualistic or biographical narrative, which is a danger inherent to first-person narratives generally and particularly in cinematic works in which the visual image of an individual may too seamlessly be viewed as illustrative of a narrative voice. Written as a personal rather than autobiographical narrative, the film's point of view draws on the experience of so many people who, like me, were not politically active during apartheid. For us, this was a way to raise the question of complicity as structural and systemic: to broaden out from complicity as a question of individual agency alone, which autobiography may reinforce rather than destabilize. The personal voice and visual presence of the narrative guide, who appears almost as a shadow, half concealed and half revealed at the edge of the frame, attempts to avoid the danger of autobiography. Rather, the personal voice and indistinct visual presence of the narrator evoke and open a wider set of shared resonances. This may enable identification with people who have held similar affiliations to Israel and for whom questioning such visceral and psychically charged loyalties may be both necessary and difficult.

The similarities between apartheid South Africa and Israel emerge obliquely in the film, cross-referencing one another faintly as traces, echoes, and reflections. The resonances may be discerned in the movement of the crossing from here to there and back again. They emerge where they are not, as a reflection in the mirror. The movement from South Africa to Israel/Palestine and across the time between the two visits to the South Africa Forest both contains and focuses the relation of complicity and response to the unfolding of moral conscience within an embodied and personal life narrative. The narrative voice also shifts and moves in the film from first-person singular to the first-person plural and then back to the singular voice. This amplification and shrinking of voice suggest that complicity is both individual and collective, structural and embodied, proximate and at a distance. Although the frictions and overlapping of the singular and collective voices blur the distinctions, they require attention.

## Opening a Space to Think

For intellectuals, artists, activists, and scholars of South Africa and of Palestine/Israel, the politics of the analogy of settler-colonial apartheid in both contexts is a particularly complex undertaking on a fraught terrain. On the one hand, analogy may be made without much difficulty, including through recourse to legal principles and to moral categories. One only has to examine the fifty or more laws and legal amendments passed by Israel's Knesset that apportion hierarchically and qualitatively differential civil rights, entitlements, and privileges to Jewish Israelis as distinct from the prohibitions and restrictions on Palestinian citizens of Israel. The state envisions and administers Palestinian life very differently from Jewish Israeli life: one only has to mention the military administration and the multiply fractured territorial "discontiguity" of the spatial regime governing all aspects of Palestinian life on the occupied West Bank and Israel's blockade of Gaza by land, sea, and air. In contrast, as Hazem Jamjoum argues, analogy may be misplaced when its analytical focus is on the historical specificities of South Africa and Israel rather than the forms that apartheid as a state system may take.[5] Jamjoum also cautions that the optic of international legal frameworks, conventions, and principles that define apartheid as a state system based on its exclusionary and segregationist features (rather than as historical example to understand and respond to Israel's repressive structural, legal, administrative, and spatial regimes) occludes something else, something that remains at the heart of the Israeli state's ethnocratic logic: the disavowal of Palestinians as existing and existential subjects of which the Palestinian refugee stands as the exemplary figure.

The work of analogy may produce other kinds of foreclosures. In a world in which transgenerational histories and structural reproductions of Black suffering and violence against Black bodies are at once normalized, ongoing, and systemic, the stakes of direct analogy are high indeed. In contemporary South Africa, a reckoning with South African settler-colonial apartheid, the subjectivities it produced and those it constrained, is but tentatively under way with different effects and possibilities. With this work, twenty years after the defeat of "legal" apartheid, the question of how we think about the postapartheid, given that it continues to be elaborated with concepts informed by the very racial logics they are called on to think against, is a question being raised with increasing urgency. In the fractured and fractious present, the interstices in which other worlds had been imagined and other subjectivities inhabited during apartheid (and the struggle against it) are also being revisited. So analogy may risk immuring what is known and knowable about apartheid, contributing to reductionist accounts of apartheid as historical "event" or to the present conjunctures of the postapartheid as its inevitable and predetermined outcome. It may also inadvertently contribute to edifying a white redemption narrative—indeed, I am not certain if the film succeeds in avoiding the latter despite not making a direct analogy. The danger of a morally redemptive narrative of whiteness is sharpened further by the absurd proportions—and distortions—that white denialism has taken in contemporary South Africa. A South African discourse in which commitment and uncertainty are conceived of together to dismantle the racialized binaries is still incipiently being forged. This, while the external lives of those binaries also threaten to engulf thought.

With the meditative and poetic register of the narration, we tried to create a filmic space that enables thinking about complicity, about pathways of ethical response that may open, rather than be foreclosed by quantifying and measuring atrocity or prescribing a solution. This is important if we are to attend to the embodied and psychic life of implication in historical catastrophe and its erasures from collective consciousness. This is important if we are to better think about the consequences and effects of being implicated, particularly in a context in which a militant and militaristic ethnonationalism dominates. It is also important if we are to find a common space for thought, a space for thinking together and out loud. The fear of existential disintegration against which one's cognitive mind shores the self, against which one's terrified unconscious zones may be held at bay, becomes sharpened and more visceral when confronted by direct moral accusation, no matter its impeccable veracity. And without question, we are compelled, as much as we are implicated in these current conditions of urgency, to think ourselves out of the dominant logic in which "the conflict" is thought: a logic that normalizes partition and separation (the "two-state solution, for example), a logic that presents technologies of militarism as thinkable instruments of "solution"—in short, an apocalyptic logic.

Analogy can foreclose these challenges that are political, ethical, and discursive as much as they are conceptual and analytical, for it can work with assumptions of knowing in advance what is being quantified, measured, and analytically adjudicated. Today, these are more than theoretical issues as the stakes of analogy are implicated in the moral grounds of thought in times of war, at a time when the obliteration of human beings unfolds in real time, as do questions of narrative voice and authority, the location of the speaking subject, and ongoing struggles for the interpretive frame. They are implicated in the very stakes of bringing into being a future in which the unconditional sanctity of *all* human life, rather than differentiated modes of state-assigned value, can be thought and pursued. The film ends with the suggestion that in enumerating our debt to the obliterations committed in "our name," the obligation to bring such a future into being may be encountered also by daring to "walk that path: through forest and in between the ruins."

Chapter 17

# The Last Colony

Melissa Levin

November 1980. The room could be forgiven for its distinctly seven-
ties style. It was hardly into the following decade, and design could still take
a deep breath before moving on. It was also small-town South Africa—not
known for its capacity to shift with the times. The sunken lounge with
its chocolate-brown carpets and heavy cream-and-brown drapes was the
adult domain. It was a warm venue, if slightly off-limits to the children.

I must have been nine; always precocious, always delighting in the
positive attention of the adults. "Is it," I asked, "Is it good for us?" The
adults paused the conversation to notice me for the first time. They smiled
warmly. I smiled proudly back. I had cut to the chase and asked the question that was being skirted—the pivotal question that I'd based on statements I had heard often in the past.

"Yes, my darling, yes, it is good for us." I breathed deeply, satisfied, that
my people were okay in a world that was generally not.

The question was about the outcome of the election in the United
States. Ronald Reagan had won against the derisively identified "peanut
farmer," Jimmy Carter. Reagan's victory ushered in a renaissance for the
right wing that would remain secure even, or especially, through the brief
interlude of third-way politics in the 1990s, long after he was gone. At the
time, Reagan's victory was deemed "good for us." "Us" were the survivors
of the Holocaust—the children and grandchildren of the slaughtered or
near-slaughtered. "Us." We were the tribe that internalized the message of
the Nazis that we were once weak, that we had once walked like lambs to the
slaughter; we believed that we had been lulled into a sense of complacency

169

by the liberal emancipation laws of Germany. We were now the "new" Jews who understood that we were despised (always had been, always would be) by the rest of humanity. But we would meet that hatred with a vigilance and determination of reborn Macabees. That's who Ronald Reagan was good for—those muscular, anti-nebbish, Zionist new Jews in general. And he was very good for the South African new Jews in particular.

The chocolate-brown sunken lounge didn't survive the twentieth century. But this acute sense of imminent danger was only bolstered by the collapse of apartheid and the post-state twenty-first-century mode of warfare unleashed against the West. Could we be forgiven for this acute sense of danger infecting every which way we see the world? I, too, have inherited the visceral fear of annihilation. There is enough historical evidence of Jews as the perpetual scapegoat to cause some trepidation. This history has been reinforced in everyday confrontations with sometimes subtle and often explicit expressions of anti-Semitism from a variety of sources (including reconstructed and unreconstructed right-wingers and from people I have considered comrades on the left). It is this sense of imminent extinction that perpetuates the nationalist fervor of Israel today. Growing up, I believed that Zionism was the articulation of our deepest longing to return to the land of our ancestors. I thought that this was our only opportunity for Jewish survival.

This idea was bound to the myth that Israel was an empty land, waiting for our return. The accompanying yet contradictory myth was that those who were there wanted our death. The portrait of an unpopulated populated landscape was a narrative I easily understood from the other colonial education I was exposed to in 1980s South African history books. But I was never as invested in the South African story as I was in the Israeli one. South Africa, like any other place outside of Israel, could never be trusted as a refuge for Jews. We grew up with a deep sense of unbelonging and longing for places that have been stolen and other places that had been promised. The nostalgia for the shtetl did not translate into demands for its return but for the possibility of an eternal home for the Jews. And life was only possible elsewhere with the insurance policy that Israel represents.

These days, the idea that what is now Israel was unpopulated is held by only the most unread nationalists. But the notion that only Israel's existence can secure Jewish life on earth remains steadfast. Indeed, this sense of existential crisis leads latter-day Israeli nationalist historians to embrace

Israel even at the expense of its indigenous population. Posing his own question, "Is it colonialism?" Ari Shavit responds, "If it looks like a duck and walks like a duck and quacks like a duck, it probably is a duck." But it is a duck that Shavit is willing to live with because, he argues, there would be no Jews if it weren't for Israel. For him, the payment in Palestinians is worth it for Jewish survival.[1]

The argument that the existence of Jews everywhere is so intimately tied to the existence of Israel as a Jewish state has cemented a support base the world over. This is what Zionism as a nationalist project cultivated that other settler-colonialisms never had—a "diaspora." The very idea of a diaspora as a given rather than a construct of political necessity has fueled the ferocity with which Israel is shielded from criticism. It produces an "us" that extends far beyond the (unfixed) boundaries of the state. And while deep divisions mark the polity; while the seculars and Haredis fight each other, and while the right and left schism deepens; while racism is pervasive in the state (including, but not limited to the abduction of Yemeni Jewish children in the early 1950s as a project of Ashkenazi power); while prime ministers are assassinated and everyday politics of venality and corruption threaten the unity of the state, exile's purity sustains the narrative of the international obligation for a Jewish state to exist.[2] The narrative is steadfast, and no matter what happens, how it happens, why it happens, the default set of assumptions and arguments establishes itself quickly. Only a Pavlovian narrative would be able to answer in the affirmative that the current dispensation in Israel is good for "us," that the colonization of others is the only way to resolve the historic denigration of the Jews. For that set of assumptions functions to dehumanize Palestinians, and, in turn, to dehumanize the "us."

§

Edward Said has thought about the invidious position of Palestinians in the global imaginary. Palestinians struggle to find a place within a narrative of liberation in part due to the impossibility of being a victim to the ultimate victim. Auschwitz fixes the status of Jews as definitive of the wounded and, in so doing, vanishes the trauma of those who would claim to be injured by them. There are additional ways in which Palestinians' victimization is discursively refashioned into the perpetual nonvictim of

the perpetual victim. Golda Meir's refrain about how Israel can never for-
give the Palestinians for making them kill their children is often rehearsed
as justification for what would otherwise be regarded as the use of brute
force. It's a rather cynical move to steal their land, force them into exile,
and suggest that they bear responsibility for their pain. A recent incar-
nation of this is the "human shield" defense for the massacre of civilians.
Even worse is the line from the summer of 2014 that calls on peaceful people the world over to "Stand with Israel. Mourn with Gaza." No land, no
freedom. And those who maintain the landlessness and incarceration even
steal their dead. The only way for Palestinians to be viewed as victims is
if they suffer at the hands of the fighters. The image of the victim here is
the silenced, acquiescent, immobilized, and harmless. The victim does not
fight back. The victim does not lob Katyushas into Sderot. That person
resides in the domain of co-conspirator in an existential battle of wits. But
the ambiguity of victimhood remains the lifeblood of the Israeli state—to
be a Jew is to be the ultimate victim in perpetuity and only the nonvictim
(but also nonperpetrator) state can shield her from harm.

But there is also another way in which Palestinians are denied their
victimhood. Religiosity has played a large part in the colonizing impulse.
In South Africa, the Calvinists established a system of capitalist white supremacy that subscribed to the idea that Black people were designed as the
biblical "hewers of wood and drawers of water." Their own version of the
promised land divinely endorsed special privileges for the settlers and destined all who were in their way to their ordained hell on earth. While the
religious right-wing fundamentalists in Israel and the "diaspora" may be
unexceptional in regard to invoking subjugation justified by the heavens,
they stand alone in their impulse to obliterating the subjugated. The battle
for the so-called land of Israel is denied its politics, its history, its conjunctural determinants and read as a biblical battle. Palestinians in particular
and Muslims in general are cast in this script as a contemporary manifestation of biblical foes—much like the crusaders or Nazis have been. In this
sense too then, Palestinians can only ever be aggressors.

So every second summer, when Israel "mows the lawn" in Gaza, it can
count on its diasporic army to impulsively support its aggression as defensive. That same army turns a blind eye to continuous expropriation of
Palestinian land for settlement in the West Bank. Absent Pavlov, this perpetual colonization leaves open three options for Jewish life in that land:

1. A unitary, binational state in Israel/Palestine (increasingly, a two-state solution is rendered impossible by the tactics of the Israeli state); or

2. The expulsion of Palestinians from the land; or

3. The genocide of Palestinians.

And beware the person who suggests that the first option is in the interest of humanity in general and of Jews in particular. For suggesting much less—that "we" ought to consider what "we" would do if we lived our entire lives under occupation—I was recently subjected to vitriol, shaming, name-calling antidemocratic bullying that descended even into the attempt to invoke the perspective of my beloved father, who died not too long ago from a rapacious illness. The invocation of the dead is a tactic familiar to nationalism everywhere. It is obscene in its compulsive repetition of the harm done to them. We can mostly ignore the rantings of those who pit their lives above the lives of others. But what was compelling in numerous hate letters I received (for the "self-hating" imagining of Palestinians as human beings) is the argument that what Palestinians need is a Nelson Mandela.

I have thought hard about what is meant by that. The assumption must have been that I do understand, since there was no explanation forthcoming. But I don't know for sure. I have worked for Mandela, I have been an activist in the organization that he led, and I was very present as a participant in the early transition from apartheid to democracy in South Africa. So it is incredibly compelling for me to understand what that transition has meant to the many adults I shared space with in the brown, sunken lounge.

The obvious response to such a stand-alone, noncontextualized call would be: "Well, there may be dozens of Mandelas languishing in Israeli prisons. Because, recall that Mandela, too, was regarded as a terrorist who was locked away for the whole of his mid-life." But to deconstruct that further: What do previous apartheid citizens and current Zionists mean when they say we need a Mandela in the Middle East? I think they are *not* saying the following:

1. We need a Mandela who will fight for freedom for the oppressed masses.

2. We need a Mandela who will fight for freedom against colonial settlers.

3. We need a Mandela who will radicalize the youth movement and build the ANC into a fighting force for change.

4. We need a Mandela who will build a people's army.

5. We need a Mandela who will stand up in solidarity with the
   oppressed people of the globe (including the Palestinians).

6. We need a Mandela who will be nurtured by, and in turn
   help build a revolutionary anticolonial movement.

7. We need a Mandela who will negotiate a unitary, nonracial
   and democratic state relegating the Bantustan system to
   the scrap yard of history.

8. We need a Mandela who is eventually released from prison
   along with his comrades and his organization (and others) unbanned through the combined pressures of internal
   mobilization (like, for instance, the intifada) and international mobilization (like, for instance, BDS).

I think maybe they do want the Mandela who tentatively birthed the
post-colony. And in that cautiousness left so many of its institutions in-
tact. They want the Mandela who stretched out his arms to embrace us
all and helped us believe the fiction that apartheid was just about people
not being nice to each other. That Mandela who expected nothing from
the oppressors and everything from the oppressed, is the one my "inter-
locutors" want in the Middle East. By insisting on the magnanimity of the
oppressed for any kind of conciliation to occur suggests a singular refusal
to acknowledge the legitimacy of their claims or the illegitimacy of colonial counterclaims.

There were many other conversations from the chocolate-brown
sunken lounge that I recall—the demonization of the ANC fighters, the
"why are we singled out when everyone is racist" talk, the "Blacks have
so many other countries to go to" talk, the conversation about how aw-
ful the rest of Africa is and how much better off Blacks in South Africa
are. Currently, the perspectives that reject the analogy of Israel–apartheid
misrecognize not only the colonial project in Palestine, but also the character of South African apartheid itself. Ethiopian Jews are often paraded
as evidence that Israel is not an apartheid state. Or the outspoken collaborator will speak to the vicious character of Palestinian liberation organizations. These may rather be evidence of the significant reversal for the

decolonization project in South Africa. Parading Blacks whom we hold hands with and who speak on our behalf says nothing about institutions of racism and settler-colonialism that dispossess people of land, curtail their freedoms, actively endeavor to underdevelop them, and seek to redefine and limit their cultural horizons.

So is it apartheid? A little bit, but not quite. It is settler-colonial. Of that, the historical record is clear. But it is characteristically settler-colonial in a post–Cold War, postcolonial world. It is the last direct colony—a twenty-first-century aberration of a twentieth-century form of governmentality. It finds itself justified by a formidable global arms industry, its war economy holding it tightly together. It has cultivated a distinct hatred for the Other that apartheid South Africa never needed to produce. It has made nonsectarian, nonracial organizing an impossibility, in a way that could only be a wet dream of the South African white supremacists but unfeasible for its pragmatists. In that case, the colonized were disposable, but not in their entirety. This is where Israel departs from the apartheid South African experience and probably resembles more the colonization of places like Australia and the early colonization of the Cape.

Of course, settler colonies themselves have historically been produced for multiple reasons, an important one being how to dispense with Europe's own disposable people without resorting to the unhappy extreme of extermination.

And Jews, we must acknowledge, have been rendered by Europe as superfluous of a special type. The unfortunate response of Zionism to the trauma of the Shoah is that it replicates the very forms of being that sustain the modern European state's incapacity to accommodate life for too long. The terms of the oppressors become rearticulated as our terms. Some place like Zion, after all, was the solution before the final one: before Wannsee, there was expulsion. We use their solutions in an attempt to secure our own right to be in the world. It is a fool's endeavor. Because as they produced us, so we will and must produce an Other. Someday, this conflict too will end.

> And when it's all over,
> my dear, dear reader,
> on which benches will we have to sit,
> those of us who shouted "Death to the Arabs!"
> and those who claimed they "didn't know"?
> —Aharon Shabtai, "Nostalgia"

# Acknowledgments

W̲e would like to express our appreciation to the following people for advice, critical feedback, and support: *Africa Is a Country* senior editor Elliot Ross, who first proposed the ebook series in which this book has its origins, Samia Al-Botmeh, Laila Parsons, Melissa Levin, Natalie Zemon Davis, Alex Lichtenstein, Jens Hansen, Jennifer Derr, Stacy Hardy, Ntone Edjabe, Omar Badsha, Kate Elizabeth Creasey, and Jessica Blatt. Christopher Lee collaborated with us in the early stages of developing this project and provided invaluable feedback that helped shape the introduction. Yasmine Mosimann assisted in preparing the manuscript and also provided insightful comments. We would also like to thank the amazing team at Haymarket Books, especially Anthony Arnove, Jim Plank, Julie Fain, Dao X. Tran, and Caroline Luft.

Ishtiyaq Shukri's *Palestine Journey* first appeared in *Chimurenga* 8 (December 2005).

An earlier version of Arianna Lissoni's chapter appeared as "Africa's 'Little Israel': Bophuthatswana's Not-So-Secret Ties with Israel," *South African Review of Sociology* 42, no. 3 (2011): 79–93.

# About the Contributors

**Teresa Barnes** is an associate professor of history and gender/women's studies at the University of Illinois Urbana–Champaign. She received her PhD in African economic history from the University of Zimbabwe and lived for twenty-five years in Zimbabwe and South Africa. She has published on histories of urban African women in colonial Zimbabwe and on gender and higher education institutional culture in southern Africa. Her current research interests include histories of complicity and collaboration in South African universities in the apartheid era.

**Andy Clarno** is an assistant professor of sociology and African-American studies at the University of Illinois at Chicago. Andy's research focuses on the relationship between race, class, and space in an era of neoliberal globalization. He is currently completing a book manuscript that analyzes the relationship between inequality and insecurity, marginalization and securitization in contemporary South Africa and Palestine/Israel.

**Bill Freund** is professor emeritus of economic history at the University of KwaZulu-Natal and visiting professor in the Corporate Strategy and Industrial Development Programme at the University of the Witwatersrand. Books that he has authored include *The Making of Contemporary Africa* and *The African City: A History*.

**Kelly Gillespie** is a senior lecturer in anthropology at the University of the Witwatersrand (Wits). She is also a convener of the Johannesburg Workshop in Theory and Criticism (www.jwtc.org.za). Her research and writing focus on the slippages and politics between social justice and criminal justice in South Africa, and on race, sexuality, and critical pedagogy. She has been active in social movements and left campaigns in South Africa, including BDS and anti-pinkwashing work in support of a free Palestine.

**Ran Greenstein** is associate professor of sociology at the University of the Witwatersrand, Johannesburg, South Africa. His most recent book is *Zionism and Its Discontents: A Century of Radical Dissent in Israel/Palestine*. His previous books include *Genealogies of Conflict: Class, Identity and State in Palestine/Israel and South Africa* and *Comparative Perspectives on South Africa*. Currently he is working on a manuscript comparing indigenous resistance movements and Communist parties in South Africa and Israel/Palestine.

**Heidi Grunebaum** is a scholar working as senior researcher at the Center for Humanities Research, University of the Western Cape. Her work focuses on the afterlives of war, aesthetics, memory, and psycho-geographies of displacement. She is author of *Memorializing the Past: Everyday Life in South Africa after the Truth and Reconciliation Commission* and coeditor with Emile Maurice of *Uncontained: Opening the Community Arts Project Archive*; and, with Mark J. Kaplan as director, she made the 2013 documentary film *The Village under the Forest*.

**Shireen Hassim** is professor of politics, and her research interests are in the area of feminist theory and politics, social movements and collective action, the politics of representation and affirmative action, and social policy. She is coeditor of *No Shortcuts to Power: Women and Policymaking in Africa; Gender and Social Policy in a Global Context*, and *Go Home or Die Here: Xenophobia, Violence and the Reinvention of Difference in South Africa*. She is the author of *Women's Organizations and Democracy in South Africa: Contesting Authority*, which won the 2007 American Political Science Association's Victoria Shuck Award for best book on women and politics.

**Sean Jacobs** is on the international affairs faculty of The New School in New York City. He was born in Cape Town, South Africa. He has held fellowships at Harvard, The New School, and New York University, and was previously on the faculty of the University of Michigan in Ann Arbor. He founded the media and analysis site *Africa Is a Country*.

**M. Neelika Jayawardane** is associate professor of English at the State University of New York–Oswego and an honorary research associate at the Centre for Indian Studies in Africa (CISA), University of the Witwatersrand (South Africa). She is a senior editor and contributor to the online magazine, *Africa Is a Country*. Jayawardane was born in Sri Lanka, grew up in the Copperbelt Province in Zambia, and completed her university education in the United States. Her academic publications focus on the nexus between South African literature, photography, and the transnational/transhistorical implications of colonialism and apartheid on the body.

**Robin D. G. Kelley** is the Gary B. Nash Endowed Chair and Distinguished Professor of US History at UCLA. His books include *Thelonious Monk: The Life and Times of an American Original*; *Africa Speaks, America Answers: Modern Jazz in Revolutionary Times*; *Freedom Dreams: The Black Radical Imagination*; *Yo' Mama's DisFunktional!: Fighting the Culture Wars in Urban America*; and *Hammer and Hoe: Alabama Communists During the Great Depression*. His essays have appeared in several anthologies and publications, including the *Nation, Monthly Review, Mondoweiss, Electronic Intifada*, the *Voice Literary Supplement, New York Times, Counterpunch, Lenox Avenue, Radical History Review, African Studies Review, Black Music Research Journal, Callaloo, New Politics, Black Renaissance/Renaissance Noir, One World, Social Text, Metropolis, American Visions, Boston Review, Fashion Theory, American Historical Review, Journal of American History, New Labor Forum, Souls, and Metropolis*.

**Melissa Levin** is a political science scholar and teacher concerned with questions of belonging, nation-statehood, decolonization, and understanding and changing power. She worked for many years for the ANC in South Africa as an activist and as the head of research and strategy for elections. In this capacity, she wrote speeches for, among others, Nelson Mandela. She has recently coedited a book, *Domains of Freedom: Justice, Citizenship and Social Change in South Africa*, which will be published early 2016 by UCT Press.

**Arianna Lissoni** is a historian currently holding a research position in the History Workshop at the University of the Witwatersrand. She obtained her PhD, titled *The South African Liberation Movements in Exile, c. 1945–1970*, from the School of Oriental and African Studies in 2008. She is one of the editors of the *South African Historical Journal* and coeditor of the volume *One Hundred Years of the ANC: Debating Liberation Histories Today*. Her research interests are South African liberation history and politics.

**Mahmood Mamdani** is the Herbert Lehman Professor of Government at Columbia University and the director of the Makerere Institute of Social Research in Kampala, Uganda. His works explore the intersection between politics and culture, a comparative study of colonialism since 1452, the history of civil war and genocide in Africa, the Cold War and the War on Terror, and the history and theory of human rights. He has received numerous awards and recognitions, including being listed as one of the "Top 20 Public Intellectuals" by *Foreign Policy* (US) and *Prospect* (UK) in 2008. From 1998 to 2002 he served as president of CODESRIA (Council for the Development of Social Research in Africa). Mamdani's books include *Saviors and Survivors: Darfur, Politics, and the War on Terror* (2009); *Good Muslim, Bad Muslim: America, the Cold War and the Roots of Terror* (2004); *When Victims Become Killers: Colonialism, Nativism and Genocide in Rwanda* (2001); and *Citizen and Subject: Contemporary Africa and the Legacy of Late Colonialism* (1996), which was awarded the Herskovitz Prize of the African Studies Association.

**Achille Mbembe** is professor at the Wits Institute for Social and Economic Research (WISER) at the University of the Witwatersrand. Born in Cameroon, he obtained his PhD in history at the Sorbonne in Paris in 1989 and a DEA in political science at the Institut d'Etudes Politiques (Paris). He was assistant professor of history at Columbia University, New York, from 1988 to 1991; a senior research fellow at the Brookings Institute in Washington, DC, from 1991 to 1992; associate professor of history at the University of Pennsylvania from 1992 to 1996; and executive director of the Council for the Development of Social Science Research in Africa (Codesria) in Dakar, Senegal, from 1996 to 2000. He was also a visiting professor at the University of California–Berkeley in 2001 and a visiting professor at Yale University in 2003. Mbembe has written extensively on African history and politics, including *La naissance du maquis dans le Sud-Cameroun*. *On the Postcolony* was published in Paris in 2000 in French and the English translation has been published by the University of California Press.

**Marissa J. Moorman** is an associate professor in history at Indiana University. A historian of southern Africa, her research focuses on politics and culture in colonial and independent Angola. Her current book project, *Powerful Frequencies: Radio, State Power and the Cold War in Angola,*

*1933–2002,* looks at the relationship between the technology of radio and the shifting politics of southern Africa as anticolonial movements established independent states in the context of a region newly charged by Cold War politics. Her previous book, *Intonations: A Social History of Music and Nation in Luanda, Angola, 1945–Recent Times,* explored how music was a practice in and through which Angolans living under extreme political repression imagined the nation. Moorman has also written articles on fashion, cinema, and kuduro in Angola, and she serves on the editorial board of *Africa Is a Country.*

**Suren Pillay** is associate professor at the Center for Humanities Research at the University of the Western Cape in Cape Town, South Africa. He has published on issues of violence, citizenship, and justice claims. With Chandra Sriram, he is coeditor of the book, *Truth vs Justice? The Dilemmas of Transitional Justice in Africa.* His current research focuses on two areas of interest: citizenship, violence, and the politics of difference; and experiments in cultural sovereignty in postcolonial Africa in the sphere of knowledge production in the humanities and social sciences. He has been a visiting fellow at Jawarhalal Nehru University, India; the Makerere Institute for Social Research, Uganda; the Center for African Studies, University of Cape Town; and the Center for Social Difference, Columbia University. He is a previous editor of the journal *Social Dynamics,* blogs for *Economic and Political Weekly,* and has published widely in the press.

**Ishtiyaq Shukri** is the author of *The Silent Minaret* and *I See You.*

**Jon Soske** is assistant professor in the Department of History and Classical Studies at McGill University and honorary research associate at the Centre for Indian Studies in Africa (CISA), University of the Witwatersrand. He is coeditor of *One Hundred Years of the ANC: Debating Liberation Histories Today* and a contributor to *Africa Is a Country* and *Chimurenga Chronic.*

**T. J. Tallie** is assistant professor of history in the Department of History at Washington and Lee University in Lexington, Virginia. He completed his PhD at the University of Illinois at Urbana–Champaign under the direction of Dr. Antoinette Burton. His research interests include imperialism, settler-colonialism, indigeneity, African history, gender studies, queer theory, and religion. He has published articles in *GLQ; BRANCH: Britain, Representation, and Nineteenth Century History; Genderforum;* and *The Journal of Natal and Zulu History.* He is currently working on his full-length study of race, gender, and settler-colonialism in nineteenth-century Natal.

**Salim Vally** is the director of the Center for Education Rights and Transformation, an associate professor at the Faculty of Education, University of Johannesburg, and a visiting professor at the Nelson Mandela Metropolitan University. He serves on the boards of various professional and nongovernmental organizations, is active in various social movements and solidarity organizations, and is a regular commentator in the mass print and electronic media.

# Notes

## Introduction

1.  Eyal Weizman, *Hollow Land: Israel's Architecture of Occupation* (London: Verso Books, 2012).
2.  For a full portrait, see Saree Makdisi, *Palestine Inside Out: An Everyday Occupation* (New York: W. W. Norton, 2010).
3.  Palestinian sociologist Sari Hanafi has described this process as "spacio-cide." See "Spaciocide: Colonial Politics, Invisibility, and Rezoning in Palestinian Territory," *Contemporary Arab Affairs* 2, no. 1 (2009): 106–121.
4.  For the concept of apartheid in international law and its application to Israel, see John Dugard and John Reynolds, "Apartheid, International Law, and the Occupied Palestinian Territory," *European Journal of International Law* 24, no. 3 (2013): 867–913; Karine Mac Allister, "Applicability of the Crime of Apartheid to Israel," *al-Majdal* 38 (2008); and Paul Eden, "The Practices of Apartheid as a War Crime: A Critical Analysis," in *Yearbook of International Humanitarian Law 2013* (The Hague: TMC Asser Press, 2015): 89–117.
5.  Quoted in Dugard and Reynolds, "Apartheid, International Law, and the Occupied Palestinian Territory," 880.
6.  Ibid., 881.
7.  For a discussion of the BDS campaign's use of the analogy, see Hazem Jamjoum, "Not an Analogy: Israel and the Crime of Apartheid," *Electronic Intifada*, April 3, 2009, https://electronicintifada.net/content/not-analogy-israel-and-crime-apartheid/8164.
8.  This argument has been forcefully made in Virginia Tilley, ed., *Beyond Occupation: Apartheid, Colonialism, and International Law in the Occupied Palestinian Territories* (London: Pluto Press, 2012). We are indebted to this book throughout our introduction.
9.  Ibid., chap. 5.
10. Ronnie Kasrils, "Israel 2007: Worse Than Apartheid," *Mail and Guardian*, May 21, 2007, http://mg.co.za/article/2007-05-21-israel-2007-worse-than-apartheid; Desmond Tutu, "Justice Requires Action to Stop Subjugation of Palestinians," *Tampa Bay Times*, April 30, 2012, www.tampabay.com/opinion/columns/justice-requires-action-to-stop-subjugation-of-palestinians/1227722.
11. For an extended critique of this paradigm, see James L. Gelvin, *The Israel–Palestine Conflict: One Hundred Years of War* (Cambridge, UK: Cambridge University Press, 2014).
12. For a version of this argument, see Yaffa Zilbershats, "Apartheid, International Law, and the Occupied Palestinian Territory: A Reply to John Dugard and John Reynolds," *European Journal of International Law* 24, no. 3 (2013): 915–28; and the reply by Dugard and Reynolds, "Apartheid in Occupied Palestine: A Rejoinder to Yaffa Zilbershats," *EJIL TALK!: The Blog of the European Jour-*

*nal of International Law,* October 2, 2013, www.ejiltalk.org/apartheid-in-occupied-palestine-a-rejoinder-to-yaffa-zilbershats/.

13. See Oren Yiftachel's summary of a recent conference on the question of Israeli apartheid in Jerusalem, "Annexation or Apartheid: (Some) Israelis Search for a Word for Their Reality," *Jews for Justice for Palestinians,* February 28, 2013, http://jfjfp.com/?p=40161. The newspaper *Haaretz* regularly publishes articles both advocating and debating the idea of Israeli apartheid.

14. See Diana Allan's excellent *Refugees of the Revolution: Experiences of Palestinian Exile* (Palo Alto, CA: Stanford University Press, 2013).

15. See "The Discriminatory Laws Database," Adalah: The Legal Center for Arab Minority Rights in Israel, www.adalah.org/en/content/view/7771.

16. *The Inequality Report: The Palestinian Arab Minority in Israel* (Haifa: Adalah, March 2011).

17. Bangani Ngeleza and Adri Nieuwhof, "Unrecognised Villages in the Negev Expose Israel's Apartheid Policies," *Electronic Intifada,* December 20, 2005, https://electronicintifada.net/content/unrecognised-villages-negev-expose-israels-apartheid-policies/5819.

18. "Revocation of Residency in East Jerusalem," *B'Tselem - The Israeli Information Center for Human Rights in the Occupied Territories,* updated August 18, 2013, www.btselem.org/jerusalem/revocation_of_residency.

19. Teju Cole, "The White Saviour Industrial Complex," *Atlantic,* March 21, 2012, www.theatlantic.com/international/archive/2012/03/the-white-savior-industrial-complex/254843/.

20. See Lisa Brock, Van Gosse, and Alex Lichtenstein, eds., "The Global Anti-apartheid Movement, 1946–1994," special issue of *Radical History Review* 119 (Spring 2014).

21. This interweaving is captured well by Ariel Dorfman, "Whose Memory? Whose Justice? A Meditation on How and When and If to Reconcile," The Eighth Nelson Mandela Annual Lecture, July 31, 2010, www.nelsonmandela. org/images/uploads/WHOSE_MEMORY_WHOSE_JUSTICE_final_version_july_2010_for_publication_purposes.pdf.

22. See David Finkel and Dianne Feeley, "An Interview with Rabab Abdulhadi," in *Against Apartheid: The Case for Boycotting Israeli Universities,* edited by Ashley Dawson and Bill V. Mullen (Chicago: Haymarket Books, 2015).

23. For a broader discussion of the origins of US support for Israel, see Ilan Pappé, "Clusters of History: US Involvement in the Palestine Question," *Race & Class* 48, no. 3 (2007): 1–28.

24. See Samia Al-Botmeh, "The Academic and Cultural Boycott: The Internal Palestinian Story and the Role of the Academy," paper presented at the World Congress for Middle Eastern Studies Barcelona, Spain, July 19–24, 2010, www.pacbi.org/pics/file/Samia%20Botmeh.pdf.

## Chapter 1
**Palestine Journey**

1.    John Berger, "Foreword," in Arundhati Roy, *The Algebra of Infinite Justice* (London: Flamingo, 2002).
2.    Ishtiyaq Shukri, *The Silent Minaret* (Johannesburg: Jacana, 2005).


## Chapter 2
**Israel, the Apartheid Analogy, and the Labor Question**

1.    International Convention on the Suppression and Punishment of the Crime of Apartheid, New York, November 30, 1973, *United Nations Treaty Series*, vol. 1015, no. 14861, p. 243, https://treaties.un.org/pages/ViewDetails.aspx?src=TREATY&mtdsg_no=IV-7&chapter=4&lang=en.
2.    Ibid.
3.    Ibid.
4.    Rome Statute of the International Criminal Court, Rome, July 17, 1998, *United Nations Treaty Series*, vol. 2187, no. 38544, https://treaties.un.org/pages/ViewDetails.aspx?src=TREATY&mtdsg_no=XVIII-10&chapter=18&lang=en.
5.    Ibid.
6.    Ibid.
7.    Ibid.


## Chapter 3
**Solidarity with Palestine: Confronting the "Whataboutery" Argument and the Bantustan Denouement**

1.    Chris McGreal, "Worlds Apart," *Guardian*, February 6, 2006.
2.    Ilan Pappé, "Israel's Incremental Genocide in the Gaza Ghetto," *Electronic Intifada*, July 13, 2014, https://electronicintifada.net/content/israels-incremental-genocide-gaza-ghetto/13562.
3.    Mark Marqusee, "If Not Now, When? On BDS and 'Singling Out' Israel," Mark Marqusee (blog), April 1, 2014, www.mikemarqusee.com/?p=1489.
4.    Joel Kovel, *Overcoming Zionism: Creating a Single Democratic State in Israel/Palestine* (London: Pluto, 2007), 216.
5.    Ibid., 216–17.
6.    Adam Hanieh, "Palestine in the Middle East: Opposing Neoliberalism and US Power, Part 1," *MR Zine*, July 19, 2008, http://mrzine.monthlyreview.org/2008/hanieh190708a.html.
7.    Ibid.
8.    Neville Alexander, "The Moral Responsibility of Intellectuals," in *Enough Is a Feast: A Tribute to Dr. Neville Alexander, 22 October 1936–27 August 2012* (Johannesburg: Foundation for Human Rights, 2012), 36.
9.    Palestinian Grassroots Antiapartheid Wall Campaign, "Democratic South Africa's Complicity In Israel's Occupation, Colonialism, and Apartheid," June 11,

2009, www.stopthewall.org/democratic-south-africa-s-complicity-israel-s-oc-cupation-colonialism-and-apartheid.

10. "South Africa Not Cutting Ties with Israel," *Times of Israel*, August 28, 2014, www.timesofisrael.com/liveblog_entry/south-africa-not-cutting-ties-with-israel/.

11. Rajini Srikanth, "South African Solidarity With Palestinians: Motivations, Strategies, and Impact," *New England Journal of Public Policy* 27, no. 1 (2015): 2.

12. Virginia Tilley, "The Case for Boycotting Israel," *Counterpunch*, August 5–7, 2006, www.counterpunch.org/2006/08/05/boycott-now/.

Chapter 4
**Apartheid's "Little Israel": Bophuthatswana**

1. During the months of the 2010 FIFA World Cup, a group of international and South African artists, in collaboration with local participants, worked on a project in and around the Mmabatho stadium aimed at revitalizing underutilized architecture for the benefit of local communities. See www.cascoland. com/2009/index2.php?cat=1&casco_cat=projects.

2. A giant billboard that used to welcome motorists entering Mafikeng to "the city of culture and entertainment" has been replaced with advertising by South African Breweries—perhaps as a final, tacit acknowledgement of the city's changed fortunes.

3. For early studies about the so-called Jerusalem–Pretoria axis, see for example James Adams, *The Unnatural Alliance* (London: Quartet, 1984); Richard P. Stevens and Abdelwahab M. Elmessiri, *Israel and South Africa: The Progression of a Relationship* (New York: New World, 1976); and Rosalynde Ainslie, *Israel and South Africa: An Unlikely Alliance* (New York: UN Department of Political and Security Council Affairs Centre Against Apartheid, 1981).

4. See Sasha Polakow-Suransky, *The Unspoken Alliance: Israel's Secret Relationship with Apartheid South Africa* (Auckland Park, South Africa: Jacana, 2010).

5. Researcher and activist Jane Hunter is one of the few writers to have published on the subject of Israel's ties with the Bantustans. See Jane Hunter, *Undercutting Sanctions: Israel, the US and South Africa* (Washington, DC: Washington Middle East Associates, 1986); *Israeli Foreign Policy: South Africa and Central America* (Nottingham: Spokesman, 1987); "Israel and the Bantustans," *Journal of Palestine Studies*, 15 (1986): 53–89.

6. See for example Chris McGreal, "Worlds Apart" and "Brothers in Arms—Israel's Secret Pact with Pretoria," *Guardian*, February 6–7, 2006.

7. Ran Greenstein, "Israel/Palestine: Apartheid of a Special Type," *Johannesburg Salon* 3 (2010): 9–18.

8. For an account of Israel's relations with African states in this period, see Joel Peters, *Israel and Africa: The Problematic Friendship* (London: British Academic Press, 1992).

9. See Mobutu Sese Seko, "Foreword: '. . .Why I Normalised with Israel,'" in N. Enuma el Mahmud-Okereke, *Israel and Black Africa: Time to Normalize* (La-

gos: Emmcon [Tworf] Books, 1987), xxvii–xxx. Mobutu's diplomatic overture was based on material military interests, as Israel sold weapons to and provided training for Zaire's army. See Polakow-Suransky, *The Unspoken Alliance*, 77.

10.  Polakow-Suransky, *The Unspoken Alliance*, 95.
11.  Ibid.,105.
12.  This was cemented with Pik Botha's "red carpet" visit to Israel in 1984.
13.  "Bantustans: A Zionist Dream," *Democratic Palestine* 3, May 1984.
14.  Quoted in Hunter, "Israel and the Bantustans," 75.
15.  "Bantustans: A Zionist Dream."
16.  Quoted in Polakow-Suransky, *The Unspoken Alliance*, 278, note 10.
17.  "Heavy Investments in Bophuthatswana," *Hadashot*, June 20, 1984.
18.  See North West Provincial Archives Mafikeng (hereafter NWPA), Bophuthatswana Papers, Trade Mission Office (Tel Aviv), Annual Report: 1984; and Annual Report: 1985.
19.  NWPA, Bophuthatswana Papers, 7/3/6, Letter from the Secretary for Public Works to the Secretary for Finance, March 27, 1985.
20.  NWPA, Bophuthatswana Papers, CN 13/2, Letter from Barchana Architects, translated from Hebrew into English, October 28, 1984.
21.  Ibid.
22.  NWPA, Bophuthatswana Papers, CN 13/2, Letter from Shabtai Kalmanow-itch to D. Mosupye (Secretary for Public Works), October 8, 1984.
23.  NWPA, Bophuthatswana Papers, Trade Mission Office (Tel Aviv), Annual Report: 1985.
24.  Hunter, "Israel and the Bantustans," 60.
25.  Polakow-Suransky, *The Unspoken Alliance*, 157.
26.  In 1985 a group of Israeli businessmen were expelled from the Ciskei as a result of their involvement in a corruption scandal, which led to the firing of Ciskei's representatives to Israel Schneider and Rosenwasser and the suspension of economic ties between the two countries. See ibid.,158; Hunter, "Israel and the Bantustans," 60.
27.  Polakow-Suransky, *The Unspoken Alliance*.
28.  NWPA, Bophuthatswana Papers, Trade Mission Office (Tel Aviv), Annual Report: 1984; and Annual Report: 1985.
29.  Mmabatho International Airport, which was built by the British company Plessey, was officially opened in June 1984.
30.  NWPA, Bophuthatswana Papers, Trade Mission Office (Tel Aviv), Annual Report: 1984; and Annual Report: 1985.
31.  NWPA, Bophuthatswana Papers, Trade Mission Office (Tel Aviv), Annual Report: 1985.
32.  "Many Israelis Interested in Investments in Bophuthatswana," *Ma'ariv*, June 20, 1984.
33.  NWPA, Bophuthatswana Papers, Trade Mission Office (Tel Aviv), Annual Report: 1984.
34.  Corresponding to about €22,000. NWPA, Bophuthatswana Papers, 7/3/6,

Italy Trade Mission, Report, February 12, 1985.

35.  NWPA, Bophuthatswana Papers, CN 13/2, 1984/5 estimates of expenditure submitted by the Secretary for Economic Affairs to the President, March 28, 1985.

36.  "Israeli Stadium in Bophuthatswana," *Hadashot*, June 19, 1984.

37.  "Reserve Army Service in Bophuthatswana," *Hadashot*, May 25, 1984.

38.  Carole Cooper, "The Militarisation of the Bantustans: Control and Contradictions" in *War and Society: The Militarisation of South Africa*, edited by Jaclyn Cock and Laurie Nathan (Claremont, South Africa: David Philip, 1989), 184.

39.  K. Magyar, quoted in Anthea J. Jeffrey, *Conflict at the Crossroads in Bophuthatswana* (Johannesburg: South African Institute of Race Relations, 1993), 26.

40.  Jonathan Hyslop, "Political Corruption: Before and After Apartheid," *Journal of Southern African Studies* 31 (2005): 783.

41.  R. Thomas Naylor, *Economic Warfare: Sanctions, Embargo Busting, and their Human Cost* (York, PA: Northeastern University Press, 2001), 169–170.

42.  Jane Hunter, "Cocaine and Cutouts: Israel's Unseen Diplomacy," *The Link* 22 (1989), 8–9.

43.  William Reno, *Warlord Politics and African States* (Boulder, CO: Lynne Rienner, 1998), 119–20.

44.  See Hunter, "Israel and the Bantustans," 57.

45.  Hunter, "Cocaine and Cutouts," 8–9.

46.  "Former KGB Spy Shot Dead in Moscow," *Guardian*, November 3, 2009.

47.  Polakow-Suransky, *The Unspoken Alliance*, 200.

48.  See ibid.

49.  Quoted in Bertil Egerö, *South Africa's Bantustans: From Dumping Grounds to Battlefronts* (Uppsala: Nordiska Afrikainstitutet, 1991), 6.

50.  In 1992 Bophuthatswana representatives were operating in Israel, Germany, Italy, France, Hong Kong, Taiwan, the UK, the United States, and South Africa. In 1993 a trade mission office was opened in Latvia during a state visit by Mangope, in the course of which he received a standing ovation. See *Bophuthatswana Pioneer* 15 (1993): 2–5.

51.  Hunter, *Israeli Foreign Policy*, 77.

52.  Tova P. Maori, quoted in "Israeli Friendship & Co-operation," *Bophuthatswana Pioneer* 14 (1992): 20.

53.  "Africa's 'Little Israel,'" *Bophuthatswana Pioneer* 14 (1992): 24.

54.  "Israeli Friendship & Co-operation," 20–21.

55.  Quoted in ibid.

56.  Ibid.

57.  Ibid.

58.  "Mmabana Thaba 'Nchu," *Bophuthatswana Pioneer* 15 (1993): 29–31.

59.  "Mmabana—Cultural Success," *Bophuthatswana Pioneer* 14 (1992): 10.

60.  Ibid., 11.

61.  "Stanbo National Junior Tennis Tournament," *Bophuthatswana Pioneer* 12

(1990): 12.
62. "Youth, the Key," *Bophuthatswana Pioneer* 15 (1993): 35.
63. "Mmabatho Kicks Retains the S.I.L. Trophy," *Bophuthatswana Pioneer* 12 (1990): 12.

## Chapter 5
**Neoliberal Apartheid**

1. Neville Alexander, *An Ordinary Country: Issues in the Transition from Apartheid to Democracy in South Africa* (Scottsville: University of Natal Press, 2002), 64.

## Chapter 6
**Apartheid as Solution**

1. Sasha Polakow-Suransky, *The Unspoken Alliance: Israel's Secret Relationship with Apartheid South Africa* (New York: Pantheon Books, 2010). One of the blurbs is written by a former Israeli foreign minister.
2. "Golda Meir 1898–1978," *Israel and Judaism Studies*, June 18, 2015, www.ijs. org.au/Golda-Meir/default.aspx.
3. The Communist system tried to harmonize the two, not always with success.
4. In the right circumstances, nationalism, even with a strongly racist charge, can coexist with progressive ideas about social organization and the politics of the in-group. After all, the white Voortrekkers in the Orange Free State adopted a constitution modeled not on old Holland or Britain but the new US republic.
5. Yasser Arafat, "Nobel Lecture," Nobel Peace Prize, accessed June 18, 2015, www.nobelprize.org/nobel_prizes/peace/laureates/1994/arafat-lecture.html.

## Chapter 7
**The Historian and Apartheid**

1. "Desmond Tutu: Israel Guilty of Apartheid in Treatment of Palestinians," *Jerusalem Post,* April 28, 2015, www.jpost.com/Diplomacy-and-Politics/Desmond-Tutu-Israel-guilty-of-apartheid-in-treatment-of-Palestinians-344874; "Tutu Condemns Israeli 'Apartheid,'" *BBC*, April 29, 2002, http://news.bbc. co.uk/2/hi/africa/1957644.stm.
2. *Die Burger*, Cape Town, May 29, 1968.
3. Alfred T. Moleah, *Israel and South Africa: Ideology and Practice*, 2nd ed. (Washington, DC: The International Organization for the Elimination of All Forms of Racial Discrimination [EAFORD], 1987), 10.
4. Harold Scheub, *There Was No Lightening: A Conversation about Race Amongst South Africa's Storytellers* (Madison, WI: University of Wisconsin–Madison Libraries Parallel Press, 2010), 56.
5. Anne Barnard, "Boys Drawn to Gaza Beach, and Into Center of Mideast Strife," *New York Times*, July 16, 2014, www.nytimes.com/2014/07/17/world/mid-

dleeast/gaza-strip-beach-explosion-kills-children.html; George Azar, "Errant Shell Turns Girl into Palestinian Icon," *New York Times*, June 12, 2006, www. nytimes.com/2006/06/12/world/middleeast/12huda.html.

6.   Jodi A. Byrd, *The Transit of Empire: Indigenous Critiques of Colonialism* (Minneapolis: University of Minnesota Press, 2011), 37.

7.   Patrick Wolfe, "Settler Colonialism and the Elimination of the Native," *Journal of Genocide Research* 8, no. 4 (2006): 387–409.

8.   Mimi Thi Nguyen, *The Gift of Freedom: War, Debt, and Other Refugee Passages* (Durham, NC: Duke University Press Books, 2012).

9.   Rania Khalek, "Israel-Trained Police 'Occupy' Missouri after Killing of Black Youth," *Electronic Intifada*, August 15, 2014, http://electronicintifada. net/blogs/rania-khalek/israel-trained-police-occupy-missouri-after-killing-black-youth.

10.  Rana Baker, "Palestinians Express 'Solidarity with the People of Ferguson' in Mike Brown Statement," *Electronic Intifada*, August 15, 2014, https://electronicintifada.net/blogs/rana-baker/palestinians-express-solidarity-people-ferguson-mike-brown-statement.

11.  Richard Pithouse, "South Africa: Marikana, Gaza, Ferguson—'You Should Think of Them Always as Armed,'" allAfrica.com, http://allafrica.com/stories/201408191581.html?viewall=1.

Chapter 8
**Teach for Your Life**

1.   Robert Warrior, "Native Critics in the World: Edward Said and Nationalism," in *American Indian Literary Nationalism*, edited by Jace Weaver, Craig Womack and Robert Warrior (Santa Fe: University of New Mexico Press, 2006), 179–223.

2.   For a chillingly prescient essay, see Steven Salaita, "Manifest Knowledges. Normatizing State Power: Uncritical Ethical Praxis and Zionism," in *The Imperial University: Academic Repression and Scholarly Dissent*, edited by Piya Chatterjee and Sunaina Maira (Minneapolis: University of Minnesota Press, 2014), 217–35.

3.   See http://cfaillinois.org/2014/12/24/caft-report-on-the-steven-salaita-case-serious-violations-of-shared-governance-and-due-process/.

4.   The AAUP censure decision was announced at http://aaup.org/media-release/ aaup-censures-four-removes-censure-one. The facts of the case are set out at www.aaup.org/report/UIUC.

5.   Fred Hendricks, "The Mafeje Affair: The University of Cape Town and Apartheid," *African Studies* 67, no. 3 (2008): 428.

6.   Daniel Massey, *Under Protest: The Rise of Student Resistance at the University of Fort Hare* (Pretoria: University of South Africa Press, 2010), 150–51.

7.   Walter J. Moore, *A Life of Erwin Schrodinger* (Cambridge: Cambridge University Press, 1994), 189–91.

8.   Teresa Barnes, "The University of Cape Town and Complicity with Apartheid,"

paper presented to the African Studies Association annual meeting, November 2014.

9.   See "AAUP and AFT-Wisconsin Stand Together," American Association of University Professors, July 20, 2015, www.aaup.org/news/aaup-and-aft-wisconsin-stand-together.

10.  See "Utah Brings Back Firing Squad Executions: Witnesses Recall the Last One," NPR, April 5, 2015, www.npr.org/2015/04/05/397672199/utah-brings-back-firing-squad-executions-witnesses-recall-the-last-one.

## Chapter 9
### Along the Edges of Comparison

1.   Rafael Marques de Morais, *Diamantes de Sangue* (Lisbon: Tinta da China, 2011).

2.   Micol Seigel, "Beyond Compare: Comparative Method after the Transnational Turn," *Radical History Review* 91 (2005): 65.

3.   Jan Nederveen Pieterse, *Israel's Role in the Third World* (Amsterdam: Emancipation Research, 1984).

4.   For more on this, see Tony Hodges, *Angola: Anatomy of an Oil State* (Bloomington: Indiana University Press, 2004): 181–82 and the UN Angola Sanctions Monitoring Mechanism Report, 2000.

5.   To learn about the Isabel dos Santos fortune, see Kerry A. Dolan and Rafael Marques de Morais, "Daddy's Girl: How an African 'Princess' Banked $3 Billion in a Country Living on $2 a Day," *Forbes*, September 2, 2013, www.forbes.com/sites/kerryadolan/2013/08/14/how-isabel-dos-santos-took-the-short-route-to-become-africas-richest-woman/.

6.   See de Morais, *Diamantes de Sangue,* 14–18.

## Chapter 11
### Toward a Queer Palestine

1.   Toronto City Council, Major Cultural Organizations Allocation, June 6, 2012, http://app.toronto.ca/tmmis/viewAgendaItemHistory.do?item=2012.ED14.4.

## Chapter 12
### Cultural Weapons Against Apartheid: Art, Artists, Cultural Boycotts

1.   The exhibition, organized in cooperation with the Center for Documentary Photography at Duke University, subsequently traveled to other cities in the United States, and 136 of the photographs were collected in *South Africa: The Cordoned Heart.* The exhibition included photographs by Paul Alberts, Joseph Alphers, Michael Barry, Omar Badsha, Bee Berman, Michael Davies, David Goldblatt, Paul Konings, Lesley Lawson, Rashid Lombard, Chris Ledechowski, Jimi Matthews, Ben Maclennan, Gideon Mendel, Cedric Nunn, Myron Peters, Berney Perez, Jeeva Rajgopaul, Wendy Schwegmann, and Paul Weinberg. It

was curated by Alex Harris and Margaret Sartor. See www.icp.org/exhibitions/south-africa-the-cordoned-heart.

2.  Okwui Enwezor and Rory Bester, eds., *Rise and Fall of Apartheid: Photography and the Bureaucracy of Everyday Life* (New York: Prestel, 2013).

3.  "Picks and Pans Review: South Africa: The Cordoned Heart," *People*, June 9, 1986, www.people.com/people/archive/article/0,,20093803,00.html.

4.  Michael C. Beaubien, "The Cultural Boycott of South Africa," *Africa Today* 29, no. 4 (1982): 7–8.

5.  "Front Flap," in *Made in Palestine*, edited by Gabriel Delgado, James Harithas, Tex Kerschen (Houston: Ineri Publishing, 2004).

6.  Tarif Abboushi, "Preface," in ibid., 9.

7.  Ibid.

8.  James Harithas, "Introduction," in ibid., 12.

9.  Ibid.

10.  Ibid., 13.

11.  "Israel's Exceptionalism: Normalizing the Abnormal," Palestinian Campaign for the Academic and Cultural Boycott of Israel (PACBI), October 31, 2011, www.pacbi.org/etemplate.php?id=1749.

12.  Raja Shehadeh, "Without Vision We Can Never Get Anywhere," *Wasafiri*, 29, no. 4 (2014): 4–7.

13.  Miriam Aronowicz, "Terra Nulla: Contesting the South African Colonial Landscape," *University of Toronto Art Journal* 2 (2009): 1–25.

14.  J. M. Coetzee, *White Writing: On the Culture of Letters in South Africa* (New Haven, CT: Yale University Press, 1988), 3.

15.  Ibid., 13.

16.  Ibid., 3.

17.  Gabeeba Badaroon, *Regarding Muslims: From Slavery to Post Apartheid* (Johannesburg: Wits University Press, 2014), 39.

18.  Ibid., 39.

19.  Githa Hariharan and Raja Shehadeh, *From India to Palestine: Essays in Solidarity* (New Delhi: LeftWord Books, 2014), 17.

20.  Ibid., 18.

21.  Ibid.

22.  Ibid.

23.  Ibid., 19.

24.  Ibid., 19–20.

25.  Ibid.

26.  Omar Badsha, Facebook correspondence with author, January 8, 2015.

27.  "History," Palestinian Campaign for the Academic and Cultural Boycott of Israel (PACBI), December 21, 2008, http://pacbi.org/etemplate.php?id=868.

28.  "Israel's Exceptionalism."

29.  Gillian Slovo, "An Interview with Omar Barghouti," *Wasafiri* 29, no. 4 (2014): 36.

30.  "PACBI Issues Guidelines for Applying the International Cultural Boycott of Israel," BDS Movement, August 11, 2009, www.bdsmovement.net/2009/

pacbi-issues-guidelines-for-applying-the-international-cultural-boycott-of-isra-el-500#sthash.zzyvnPOd.dpuf.

31.   Enuga Reddy, "Cultural Boycott: Statement by Enuga S. Reddy, Director of U.N. Centre Against Apartheid at a Press Briefing (1984)," January 11, 1984, Palestinian Campaign for the Academic and Cultural Boycott of Israel (PACBI), last modified November 24, 2010, http://pacbi.org/etemplate. php?id=1417.
32.   Ibid.
33.   Ibid.
34.   Ibid.
35.   Ibid.
36.   Omar Barghouti, "Israel vs. South Africa: Reflecting on Cultural Boycott," *Electronic Intifada,* May 8, 2008, http://electronicintifada.net/content/isra-el-vs-south-africa-reflecting-cultural-boycott/7496.
37.   Ibid.
38.   "History," PACBI.
39.   Omar Barghouti, "The Cultural Boycott: Israel vs. South Africa," in *The Case for Sanctions Against Israel,* ed. Audrea Lim (New York: Verso, 2012), 33.
40.   Barghouti, "The Cultural Boycott," 37.
41.   Sama Alshaibi, Facebook correspondence with author, November 28, 2014.
42.   Ibid.
43.   Slovo, "An Interview with Omar Barghouti," 40.
44.   Ibid.
45.   "Israel's Exceptionalism: Normalizing the Abnormal."
46.   Slovo, "An Interview with Omar Barghouti," 36.
47.   Sama Alshaibi, Facebook correspondence.
48.   Ibid.
49.   Barghouti, "The Cultural Boycott," 36.
50.   Ibid., 37–38.
51.   Slovo, "An Interview with Omar Barghouti," 39.
52.   Ibid.

Chapter 13
**Apartheid's Black Apologists**

1.    See Yaman Salahi, "Truth Matters: The Vanguard Leadership Group Is Wrong," *Mondoweiss,* April 11, 2011, http://mondoweiss.net/2011/04/truth-matters -the-vanguard-leadership-group-is-wrong.html; Gary Rosenblatt, "Black Group Defends Israel against Charge of Apartheid," *The Jewish Week,* October 11, 2011, www.thejewishweek.com/news/new_york/black_group_defends _israel_against_charge_apartheid; Seth Freed Wessler, "The Israel Lobby Finds a New Face: Black College Students," *Colorlines,* January 18, 2012, http:// colorlines.com/archives/2012/01/why_the_israel_lobby_looks_to_black _students_for_support.html.

2.   Katie Hesketh, et al., *The Inequality Report: The Palestinian Arab Minority in Israel* (Adalah: The Legal Center for Arab Minority Rights in Israel, Yaffa, March 2011).

3.   "Israeli Military Orders Relevant to the Arrest, Detention and Prosecution of Palestinians," Addameer: Prisoner Support and Human Rights Association, May 15, 2015, www.addameer.org/israeli_military_judicial_system/military_ orders; see also United Nations General Assembly, *Human Rights Council, Human Rights in Palestine and Other Occupied Arab Territories: Report of the United Nations Fact-Finding Mission on the Gaza Conflict* (A/HRC/12/48, United Nations, 2009), 308–309 for earlier military orders that set precedent for military detentions that circumvent international law.

4.   Harriet Sherwood, "Israel Passes Law Banning Citizens from Calling for Boy-cotts," *Guardian*, July 11, 2011, www.theguardian.com/world/2011/jul/11/ israel-passes-law-boycotts.

5.   Stephen Lendman, "Israel Persecuting Palestinian Knesset Member Hanin Zoabi," *Global Research*, March 7, 2013, www.globalresearch.ca/israel-persecut-ing-palestinian-knesset-member-hanin-zoabi/5325683; Sophie Crowe, "Isra-el's Political Persecution of Palestinian Parliamentarians," *Palestine Monitor*, February 27, 2012, reposted on www.uruknet.info/?p=86077; "Hanin Zoabi Suspended from Knesset for Six Months," *Times of Israel*, July 29, 2014, www. timesofisrael.com/hanin-zoabi-suspended-from-knesset-for-six-months; Revita Hovel, "MK Hanin Zoabi Must Report for Questioning," *Haaretz*, August 5, 2014, www.haaretz.com/news/national/.premium-1.609077.

6.   Shiri Raphaely, "The 'Nakba Law' and Erasing History," March 31, 2011, http://mondoweiss.net/2011/03/the-nakba-law-and-erasing-history.

7.   For an overview of apartheid in South Africa, see Nancy L. Clark and William H. Worger, *South Africa: The Rise and Fall of Apartheid* (New York: Routledge, 2013); Philip Bonner, Peter Delius and Deborah Posel, eds., *Apartheid's Gene-sis, 1935–1962* (Braamfontein, South Africa: Ravan Press, 1993).

8.   International Convention on the Suppression and Punishment of the Crime of *Apartheid*, G.A. res. 3068 (XXVIII)), 28 U.N. GAOR Supp. (No. 30) at 75, U.N. Doc. A/9030 (1974), 1015 U.N.T.S. 243, entered into force July 18, 1976, www1.umn.edu/humanrts/instree/apartheid-supp.html. For an elaboration on Israeli apartheid, see Uri Davis, *Apartheid Israel: Possibilities for the Struggle Within* (London and New York: Zed Books, 2003). See also Nima Shirazi, "Defending Apartheid: Then in South Africa, Now in Palestine," *Mondoweiss*, September 5, 2014, http://mondoweiss.net/2014/09/defend-ing-apartheid-palestine.html; Musa Keilani, "Apartheid in Israel," *Jordan Times*, January 14, 2012, http://jordantimes.com/apartheid-in-israel; Ben White, *Israeli Apartheid: A Beginner's Guide* (London: Pluto Press, 2014); Saree Mak-disi, *Palestine Inside Out: An Everyday Occupation* (New York: W. W. Norton); Ilan Pappé, *The Ethnic Cleansing of Palestine* (Oxford: Oneworld Publications, 2007); Nur Masalha, *The Palestine Nakba: Decolonising History, Narrating the Subaltern, Reclaiming Memory* (London: Zed Books, 2012); Palestine Solidari-ty Committee, *Declaration by South Africans on Apartheid Israel and the Strug-*

*gle for Palestine* (Durban, South Africa, August 31, 2001).

9. Nathan Guttman, "Christian Backers of Israel Reach Out to Blacks," *Forward*, October 19, 2011, http://forward.com/articles/144558/christian-backers-of-israel-reach-out-to-blacks; Ira Glunts, "The Pro-Israel Lobby Courts African Americans," *Truthout*, November 6, 2011, http://www.truth-out.org/news/item/4583:the-proisrael-lobby-courts-africanamericans.

10. Eddie Glaude, *Exodus! Religion, Race and Nation in Early Nineteenth-Century Black America* (Chicago: University of Chicago Press, 2000); Keith P. Feldman, "Representing Permanent War: Black Power's Palestine and the End(s) of Civil Rights," *New Centennial Review* 8, no. 2 (Fall 2008): 199. There is a very long history of Black Zionism beyond the scope of this short essay. Just on Marcus Garvey's Zionist leanings and influences, see, for example, Robert A. Hill and Barbara Bair, eds., *Marcus Garvey: Life and Lessons* (Los Angeles and Berkeley: University of California Press, 1987), lv–lvi; and see also Jacob S. Dorfman, *Black Israelites: The Rise of American Black Israelite Religions* (New York and Oxford: Oxford University Press, 2014), 113–34; Shana L. Redmond, *Anthem: Social Movements and the Sound of Solidarity in the African Diaspora* (New York: New York University Press, 2014), 32–34.

11. Keith P. Feldman, "Representing Permanent War: Black Power's Palestine and the End(s) of Civil Rights," *New Centennial Review* 8, no. 2 (Fall 2008): 199.

12. Hill and Bair, *Marcus Garvey*, lv–lvi; and see also Dorfman, *Black Israelites*, 113–134; Redmond, *Anthem*, 32–34.

13. Alaine Locke, ed., *The New Negro: Voices of the Harlem Renaissance* (New York: Touchstone, 1999), 4.

14. "Randolph Urges Negro Support Palestine Jews," *Amsterdam News*, March 6, 1948.

15. Quoted in Melani McAlister, *Epic Encounters: Culture, Media, and U.S. Interests in the Middle East Since 1945* (Berkeley and Los Angeles: University of California Press, 2005), 89.

16. Quoted in Alex Lubin, *Geographies of Liberation: The Making of an Afro-Arab Political Imaginary* (Chapel Hill: University of North Carolina Press, 2014), 105. See also W. E. B. DuBois, "The Winds of Time," *Chicago Defender*, May 15, 1948; see also Du Bois, "The Case for the Jews," *Chicago Star*, May 8, 1948.

17. Charles A. Davis, "Palestine Educator Seeks Model for Jewish Schools," *Chicago Defender*, May 15, 1948.

18. *Atlanta Daily World*, March 3, 1948.

19. "Flourishing State in Palestine, Domas Tells A.U. Students," *Atlanta Daily World*, July 27, 1948.

20. See, for example, Jonathan Cook, "Israel and the Dangers of Ethnic Nationalism," *Global Research*, November 3, 2013, www.globalresearch.ca/israel-and-the-dangers-of-ethnic-nationalism/5356677; Juan Cole, "Israel Declares for Ethnic Nationalism," *Informed Comment* (blog), October 11, 2010, www.juancole.com/2010/10/israel-declares-for-ethnic-nationalism.html.

21. "They're on Their Way to Palestine," *Chicago Defender*, July 3, 1948.

22. Theodore Stanford, "Palestine Question Important to Negroes Throughout the World—Bunche," *Pittsburgh Courier*, February 21, 1948.
23. "The New Jewish State," *Amsterdam News*, May 22, 1948.
24. Robert Durr, "Speaking Out," *Chicago Defender*, July 10, 1948.
25. George S. Schuyler, "Views and Reviews," *Pittsburgh Courier*, June 19, 1948. This was not Schuyler's only column on Palestine. See "Views and Reviews," *Pittsburgh Courier*, March 27, 1948. *Courier* columnist P. L. Prattis held a diametrically opposing view. He compared Israel's fight for independence with African colonies under British rule and excoriated the Truman administration for balking on its support for partition. Prattis, "The Horizon," *Pittsburgh Courier*, April 3, 1948.
26. "What You Buy with Blood," *Pittsburgh Courier*, July 17, 1948.
27. Amy Kaplan's excellent essay, "Zionism as Anticolonialism: The Case of Exodus," *American Literary History* 25, no. 4 (Winter 2013): 870–895, makes a similar point about how Leon Uris's novel *Exodus* and the subsequent Hollywood interpretation of the book produced a narrative of Israel's founding as an anticolonial struggle against British domination.
28. Keith P. Feldman adds yet another layer to this argument by revealing how postwar racial liberalism and the promise of an integrated democracy undermined a radical critique of Israel's emerging racial/colonial order. Israel was represented as a modern, integrated democracy along US lines, and the ideology of racial liberalism erased historical and contemporary racial violence. Feldman, "Representing Permanent War," 200–201. Also see Feldman's brilliant forthcoming book, *A Shadow over Palestine: The Imperial Life of Race in America* (Minneapolis: University of Minnesota Press, 2015).
29. Melani McAlister, "One Black Allah: The Middle East in the Cultural Politics of African American Liberation, 1955-1970," *American Quarterly* 51, no. 3 (September 1999): 622–656; Vijay Prashad, *The Darker Nations: A People's History of the Third World* (New York: The New Press, 2009), 51–52, 99–100.
30. Quoted in Gerald Horne, *Black Liberation/Red Scare: Ben Davis and the Communist Party* (London and Toronto: University of Delaware Press, 1994), 284. Davis and Strong were primarily responding to articles written by another Black comrade, Abner W. Berry, defending Israel's position and suggesting that the African American community was torn between its loyalties to Israel and its general opposition to imperialism. *Daily Worker*, February 26, 1957.
31. Letter from "C.B.," *Daily Worker*, April 2, 1957; Horne, *Black Liberation/Red Scare*, 283; also see Paul Buhle and Robin D. G. Kelley, "Allies of a Different Sort: Jews and Blacks in the American Left," in *Struggle in the Promised Land: The History of Black/Jewish Relations in the U.S.*, edited by Jack Salzman and Cornel West (New York: Oxford University Press, 1997), 215; Feldman, "Representing Permanent War," 201-202.
32. Benny Morris, *Righteous Victims: A History of the Zionist-Arab Conflict, 1881–1998* (New York: Vintage Books, 2001), 275.
33. "Zionist Logic," *Egyptian Gazette*, September 17, 1964, www.malcolm-x.org/

docs/gen_zion.htm. See also Sohail Daulatzai, *Black Star, Crescent Moon: The Muslim International and Black Freedom Beyond America* (Minneapolis: University of Minnesota Press, 2012), 40–45.

34. Quoted in Uri Davis, *Apartheid Israel: Possibilities for the Struggle Within* (London and New York: Zed Books, 2003), 87.

35. Quoted in Sasha Polakow-Suransky, *The Unspoken Alliance: Israel's Secret Relationship with Apartheid South Africa* (New York: Random House, 2010), 5.

36. Quoted in Gary E. Rubin, "African Americans and Israel," in Jack Salzman and Cornel West, eds., *Struggles in the Promised Land*, 357. Of course, Ozick is not alone. The idea that the 1967 War caused an uptick in Black anti-Semitism originated immediately after Israel's occupation and is still fairly commonplace. See Robert G. Weisbord and Arthur Stein, "Black Nationalism and the Arab-Israeli Conflict," *Patterns of Prejudice* 3 (November–December, 1969): 1–9.

37. See Lubin, *Geographies of Liberation*, 119–30.

38. Student Nonviolent Coordinating Committee, "Third World Round-up: The Palestine Problem: Test Your Knowledge," *SNCC Newsletter* 1, no. 2 (July–August 1967): 5–6. Feldman, "Representing Permanent War," 210–21, provides the most comprehensive discussion of the SNCC essay. Also see Lubin's excellent treatment in *Geographies of Liberation*, 117–19.

39. The published interview appeared in "Conversation with Martin Luther King," *Conservative Judaism* 22, no. 3 (Spring 1968): 1–19.

40. Ibid., 9–10.

41. Ibid., 11.

42. Ibid., 12.

43. Ibid., 12.

44. "African American Vanguard Steps Forward for Israel," Birmingham Jewish Foundation, press release, www.bjf.org/daily-updates/134-african-american-vanguard-steps-forward-for-israel.html.

45. Gary Rosenblatt, "Black Group Defends Israel Against Charge of Apartheid," *Jewish Week*, October 11, 2011, www.thejewishweek.com/news/new_york/black_group_defends_israel_against_charge_apartheid.

46. Darius Jones, "Compete or Die!" 9EtherNews (blog), October 4, 2006, http://9ethernews.blogspot.com.

47. Omar Barghouti, *BDS: Boycott, Divestment, Sanctions: The Global Struggle for Palestinian Rights* (Chicago: Haymarket Books, 2011).

48. Tutu quoted in Barghouti, *BDS: Boycott, Divestment, Sanctions*, 21.

49. Ali Abunimah, *One Country: A Bold Proposal to End the Israeli–Palestinian Impasse* (New York: Metropolitan Books, 2006), 149.

## Chapter 14
### Checkpoints and Counterpoints: Edward Said and the Question of Apartheid

1. Edward W. Said, *Identity, Authority and Freedom: The Potentate and the Traveller*, 31st T B Davie Memorial Lecture May 22 (Cape Town: University of Cape

Town Press, 1991).

2.  Edward W. Said, "Zionism from the Standpoint of Its Victims," in *The Edward Said Reader*, edited by Mustapha Bayoumi and Andrew Rubin (New York: Vintage Books, 2000), 114–68.

3.  Said, "Zionism from the Standpoint of Its Victims," 144. In another part of essay he pointed out, "On the other hand, it would be totally unjust to neglect the power of Zionism as an idea for Jews, or to minimize the complex internal debates characterizing Zionism, its true meaning, its messianic destiny, etc. Even to speak about this subject, much less than attempting to 'define' Zionism, is for an Arab quite a difficult matter, but it must be honestly looked at." Ibid, 118.

4.  Edward W. Said, *Orientalism* (New York: Vintage Books, 1978).

5.  Partha Chatterjee, *Nationalist Thought and the Colonial World, A Derivate Discourse* (London: Zed Books, 1986), 41.

6.  "An Interview with Edward Said," in *The Edward Said Reader*, edited by Mustapha Bayoumi and Andrew Rubin (New York: Vintage Books, 2000), 433.

7.  Edward W. Said, *Power, Politics and Culture, Interviews with Edward W. Said* (New York: Vintage Books, 2002), 435.

8.  Mahmood Mamdani, *Define and Rule: Native as Political Identity* (Cambridge, MA: Harvard University Press, 2012).

9.  Stuart Hall, et al., *Policing the Crisis: Mugging, the State, and Law and Order* (London: Macmillan, 1978).

10. Rian Malan, *My Traitor's Heart, A South African Exile Returns to Face his Country, his Tribe and his Conscience* (New York: Grove Press, 1990).

11. Said traces this historically conjunctural and contingent aspect of Zionism's "success" in *The Question of Palestine*. It emerged when the legitimacy of settler-colonialism was still in place, but barely just, as a racially legitimate project that enabled Europeans to settle the rest of the world was reaching its twilight phase in that form.

12. Tony Judt, "Israel: 'The Alternative,'" *The New York Review of Books*, October 23, 2003.

13. Edward W. Said, *Reflections on Exile and Other Essays* (Cambridge: Harvard University Press, 2002), 147–148.

14. John Rahn, *Music Inside Out: Going Too Far in Musical Essays* (Amsterdam: G+B Arts International, 2000), 177.

Chapter 16
### Reflections in a Mirror: From South Africa to Palestine/Israel and Back Again

1.  Michael Rothberg, "Trauma Theory, Implicated Subjects, and the Question of Israel/Palestine" *Profession* (2014), https://profession.commons.mla.org/2014/05/02/trauma-theory-implicated-subjects-and-the-question-of-israelpalestine/.

2.  Mahmoud Issa, "Resisting Oblivion: Historiography of the Destroyed Palestin-

ian Village of Lubya," *Refuge* 21, no. 2 (2003): 14–22.

3. Mahmoud Issa, *Lubya var en landsby I Palæstina* [Lubya: A Palestinian Village in the Middle East] (Copenhagen: Tiderne skifter, 2005). I am deeply grateful to Mahmoud Issa for sharing the unpublished manuscript of the English translation of his book with me.

4. Meron Benvenisti, *Sacred Landscape: The Buried History of the Holy Land since 1948*, trans. by M. Kaufman-Lacusta (Berkeley: University of California Press, 2000).

5. Hazem Jamjoum, "Not an Analogy: Israel and the Crime of Apartheid," *Electronic Intifada*, April 3, 2009, http://electronicintifada.net/content/not-analogy-israel-and-crime-apartheid/8164.

## Chapter 17
### The Last Colony

1. Ari Shavit, *My Promised Land: The Triumph and Tragedy of Israel* (New York: Spiegel and Grau, 2013).

2. Ruth Amir, "Transitional Justice Accountability and Memorialisation: The Yemeni Children Affair and the Indian Residential Schools," *Israel Law Review* 47, no. 1 (2014): 3–26.

# Index

# About Haymarket Books

Haymarket Books is a nonprofit, progressive book distributor and publisher, a project of the Center for Economic Research and Social Change. We believe that activists need to take ideas, history, and politics into the many struggles for social justice today. Learning the lessons of past victories, as well as defeats, can arm a new generation of fighters for a better world. As Karl Marx said, "The philosophers have merely interpreted the world; the point, however, is to change it."

We take inspiration and courage from our namesakes, the Haymarket Martyrs, who gave their lives fighting for a better world. Their 1886 struggle for the eight-hour day reminds workers around the world that ordinary people can organize and struggle for their own liberation.

For more information and to shop our complete catalog of titles, visit us online at www.haymarketbooks.org.

## Also Available from Haymarket Books

**Against Apartheid: The Case for Boycotting Israeli Universities**
Edited by Ashley Dawson and Bill V. Mullen, Foreword by Ali Abunimah

**Boycott, Divestment, Sanctions:**
**The Global Struggle for Palestinian Rights**
Omar Barghouti

**Freedom Is a Constant Struggle:**
**Ferguson, Palestine, and the Foundations of a Movement**
Angela Y. Davis, Edited by Frank Barat, Foreword by Dr. Cornel West

**Lineages of Revolt: Issues of Contemporary Capitalism**
**in the Middle East**
Adam Hanieh

**On Palestine**
Noam Chomsky and Ilan Pappé, Edited by Frank Barat

**Shell-Shocked: On the Ground Under Israel's Gaza Assault**
Mohammed Omer

**The Battle for Justice in Palestine**
Ali Abunimah

**Uncivil Rites: Palestine and the Limits of Academic Freedom**
Steven Salaita

# About the Authors

**Jon Soske** is an assistant professor of modern African history at McGill University and the coeditor of *One Hundred Years of the ANC: Debating Liberation Histories Today*.

**Sean Jacobs** is an assistant professor of international affairs at the New School in New York City and the founder of the popular website Africa Is a Country.

Printed in the USA
CPSIA information can be obtained
at www.ICGtesting.com
JSHW020530280224
58085JS00003B/5

9 781608 465187